W9-AJM-432

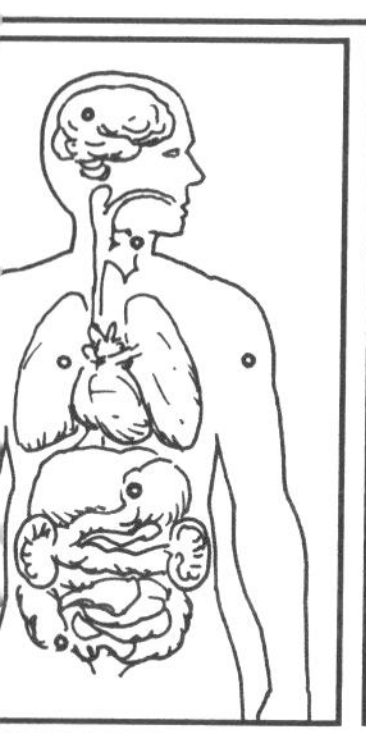

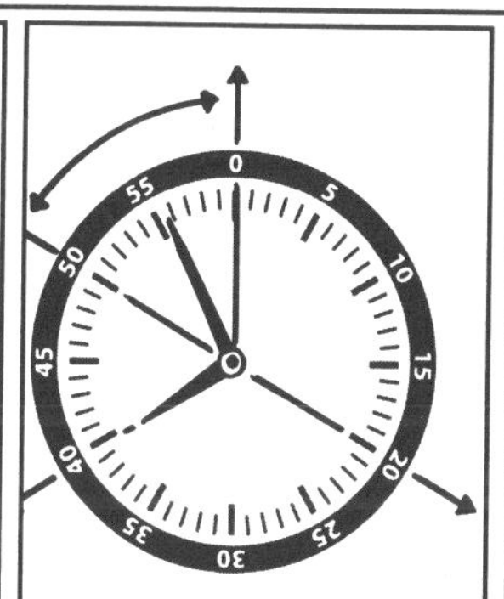
0
5
10
15
20
25
30
35
40
45
50
55

100 DEADLY SKILLS

SURVIVAL EDITION

The SEAL Operative's Guide
to Surviving in the Wild and Being
Prepared for Any Disaster

Clint Emerson, retired Navy SEAL

Illustrations by Ted Slampyak

TOUCHSTONE

New York London Toronto Sydney New Delhi

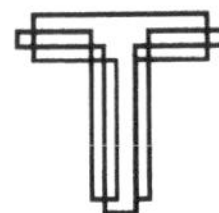

Touchstone
An Imprint of Simon & Schuster, Inc.
1230 Avenue of the Americas
New York, NY 10020

First Touchstone trade paperback edition October 2016

TOUCHSTONE and colophon are registered trademarks of Simon & Schuster, Inc.

For information about special discounts for bulk purchases, please contact Simon & Schuster Special Sales at 1-866-506-1949 or business@simonandschuster.com.

The Simon & Schuster Speakers Bureau can bring authors to your live event. For more information or to book an event, contact the Simon & Schuster Speakers Bureau at 1-866-248-3049 or visit our website at www.simonspeakers.com.

Skill testing by Kenzie Emerson
Interior design by Erich Hobbing

Manufactured in the United States of America

10 9 8 7 6 5 4 3 2 1

Library of Congress Cataloging-in-Publication Data
Names: Emerson, Clint, author. | Slampyak, Ted, illustrator.
Title: 100 deadly skills : survival edition : the SEAL operative's guide to surviving in the wild and being prepared for any disaster / Clint Emerson, retired Navy SEAL ; illustrations by Ted Slampyak.
Other titles: One hundred deadly skills | SEAL operative's guide to surviving in the wild and being prepared for any disaster
Description: Survival edition. | New York : Touchstone, [2016] | Includes index.
Identifiers: LCCN 2016026472 (print) | LCCN 2016027382 (ebook) | ISBN 9781501143908 (pbk.) | ISBN 9781501143939 (Ebook)
Subjects: LCSH: Combat survival—Handbooks, manuals, etc. | Survival—Handbooks, manuals, etc. | United States. Navy. SEALs.
Classification: LCC U225 .E64 2016 (print) | LCC U225 (ebook) | DDC 613.6/9—dc23 LC record available at https://lccn.loc.gov/2016026472

ISBN 978-1-5011-4390-8
ISBN 978-1-5011-4393-9 (ebook)

A Note to Readers

The skills described in the following pages are called "deadly" for a reason. Many were inspired by the missions and training of Special Forces personnel, operatives who are routinely pushed to the limits of their endurance, precision, and ingenuity under life-threatening conditions. But unlike the original *100 Deadly Skills*, a manual intended to expose civilians to a shadowy special ops world filled with subterfuge, surveillance, and surreptitious infiltration, this survival edition is geared toward actions that will save lives—yours and those of the people around you. The skills in this book are meant to help you overcome a range of deadly situations, from getting lost at sea to being caught in the crosshairs of an active shooter or the tusks of a wild boar.

Still, some of these skills are extremely dangerous, and many should only be attempted in the direst of situations. All require the application of personal judgment, their necessity in any given situation highly dependent on context. A cricothyrotomy (see page 252) should be performed by an untrained bystander only in the event that a massive trauma has mangled a victim's upper airway, less invasive attempts to restore breathing have failed, and an emergency dispatcher agrees that the benefits outweigh the risks. A botched attempt could result in spinal injury or the laceration of a major vessel or artery, eventualities for which even the most well-meaning bystander might be liable. Starting a signaling fire with a cell phone battery (see page 68) should only be undertaken in extreme situations. And attempting to thwart a pirate attack (see page 102) or take out a hijacker (see page 174) is a brave act of intervention with an extremely high level of risk.

The author and publisher disclaim any liability from any injury that may result from the use, proper or improper, of the information contained in this book. The stated goal of the book is not to enable deadly actions but to entertain while simultaneously imparting a body of knowledge that may come in handy in the absolute direst of emergencies.

Be deadly in spirit, but not in action. Respect the rights of others and the laws of the land. May the strongest survive.

Extinction is the rule. Survival is the exception.

—Carl Sagan

CONTENTS

PART IX: EMERGENCY MEDICINE 233

INTRODUCTION

The state of survival isn't what it used to be. Scroll back several hundred years, and the living was harder, but the environment was a known quantity. Though our ancestors could still be felled by illness, natural disaster, or marauding troops, they knew the lay of their land. They probably hadn't roamed far, from birth through old age, but they understood the risks they faced, and prepared for those they could control.

Too often these days we're lulled into a false sense of security, an easy complacency born of a matrix of assumptions about the modern world. The trains run on time (or are predictably delayed), we hit the brakes at red lights, we plan adventure treks and travel freely around the globe. If anything goes wrong, we reach for the tiny computers in our pockets and find the answer we're looking for or summon the help we need. But the same conveniences that make our lives run so smoothly—the top-of-the-line gear that is meant to make outdoor exploration even cushier, the cars that whisk us to our offices, the computers that research our queries and crunch our complex algorithms, the planes that vault us thousands of feet through the air toward our final destinations—render us soft on survival skills and vulnerable to predators.

With a change of perspective, our modern conveniences start to look a lot like security loopholes.

Perhaps worst of all, their convenience is a double-edged sword. Our reliance on automated, networked, "smart" devices and machines has also made us more dependent, less smart—unable to find our way around our own cities without the aid of pinging cellular towers or satellites tracking our positioning from outer space, much less make our way around in unfamiliar territory.

If a catastrophic event occurs, will you have amassed the knowledge and undertaken the preparations necessary to survive? What does survival look like in a time when borders are porous and threats are varied, ever-changing, and sometimes unknowable?

An increasingly global, networked society demands a new prototype for survival. A blueprint that brings us back to a core arsenal of lost skills, teaching us how to navigate a landscape devoid of street signs or satellite signals while preparing us for the newest and most up-to-date threats emerging in our urban environments—from lightning-fast pandemics to social media–enabled kidnapping scams.

A new blueprint for survival understands that the line between war and peace can be fractured in an instant, not by a marauding horde but by a lone actor carrying out the delusional fantasies of a self-proclaimed world order. This blueprint understands that in order to survive such an attack, each and every citizen must be prepared to fight. And it also understands that though the natural world around us sometimes seems to have been tamed, Mother Nature still has the power to surprise and shock.

Take it from a retired Navy SEAL with twenty years of special ops service and extensive experience in identifying and fortifying security loopholes: The only elements of crisis under our control are our own preparation and response. A true warrior is prepared to fight in any environment on earth, protecting his or her loved ones from threats as varied as gunshot wounds and home intruders. And whether a crisis is medical, man-made, natural, urban, or rural, a base layer of knowledge and forethought can make the difference between life and death.

Only the strong survive. Only the knowledgeable prosper.

The world isn't getting any safer. Be ready to stand your ground.

PART I

PERSONAL PREPAREDNESS

001 Become Crisis Proof

Survivability isn't just a matter of carrying the right tools or following the most punishing physical training regimen available. Beyond muscle, brawn, and a crisis-oriented readiness kit, the most important element of survival training begins with the adoption of a preemptive, proactive mindset.

Most civilians living in relatively peaceful modern societies move through their days in a haze of passivity, assuming the worst that will happen is a missed deadline, a parking ticket, an argument with a loved one. The ground is solid beneath their feet. The only risk entailed by a Saturday night movie or ballgame is that the newest superhero sequel disappoints or their favorite team loses. But as we've learned, sophisticated urban centers aren't immune to the threat of global conflict or to the unpredictable menace caused by lone actors whose sinister plans may escape the notice of their closest friends and family.

A survival mindset rejects the lure of passivity and instead prepares for a range of undesirable possibilities—whatever their nature and wherever they may occur, from a mountaintop to your local cineplex. A survival mindset isn't paranoid, but realistic. And it begins with a multipronged strategy for awareness and response to crises of all kinds, comprised of situational awareness, personal and cultural awareness, active threat reduction techniques, and the adoption of an offensive—and not defensive—mindset.

Situational Awareness: Whether you're traveling or on home ground, reduce your vulnerability to threats by adopting situational awareness as a personal philosophy. Look outside the three-foot bubble most civilians inhabit as they transit through their surroundings. Look up, look down, stay off your mobile device. Orient yourself to your surroundings and to potential threats you may spot in the vicinity, and make advance decisions about your potential response to these threats as you see them. Set thresholds for defensive or offensive responses. *If the man who seems to be following*

No. 001: Become Crisis Proof

CONOP: Adopt dress, tools, and mindset that will increase survivability in crisis.

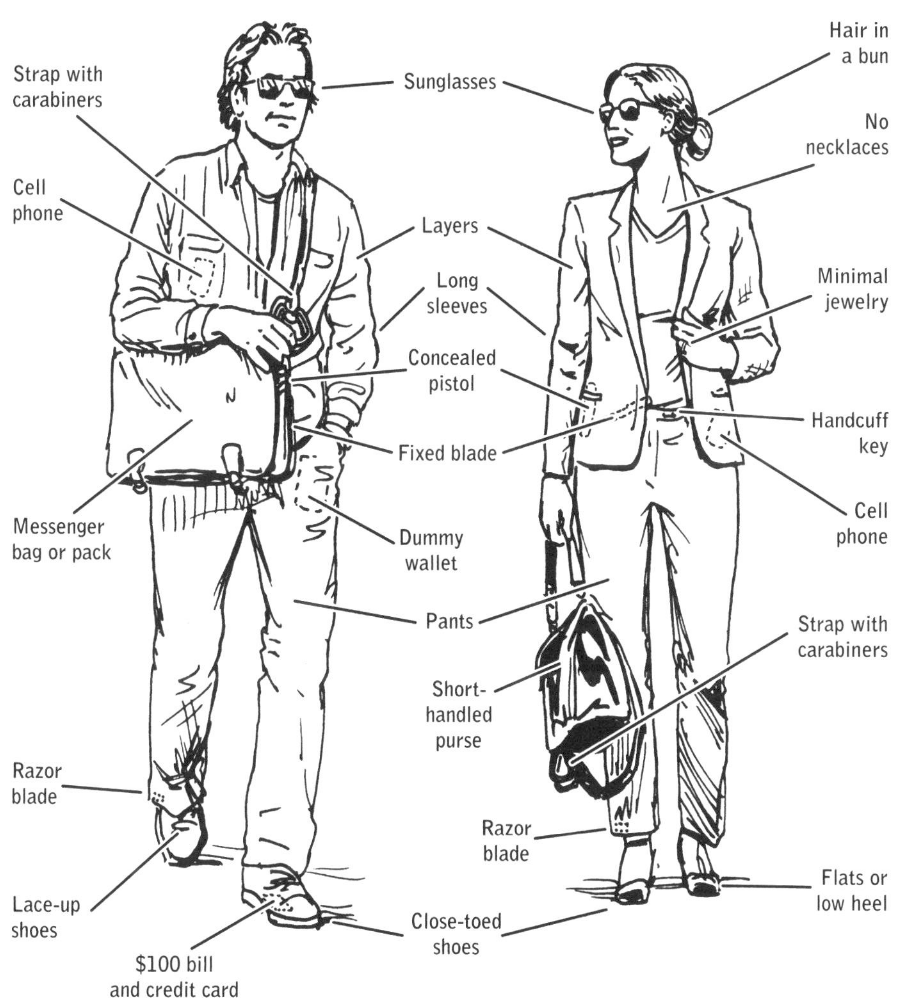

BLUF: Never assume it won't happen to you.

me crosses over to my side of the street, I will duck into the next place of business to call 911 and get help from bystanders. Identify exits in enclosed, crowded public spaces in advance. Identifying situational risks and thinking through crisis response in advance allows you to act without hesitation when emergencies strike. If and when chaos descends, you'll be making your way to safety while others are still scrambling to determine a response.

Personal and Cultural Awareness: Combine *personal awareness* with *cultural awareness* to reduce the odds of being targeted as a potential victim. Personal awareness involves scanning your self-presentation and demeanor from a predator's perspective. What does your look telegraph to thieves or violent criminals? Flashing expensive brands and logos only draws attention to you as a potentially lucrative target, so favor generic clothing and accessories. No matter the scenario, you stand to benefit by being the gray man or woman, a figure who passes unnoticed through a variety of contexts. Cultural awareness involves scanning your self-presentation and demeanor against the prevailing customs of any given environment. When you are traveling, an aversion to ostentation should be combined with a preference for assimilation. Tourists and travelers are frequently targeted as easy marks for a variety of crimes, scams, and heists. Altering your everyday appearance in order to blend in with the local population is one simple way to reduce your visibility.

Threat Reduction: Women looking to protect themselves from predators can start with a few very simple measures that may lessen their chances of being targeted. Wear long hair in a bun rather than loose or in a ponytail, to avoid giving predators a handle to hold on to. Necklaces and IDs worn on lanyards around your neck could also be used by a predator seeking to gain control over you. Wear pants—predators are known to target women wearing skirts and dresses, and pants offer maximum mobility and protection in any kind of crisis.

An Offensive Mindset: When it comes to survival, "self-defense" is a natural association. But in most crisis scenarios, a defensive mindset won't do you much good. If the crisis threshold has been crossed and the moment for action has arrived, it's time for you to flip a mental switch and move into offensive mode. In confrontations with violent adversaries, you must match or exceed the level of aggression you are presented with. Assume the worst-case scenario—that your aggressor is trained in mixed martial arts or very accurate with his or her weapon—and fight back with everything you've got. Your life depends on it.

This spirit of aggressive counteraction is just as applicable to natural disasters or survival in the wild. In any crisis or disaster scenario, your goal is to aggressively move away from the danger as quickly and efficiently as possible, remaining in control of your emotions and refraining from letting hysteria take over. The fight-or-flight instinct is powerful, but it must be combined with clear-headed thinking for optimal response.

Note: Each skill in this book is broken down into its most critical parts, or Courses of Action (COAs), introduced by a Concept of Operation (CONOP) and then summed up by a BLUF (Bottom Line Up Front) that spells out the skill's key takeaway.

002 Build a Personal EDC Kit

Survival is a game of adaptability, and many of the skills in this book focus on improvised tools created from available materials at the last minute. But a small amount of well-chosen gear goes a long way. Every man or woman must tailor his or her own EDC (everyday carry) kit to the environment and to personal habits, but whether you're looking to fine-tune your kit or starting from scratch, a few small, lightweight items should be considered baseline necessities (see opposite).

A bulletproof insert, custom-fitted or ordered to fit a variety of bag sizes, can transform your bag into a quick shield against a gun-toting assailant. A small flashlight has endless uses as a navigational tool or signaling device (page 114). A steel-barreled pen works overtime as both a writing device and (when stabbed into an opponent's eye or neck) a weapon of self-defense. A roll of coins can be folded into a bandana and turned into a bone-crushing tool. The same bandana can be used as a tourniquet, while a tube of super glue can be used to create improvised sutures (page 246). A pair of Kevlar shoelaces, worn or carried, can be used to saw through metal. And medical shears will cut through clothing or metal wire.

In combination with the weapons a civilian might regularly carry, a small can of Mace provides a nonlethal means of self-defense.

A GPS device provides navigational backup in the event that cell phone service is interrupted during a natural or urban disaster, and a printed map adds an extra layer of insurance should both devices fail or be stolen.

Reattach purse or bag straps with carabiners if you can—a removable strap can be of great use during a crisis (see page 200), as can a length of tubular nylon (page 96).

No. 002: Build a Personal EDC Kit

CONOP: Gather everyday carry items that promote safety and survival.

Bulletproof insert

Carabiners (2)

Medical shears

Map

Altoids tin with Band-Aids, super glue, Kevlar laces, and lighter

Zebra pen

Nalgene bottle

Mace

Ten feet of one-inch tubular nylon

Small flashlight

Key ring with LED, glass break, whistle, and keys

Energy bars

GPS

Roll of coins

Bandana

BLUF: Complacency is only identified after consequences are served.

003 Train to Survive

If you don't have the physical conditioning necessary to get yourself out of trouble, the skills in this book won't do you much good. Whether you're exiting a burning building or knocking a dangerous assailant unconscious, the ordeal will consist of surmounting the initial crisis and then running or crawling your way to safe ground some distance away. At a minimum, you want to be able to push, pull, and lift your own body weight. Ideally, you'll have the strength to lift your own body weight while *also* carrying a loved one to safety.

Full-body strength and cardiovascular endurance are two prongs of a solid functional workout that will give you the initial fortitude to pull yourself out of a crisis—and then the endurance you'll need to get out of harm's way. An adaptable workout based on hauling, pushing, punching, and pulling a heavy weighted mass will have the best chance of approximating real-life survival scenarios.

Work through the phases of the workout in thirty-second intervals, starting with the Heavy Bag Sprints (see opposite). Working the core and the legs, these will inevitably resemble more of a forced march than an actual sprint. Proceed to Heavy Bag Ground Pounds, which work arm and back strength while engaging core rotational force. Ground your legs during Heavy Bag Pulls, pulling the rope hand-over-hand to bring the bag toward you. Alternate sides after ten reps or thirty seconds of Heavy Bag Squats. Proceed to another Heavy Bag Ground Pound, this time letting the rotational power exit through your knees as you push the heavy bag across the floor.

End the interval series with a quarter- or half-mile full-speed sprint. Rest for thirty seconds to one minute, then repeat the sequence up to five times.

No. 003: Train to Survive

CONOP: Engage in functional workouts that increase performance in crisis.

COA 1: Heavy Bag Sprints

COA 2: Heavy Bag Ground Pound

COA 3: Heavy Bag Pulls

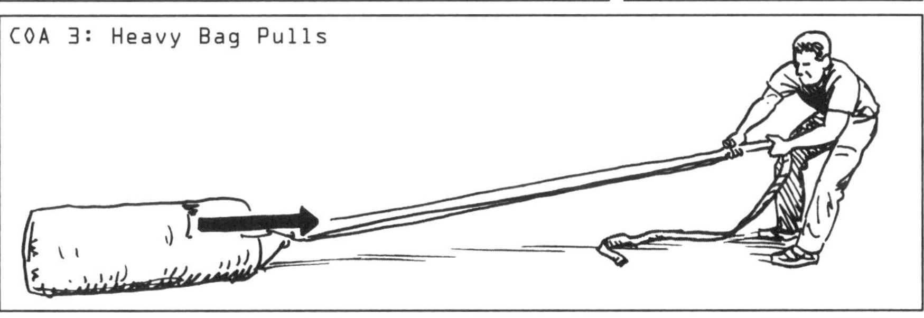

COA 4: Heavy Bag Squat (L/R)

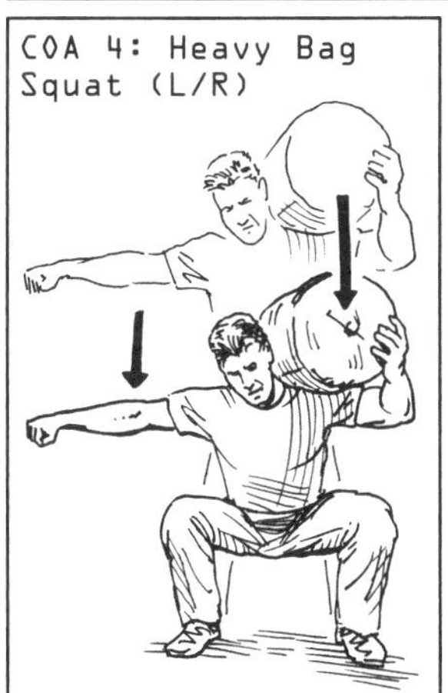

COA 5: Heavy Bag Ground Pound (knees)

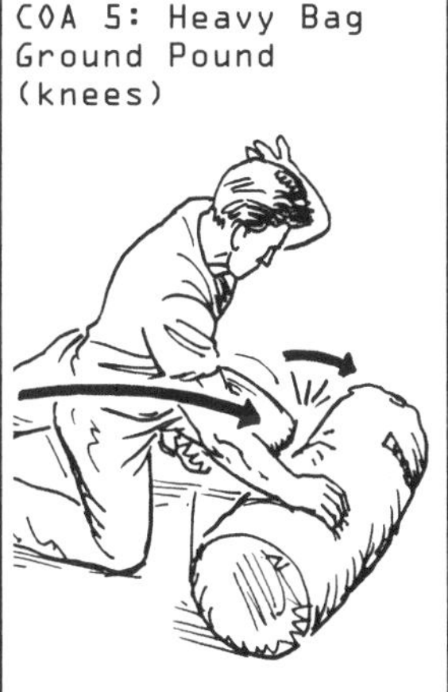

COA 6: Sprint

BLUF: Train like your life depends on it.

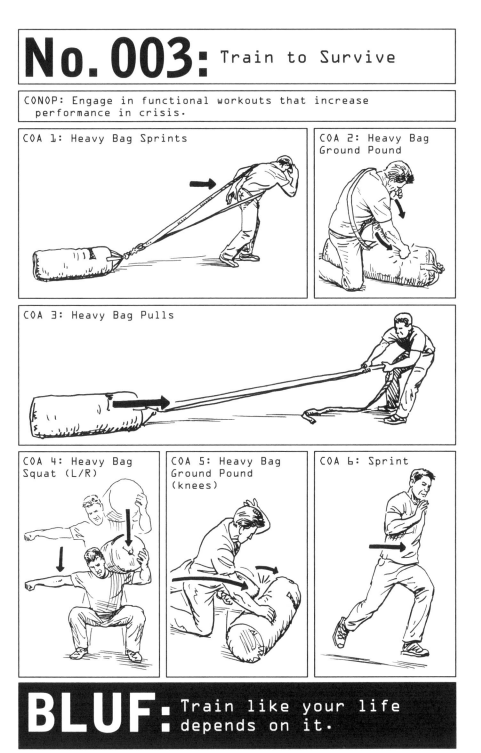

004 Prepare a Vehicle Go-Bag

A basement full of emergency supplies is an excellent starting point for disaster preparation, but the trunk of your car is an underutilized resource. Crisis is unpredictable, and a nimble response should be mobile-adapted. Conceal a vehicular go-bag beneath or beside your spare tire to surmount not only a flat but also a plunge into a sinkhole (see page 196) or an unexpected cold-weather trek toward roadside assistance. Stock your go-bag with items crucial for life-support and self-defense, including but not limited to:

Carabiners. Strap down gear in a maritime environment, hang food supplies in the mountains, or make an improvised seat belt.

Concealed Razor Blade. An undetectable weapon can be a very powerful tool.

Duct Tape. Splint a fractured bone (see page 250) or create an Improvised Magnetic Compass (page 20).

Dynamic Rope. Haul yourself out of a sticky situation.

First-aid Kit. Temporarily stop bleeding in the event of a collision.

Flares, Flare Gun, Air Horn, Whistle. The ability to signal for help may get you out of a very tight squeeze.

Flashlight, Lighter. A large flashlight has a multitude of uses, and a lighter ensures you'll never be without fire.

Food and Water. Maintain a three-day supply to prepare for a lengthy drive out of town in the event of a large-scale urban crisis or natural disaster.

No. 004: Prepare a Vehicle Go-Bag

CONOP: Collect and store lifesaving gear when away from home.

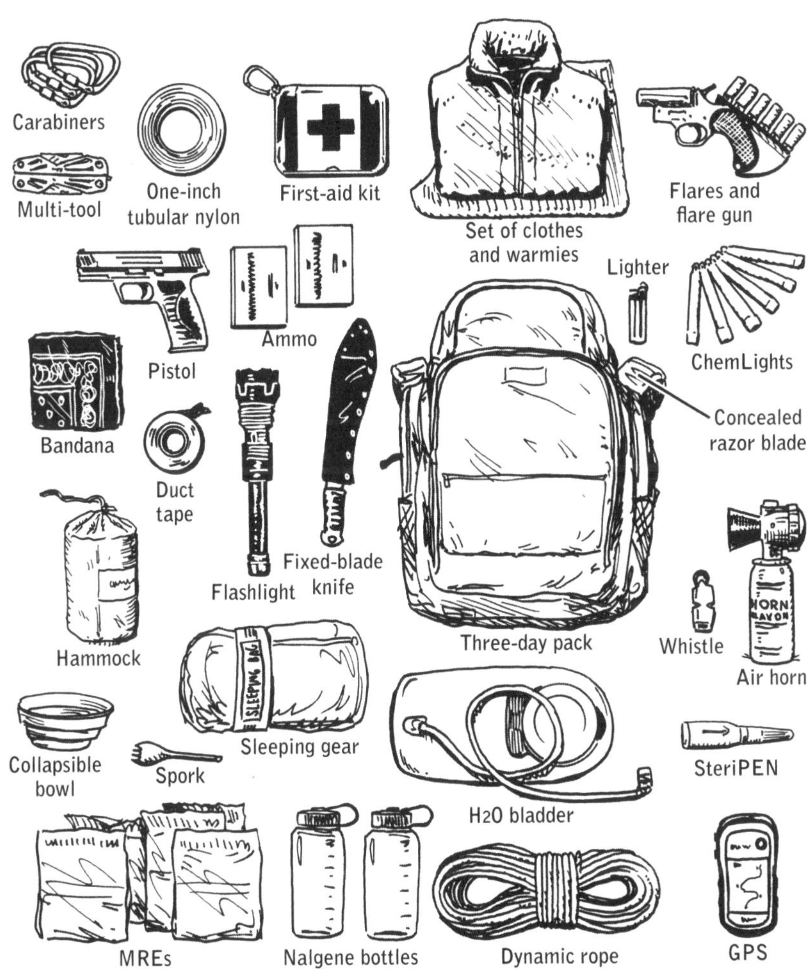

BLUF: Never leave home without your go-bag.

Handheld GPS Device. Supplement your cell phone and/or built-in GPS system in case both systems fail.

Multi-tool. Cut through wire, loosen screws, or saw down metal with a single tool.

Pistol, Ammo, Fixed-blade Knife. Arm yourself in case things go sideways.

Sleeping Bag, Hammock, Poncho Liner. Increase your comfort and endurance in survival conditions.

Warm Layers. Cars can break down anywhere, and running your heater overnight is a great way to wear out your battery.

PART II

NAVIGATION

005 Environmental Navigation

In a survival scenario, an overreliance on your GPS system can be a liability. Devices can be lost or destroyed. Under a triple canopy or in inclement weather, they may not be able to contact the three or more satellites needed for positioning. And most important, in the absence of street names, being able to pinpoint your position won't help you if you don't have a context for the environment's topographical landmarks.

To mitigate against these possibilities, carry a compass, extra batteries, and a map as backup—and perform a generalized map study prior to setting out into the wilderness. Your goal should be to familiarize yourself with the terrain within a fifteen- to twenty-mile radius of your destination. If you have the misfortune of getting lost, having memorized the direction of landmarks such as lakes, villages, mountains, and oceans will make for smarter decision-making on the fly.

So will an observant eye. Whether by design or by accident, Mother Nature provides those who pay attention with a host of clues regarding their whereabouts. Because most winds are western-prevailing, for example, trees and bushes tend to display thicker foliage on their eastern sides. A prevalence of branches (as opposed to leaves) marks the southern side of the tree, which gets the most sunlight due to planetary tilt. And moss growth generally favors the northern side of trees, because moss favors shade. This last clue only works in the aggregate, because shade may be coming from neighboring trees or plants. As with all clues, make sure you see an overall pattern before jumping to conclusions about your cardinal directions.

To create a makeshift emergency compass, see page 20.

No. 005: Environmental Navigation

CONOP: Use plants and trees to determine direction.

COA 1: Western prevailing wind will leave navigational clues on vegetation.

COA 2: Trees are naturally lopsided. The side with the most branches, leaves, and overall growth is the south side of the tree.

COA 3: Moss growth can indicate north due to its penchant for shade.

BLUF: The environment is full of clues, if you know where to look.

006 Solar Navigation

Though the satellite tracking that has pervaded so many aspects of modern life dates back only a half century, the use of celestial objects as navigational tools has been around for thousands of years. If you've performed a map study and outfitted yourself with a basic working knowledge of the environment, tracking the movements of our closest star—the sun—should help you find your way to safe ground.

The simplest way to use the sun's movements is to determine which way your shadow is being cast. Because the sun rises in the east, a morning sun will cast your shadow to the west. Past noon, when the sun is starting to set in the west, your shadow will point toward the east.

At midday, this technique will be difficult to use, as a sun that's high overhead won't cast much of a shadow at all. But if you're wearing an analog watch, you have all the tools you need in order to determine your cardinal bearings (the direction of north, south, east, and west). Raising your wrist as if you're looking at your watch, rotate your body so that the hour hand points directly toward the sun. The halfway point between the hour hand and the twelve o'clock mark on your watch indicates the way south.

If you're unsure of the time of day, create an improvised sundial and use the movement of your shadow to chart your course. To construct, place a stick in the ground, setting a rock at the end of the shadow cast by the stick. Let fifteen minutes pass, then place a second rock at the end of the new shadow. Draw one line between the two rocks, and another perpendicular to the first. The end of the perpendicular line furthest from the stick will point toward north.

No. 006: Solar Navigation

CONOP: Use the sun to determine direction.

COA 1: Use the sun's easterly rise and westerly set to determine cardinal bearings (NSEW).

Sun moving east to west

East

North

South

West

COA 2: Point the hour hand of your watch at the sun. South is halfway between the hour hand and 12:00 in the Northern Hemisphere.

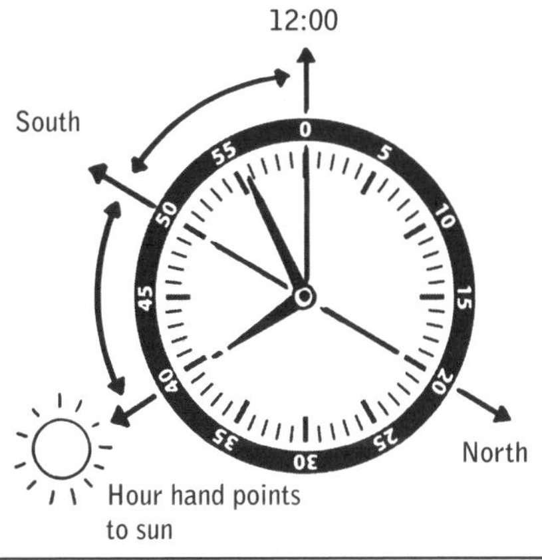

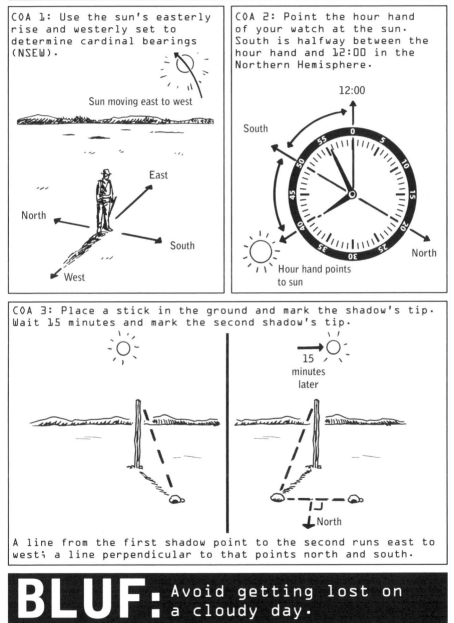

COA 3: Place a stick in the ground and mark the shadow's tip. Wait 15 minutes and mark the second shadow's tip.

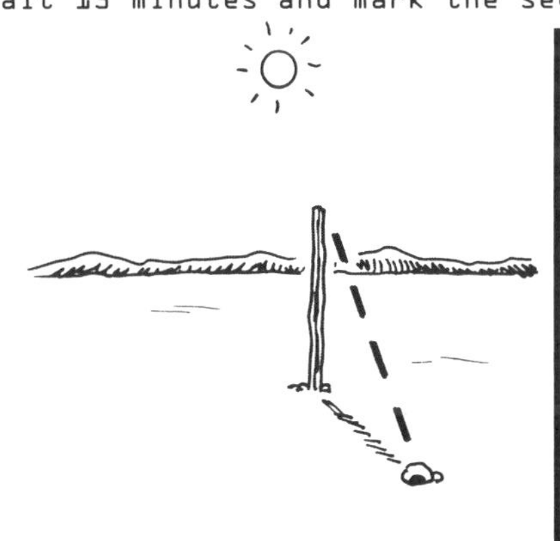

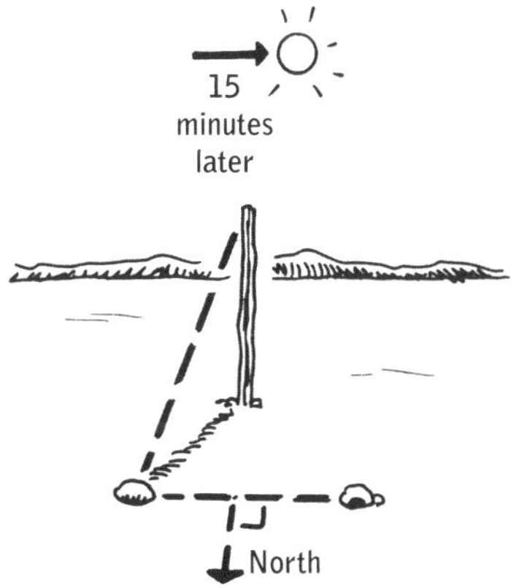

A line from the first shadow point to the second runs east to west; a line perpendicular to that points north and south.

BLUF: Avoid getting lost on a cloudy day.

007 Celestial Navigation

Guided by the ancient practice of celestial navigation—the star-gazing technique that ferried countless sailors, pirates, and explorers to distant shores and plundered treasure—any traveler should be able to determine cardinal directions, even in pitch-black darkness. Which is good news for civilians crossing a blistering desert (see page 52) or fleeing disaster, when traveling after sundown may be unavoidable.

The apparent position of the stars in the nighttime sky, and the selection of stars that will be visible to you, will depend on your latitude and longitude, the season, the cloud cover, and the time of night. In the northern hemisphere, the North Star is an effective gauge of northerly direction. Because the star sits so near the earth's north pole, its position in the sky is almost unchanging. The earth's rotation causes other stars to appear to move across the sky, but the North Star remains pinned at the globe's upper pole as the planet spins like a top. The North Star isn't the brightest in the sky, so search for it by identifying nearby constellations: the Big Dipper, the Little Dipper, and Cassiopeia. The star lies in a direct line with the two outer stars of the Big Dipper's bowl (see opposite—using the distance between those two stars as a measuring stick, it's roughly five lengths away) and with the central star or topmost point formed by the W in Cassiopeia. The North Star is also the last star in the Little Dipper's handle.

There is no consistently visible star at the southern pole, but in the Southern Hemisphere you can determine direction by locating the Southern Cross. Trace an imaginary line from the constellation's brightest star to the star directly opposite, through the longest axis of the constellation's cross; using the axis as a measure, the southern pole lies four-and-a-half lengths away, in the direction of its brightest star.

At the equator, locate Orion's Belt. The three horizontal stars that comprise Orion's belt lie along the east-west line; Orion's torso points toward the north, his legs toward the south.

No. 007: Celestial Navigation

CONOP: Use the stars to determine direction.

COA 1: In the northern hemisphere, find and use Polaris, the North Star.

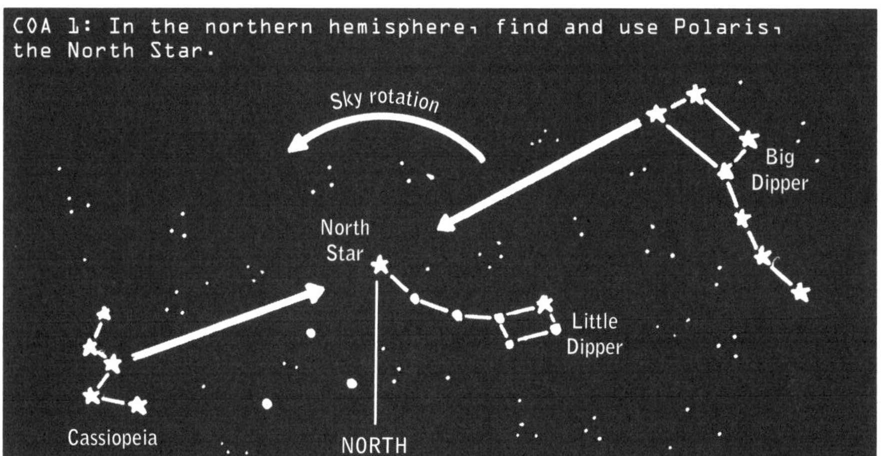

COA 2: In the southern hemisphere, find and use the Southern Cross.

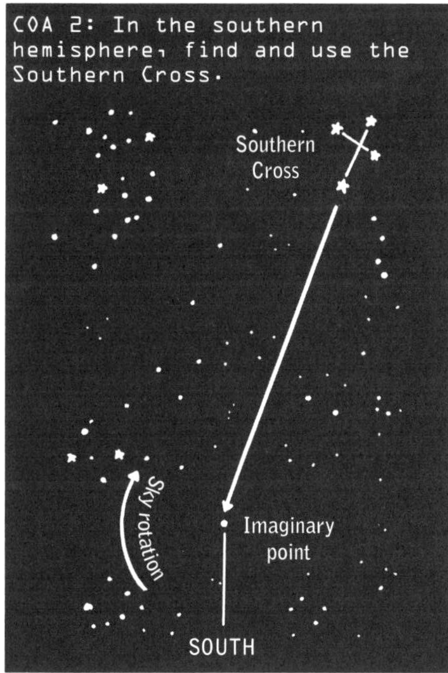

COA 3: At the equator, find and use Orion's Belt.

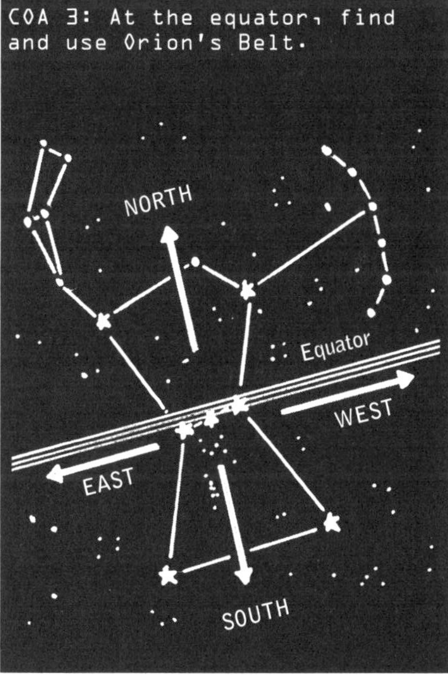

BLUF: Do not lose your compass, map, or GPS.

008 Magnetic Navigation

More than an entertaining science experiment, a DIY compass is a useful navigational aid—and like all great improvised tools, it's made from materials that can be leveraged from a variety of available sources. Electric wiring can be found in radio speakers, flashlights, the harness of a vehicle. Batteries are tucked inside an endless array of devices. And everyone should have a roll of duct tape in the back of his or her trunk. All you really need is a bit of serendipity or forethought in procuring a needle or a slender length of steel.

Using a few simple steps, a steel needle or piece of wire fencing can be magnetized and employed to similar effect as store-bought compasses, which rely on magnetized needles that align themselves with the earth's magnetic field or "magnetosphere." An electric charge will cause ions in the needle to congregate at one end, and when floated weightlessly, the needle will automatically point north-south.

One difference between the two versions is that store-bought compasses are properly magnetized so that one of their needles aligns south, the other north. Ideally, you'd want to magnetize only one end of your needle, but this can be difficult to manage when working with such a small and thin gauge. So use your needle as a source of more general information, to find the axis representing north and south. In order to determine which end is which, you'll need to confirm via another form of natural navigation. (See pages 14, 16, and 18.)

Note: The northern direction on a compass is actually the earth's northern magnetic pole, which lies about one thousand miles south of true north, the earth's geographical north pole. Improvised compasses should be combined with maps when possible, as they only provide a general sense of direction.

No. 008: Magnetic Navigation

CONOP: Make a compass to determine direction.

COA 1: Magnetize a sewing needle with a nine-volt battery and a piece of insulated wire. Strip wire at both ends.

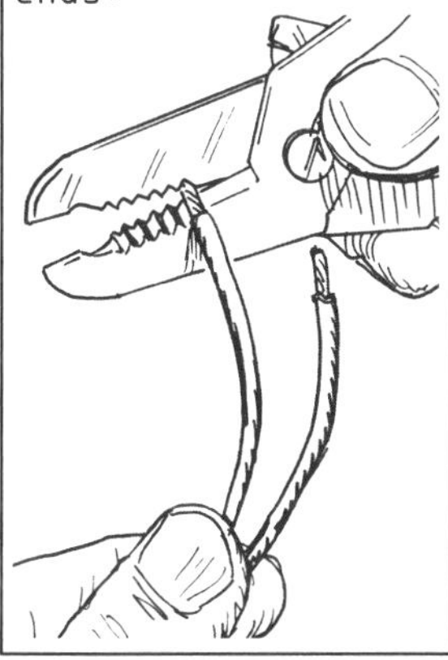

COA 2: Wrap center of wire around sewing needle.

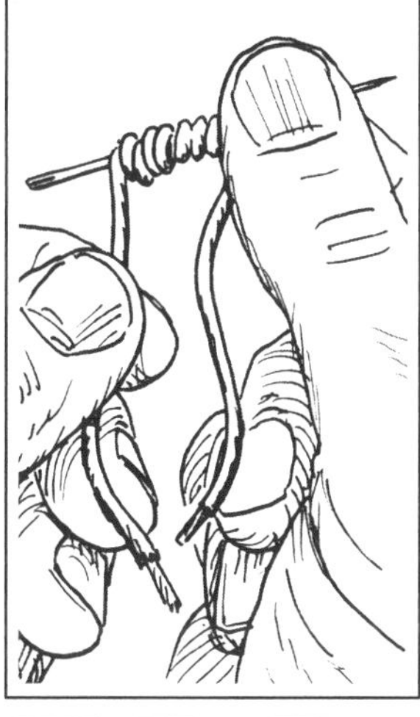

COA 3: Holding insulated part of wire, contact exposed ends to battery terminals for a few seconds.

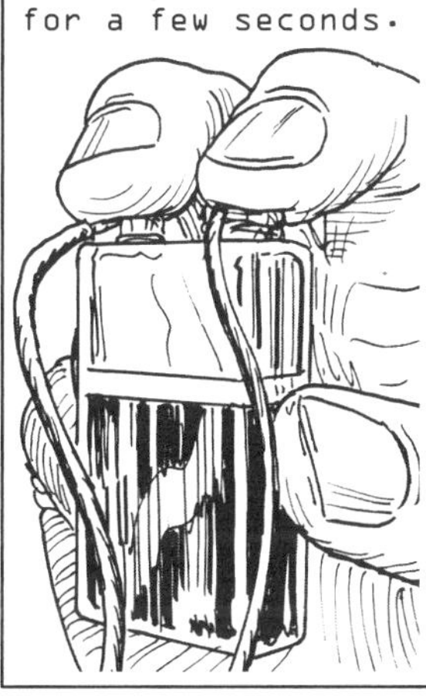

COA 4: Place needle on a leaf and float in puddle of water to find the north-south axis.

COA 5: Or float needle atop a cork in an improvised tray made of duct tape.

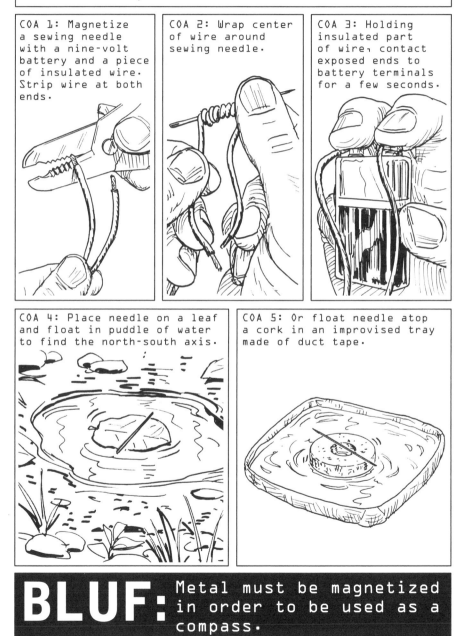

BLUF: Metal must be magnetized in order to be used as a compass.

PART III

SURVIVAL IN THE WILD

009 Minimum EDC, Jungle Environment

Dark, loud, and buzzing with dangerous life forms, a jungle can quickly become one of the most frustrating environments on earth, its terrain presenting even experienced navigators with uniquely challenging obstacles to transit and survival. Progress at ground level is often undertaken in near darkness, every step impeded by thorny, sticky, and sometimes poisonous plant life with a supernatural ability to grab onto skin or clothing. Terrain will be overshadowed by the lush canopy of trees and vines that makes jungles and rainforests appear so green and idyllic and also blocks a large portion of visible light from the dark and damp forest floor. The environment is hot and humid, yet demands full coverage for protection against insects and plant life. Discomfort is a given.

If you find yourself lost in a jungle, know that the density of your surroundings and the relentless oppressiveness of the climate are likely to increase feelings of panic and hopelessness. Keep moving. Momentum is important in a survival scenario.

How to Clear a Path Through the Jungle

Many factors can make efficient transit through a jungle a losing battle, but following streams or game trails may diminish the need for trail-clearing. Regardless of your path, a proper knife is essential for cutting your way through the jungle's thick matrix of brush, vines, and limbs, an ever-present reality that makes even a single step a challenge. The optimal tool is the Kukri, an indigenous long-bladed knife whose curved blade shortens the overall length of the tool without compromising blade length, thus making it easier to carry.

To clear a path, swing the knife in diagonal motions, using an overhand hold.

For ease of access, the knife should be worn in a leather or Kydex

No. 009: Minimum EDC, Jungle Environment

CONOP: Everyday carry requirements for rainforest operations.

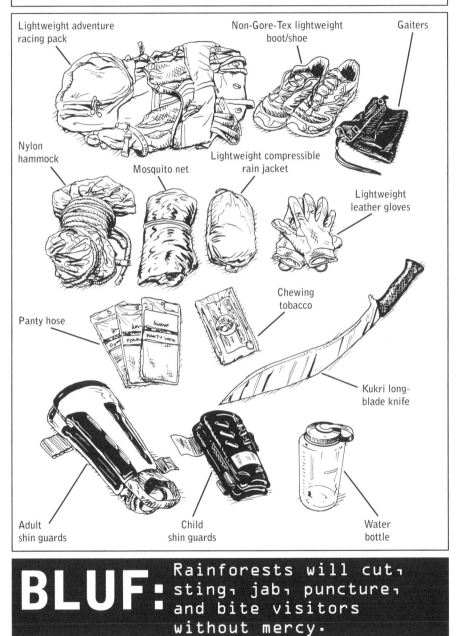

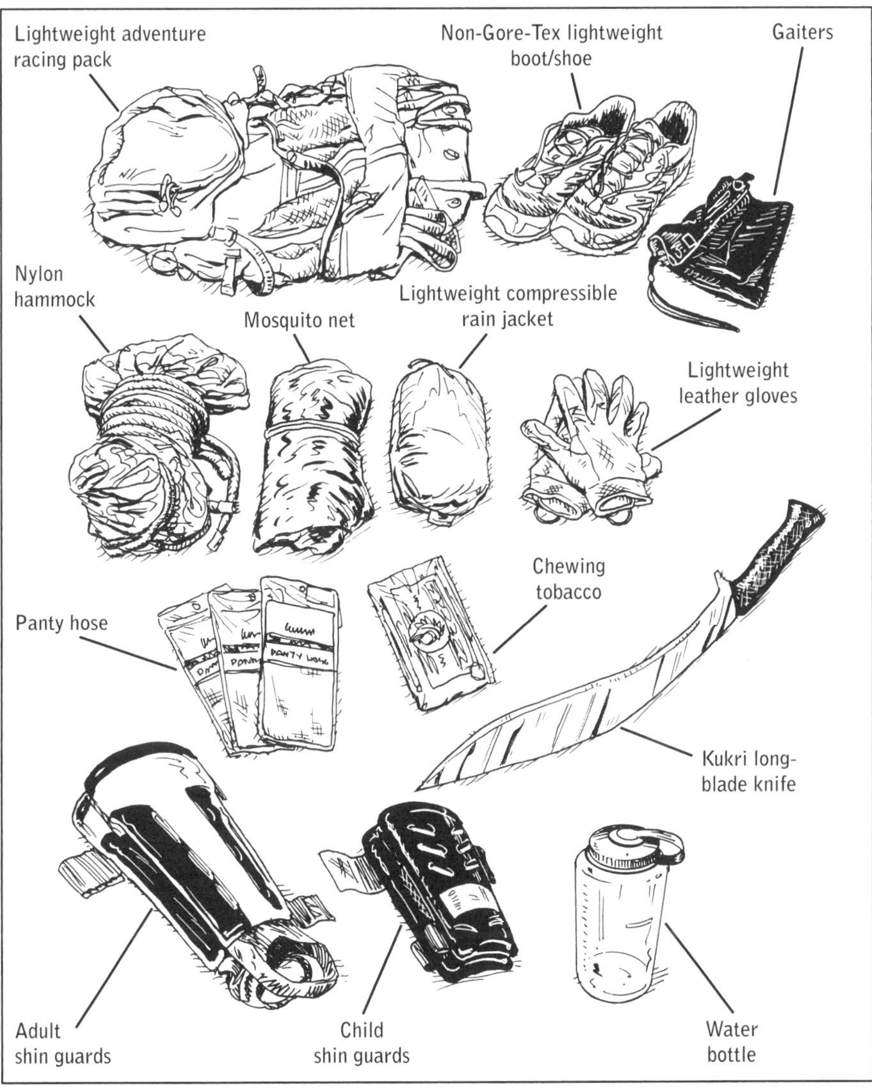

BLUF: Rainforests will cut, sting, jab, puncture, and bite visitors without mercy.

waist sheath—you'll find many uses for a sturdy knife in the jungle, from procuring and preparing food, to building a shelter, to self-defense, so you'll want it close at hand. A sharpening stone is also a must.

Though a jungle is the opposite of a desert in being so densely packed with vegetation and natural features, there are similarities when it comes to navigation. In both environments, a lack of topographical differentiation can make it easy to lose your way. Additionally, in a jungle, GPS devices are likely to fail due to the thickness of the canopy. And, unlike in desert sand, footprints may not be noticeable, increasing the likelihood of circling back on yourself. Travel with a map and a compass, and use a Sharpie or colored tape (see page 224) to mark your path as you go. This will have the added benefit of creating a trail for potential rescuers.

Protecting Yourself from the Environment

The jungle's plant life can inflict a surprising amount of damage upon unprotected flesh. Shin guards in adult and child sizes, worn on the forearms and lower legs, can help protect your limbs from sharp, thorny obstacles and over-emphatic swings of the blade as you clear your path. Forearms, shins, hands, and feet are the primary points of contact with any sharp brush and thorns you encounter, which makes a pair of lightweight leather gloves essential as well.

Any exposed skin is also vulnerable to the jungle's most persistent class of predators. With potential foes ranging from dengue- or Zika-carrying mosquitoes to army ants and poisonous centipedes, jungles are rife with critters whose bites could result in a life-threatening fever. Even a single bite from an army ant could render your hand inoperable for a day, so proper coverage is essential—from a breathable long-sleeved shirt and pants to gaiters that seal off the lower extremities and prevent leeches and spiders from crawling up pant legs. Overlap clothing and gear to create protective seals.

For additional security, layer on panty hose under clothing. Leeches cannot penetrate its tight weave or obtain traction on its slippery surface, though they have a surprising knack for fighting their way through layers of clothing. A full pair may be worn on the lower body, with a secondary pair cut off at the feet and waist to provide additional protection to arms. To deal the predatory worms a final death blow, add water to a pouch or tin of chewing tobacco and let it soak for a few minutes, then rub the solution over extremities and onto panty hose and clothing. No matter how carefully covered you are, leeches *will* find their way inside your clothing, and nicotine paralyzes and kills them faster than man-made repellents.

A panel of mosquito netting is a baseline essential. Wear a small patch over your face while you're working your way through the jungle, and drape the rest over your sleeping quarters (see page 34) at night. Failing to protect yourself is not an option.

Multiple changes of socks and a breathable shoe help keep the feet warm and dry, an issue that pertains not only to comfort but also to survival. Your choice of footwear can make or break you in the jungle. To avoid trench foot or jungle rot, the result of the environment's inescapable humidity and the high probability of wading through water, steer clear of shoes made of Gore-Tex or other non-breathable materials. These will trap in moisture, which can begin to degrade your skin in less than a day. Left untreated, trench foot can result in gangrene and the very real possibility of amputation. Remove socks at night and anytime you stop to rest, to let your feet dry. Hang wet socks on the outside of your pack to dry during transit.

010 Collect Water in a Rainforest

Perhaps the wettest non-aqueous environment on earth, the rainforest offers plenty of clean, drinkable water to visitors who know where to look—as well as many opportunities for taking in dangerous parasites and bacteria from contaminated sources. If you find a river or stream and happen to be carrying water filtration tablets or the equipment necessary to boil the water clean, you're in luck. If not, mitigate against the risk of contamination by digging into the ground a few feet from the shoreline, where you'll find water that's been filtered through the soil's rocks and sediment.

Even when you're far from rivers and streams, the humid ecosystem offers many options for hydration. Frequent rain is one such source, and a container is all you need in order to collect it. No water bottle? Cut a segment of bamboo just above and below a joint. The hollow plant is solid at the joints, creating a closed-off cylinder that can be stood upright on a level surface.

The plant can also provide a direct source of clean water, filtered by its passage through the soil and the plant's cell walls. To access, cut a hole just below a joint of live, green bamboo, then use a smaller bamboo shoot as a straw to drink the water that courses through the stalk.

The rainforest's abundant vines can be tapped similarly in the name of survival. The key to success is to cut two notches in a vine, the first high, the second (the "bitter end") low to the ground. The higher notch allows air to flow in, pushing water down to the collection point below.

A more labor-intensive but plentiful source can be found in plantain and banana palms, whose root systems are shaped like giant bowls—full of clean drinking water coming right up from the palm's roots. Cutting the trunk requires muscle power and a sharp blade, but the effort will be worthwhile.

No. 010: Collect Water in a Rainforest

CONOP: Finding filtered drinkable water in the rainforest.

COA 1: Cut a hole just below a bamboo joint, insert small-diameter bamboo straw and drink. Each section contains drinkable water.

COA 2: Cut notch at highest point on a vine, cut bitter end, and water will flow.

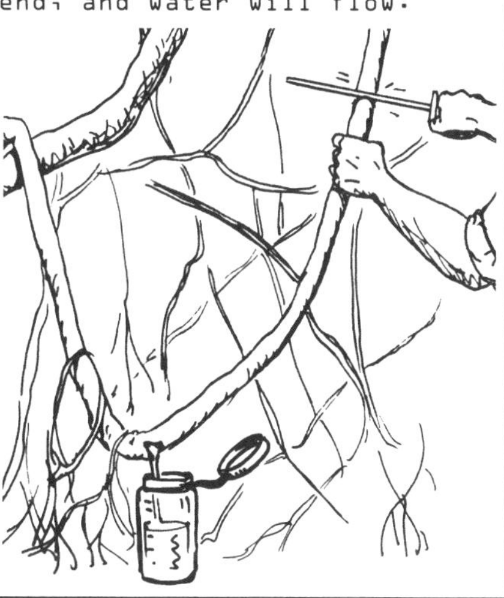

COA 3: To drink directly from banana or plantain trees, cut tree down at base and scoop out stump until bowl fills with water.

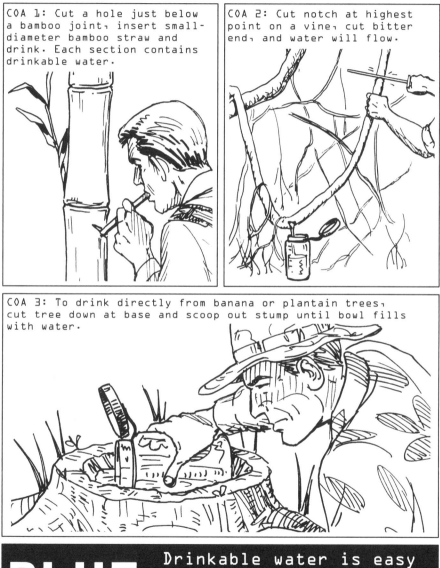

BLUF: Drinkable water is easy to find in the jungle, for those who know where to look.

011 Build a Rainforest Fire

An overnight stay in a handmade bed forged from materials found in the environment is unlikely to be extremely comfortable. But the addition of a fire may make the difference between a few hours of much needed rest and a night spent tossing and turning.

Nighttime in the jungle can be damp and cold—and it's also the time when many of the forest's insects and predators come to life. Though most insects are attracted to light, they will be repelled by the fire's smoke. Larger animals will be repelled by its flames.

Fires are obviously also essential in any survival environment as a means to cook food and purify water gathered from rivers or streams. In a jungle, you can leverage the natural abundance of highly flammable bamboo to light an easy-to-start blaze. Look for dried pieces of bamboo that have fallen to the ground and are a light tan in color, not green.

You'll need a knife (see page 24) to collect shavings from the skin of the bamboo, which will act as kindling. The plant's core will act as tinder and fuel, and friction will create the spark necessary to start any fire.

Once you've prepped your materials, it should only take about twenty strokes of your scored bamboo halves (see illustration) to create smoke. Blowing on or waving your hand above the kindling will turn that smoke into spark.

Note: Bamboo, an invasive species that is one of the rainforest's most bountiful offerings, can also be leveraged as a fish-catching spear (see page 32), a sleeping surface (see page 34), a cooking vessel, or a receptacle for food—among its many other uses for survival.

No. 011: Build a Rainforest Fire

CONOP: Make fire with a single bamboo shoot.

COA 1: Collect dead, dry bamboo shoot and shave exterior to create kindling.

COA 2: Cut and split a two-foot section. Score one section at its center, then puncture score with a small hole.

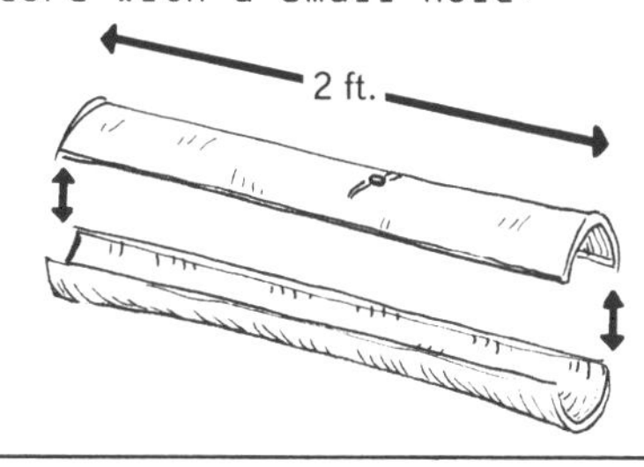

COA 3: Place hole directly over "ball" of kindling.

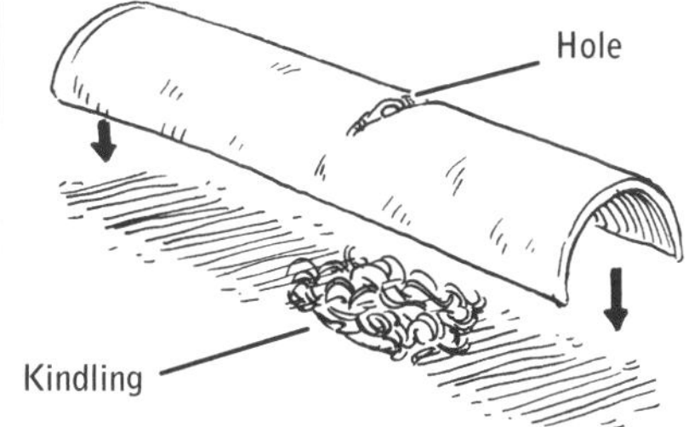

COA 4: Match edge of unscored split with scored hole and slowly saw back and forth until kindling smokes.

COA 5: Once you have smoke, blow on tinder lightly to increase burn and create flame. Add tinder to increase size of fire.

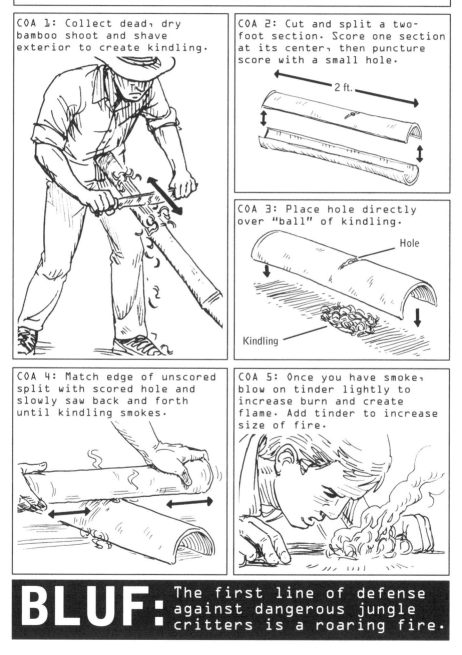

BLUF: The first line of defense against dangerous jungle critters is a roaring fire.

012 Scavenge and Spearfish Rainforest Survival Food

There are as many ways to get sick in a rainforest as there are sources of food in this rich and life-filled environment. Compounding the threat of mosquito-borne tropical illnesses like malaria, dengue fever, and the Zika virus, food-borne ailments like trichinosis, salmonellosis, and leptospirosis are just as common in a rainforest as in any natural environment. If you're unable to cook your food, seek out fish and insects such as worms, grubs, and termites. These will still be safest when cooked, but can be eaten raw, as the parasites they tend to carry are generally less life-threatening than those hosted by mammals or reptiles. They're also rich in proteins and the essential fats and nutrients needed to sustain human life.

Avoid roaches, which are well-known carriers of disease, and brightly colored insects, which stand a fair chance of being poisonous. While snakes, frogs, and other reptiles may be plentiful, they can be coated with salmonella and other bacteria and thus need to be cooked for safety (see pages 60 and 70). Snails, also common in the environment, are fond of dining on poisonous plants.

Depending on your starting condition and weight, you might be able to survive without any food for up to two months. But to avoid going into a state of semi-starvation that will make it impossible for you to find your way out of the wilderness, you'll ideally want to consume around two thousand calories per day. That translates to about 1.5 pounds of insects or 2 to 3 pounds of fish, or some combination of the two.

To catch fish using a spear carved out of bamboo (see illustration), wade into shallow waterways and stand very still. Fish will approach if you don't reveal yourself as a predator. In still water, toss blades of grass or other pieces of natural debris on the surface as you see fish approach; they will mistake the detritus for bugs and come up to bite.

No. 012: Scavenge and Spearfish Rainforest Survival Food

CONOP: Hunt and eat safest, most common foods in the rainforest.

COA 1: Worms, grubs, and termites are just beneath soil, rocks, and bark.

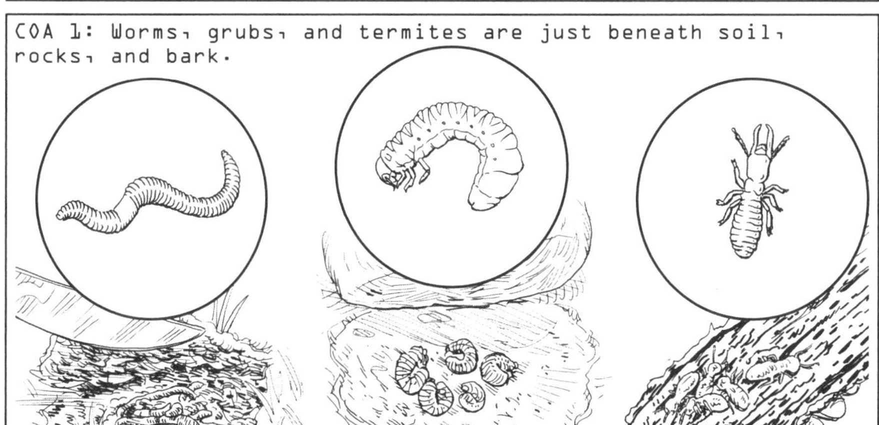

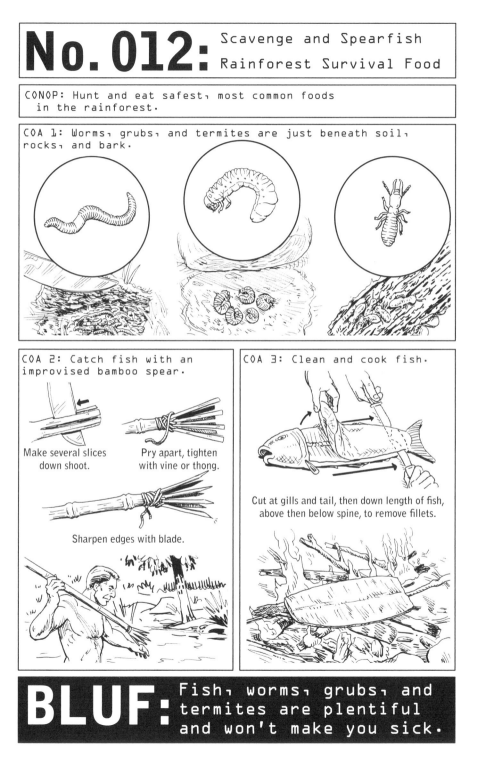

COA 2: Catch fish with an improvised bamboo spear.

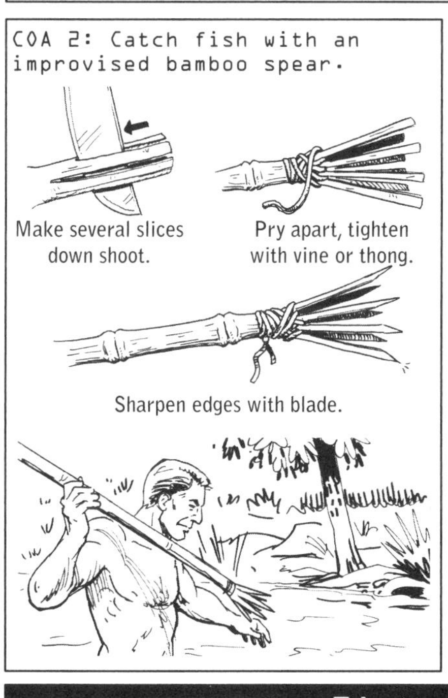

Make several slices down shoot.
Pry apart, tighten with vine or thong.
Sharpen edges with blade.

COA 3: Clean and cook fish.

Cut at gills and tail, then down length of fish, above then below spine, to remove fillets.

BLUF: Fish, worms, grubs, and termites are plentiful and won't make you sick.

013 Build a Bamboo Hammock

The ground is the last place a visitor wants to be when the sun goes down and the forests' creatures—from centipedes and spiders to snakes, bats, boars, and the big cats who reign above them all—come out to feed. A warm body on the forest floor is a perfect target for predators, large and small.

That's why the optimal temporary shelter in a jungle environment is a cocoon-style nylon hammock (see page 25) that lifts the sleeper up off the ground. Small, collapsible, and easy to set up, an adventure hammock specifically made for rainforest conditions can easily be tied from tree to tree, with a protective swath of mosquito netting dangling from a cord a few feet above it. But if your primary hammock is torn (a real possibility given the prevalence of thorny plant life in the environment), you can make a quick and surprisingly durable version from a single shoot of bamboo.

Start building your shelter well before sundown—the forest's thick canopy will muffle the jungle in darkness long before the sun actually dips below the horizon. Select a piece of green, live bamboo for strength, and leverage the plant's unique flexibility to your advantage by splitting that single shoot into long horizontal lines woven through with shorter lengths from the same shoot (see illustration). Selecting a shoot two to three feet longer than your height will leave sturdy knobs that can be attached to trees with pieces of vine, and the resulting construction will spread apart to absorb your body weight.

Sleeping in a suspended position does expose you to circulating air. If the nighttime environment is cool, layer loose brush between the hammock and your body to serve as extra insulation.

None of these measures may guarantee a comfortable night's sleep, but they will maximize your chances of waking up to see another sunrise.

No. 013: Build a Bamboo Hammock

CONOP: Construct a hammock from a single bamboo shoot.

COA 1: Collect a single, large-diameter bamboo shoot and cut a length at least two feet taller than your body height. Carve and "canoe" open middle portion of bamboo, leaving a foot at both ends of shoot whole.

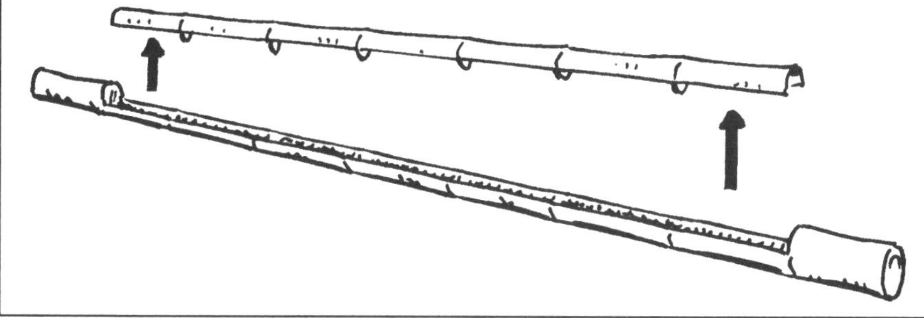

COA 2: Reinforce both ends with vine and leave plenty of slack to hang hammock.

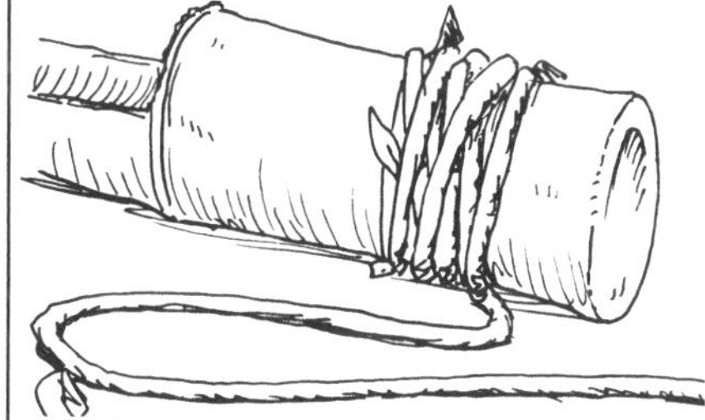

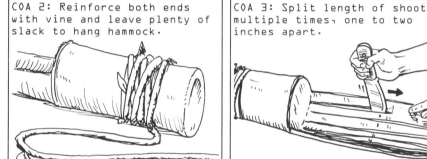

COA 3: Split length of shoot multiple times, one to two inches apart.

COA 4: Shave and weave short bamboo lengths to fan open hammock.

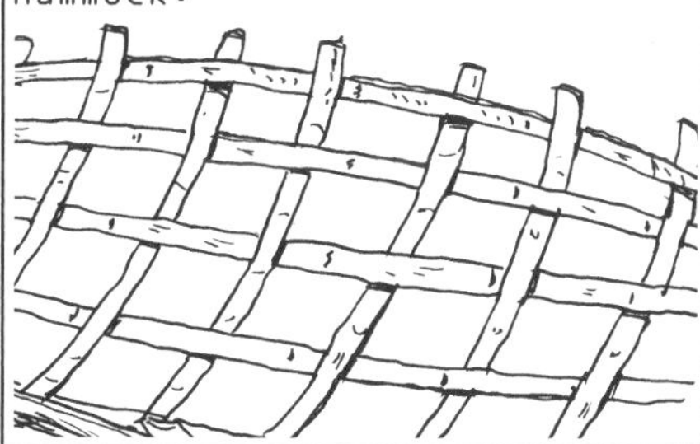

COA 5: Hang hammock from tree to tree.

BLUF: Never, ever spend a night on the jungle floor.

014 Escape a Wild Boar Attack

What are your chances of running into a wild boar? Higher than you might think, given that the animal ranges across a wider territory than almost any other mammal on earth. Wild boar attacks on humans are infrequent, and the tusked animal is more likely to run from you than charge. But when startled, especially if accompanied by its piglets, this forefather of domestically bred pigs becomes a lot less friendly than your average farm animal.

And it runs a whole lot faster, too.

Plentiful in a variety of forest types across several continents and increasingly found in suburban areas around the world, the animals are characterized by sharp tusks, tough snouts, and large, bony heads. These are the tools the wild pigs use to dig and forage for food—and the lethal weapons they recruit as a means of self-defense. The creatures are legendarily ferocious when provoked, with jaws that can easily crush bone, and massive, armored fore-bodies that make them impervious to shots fired from a standard-issue pistol. (A .308 rifle round would be the better choice.)

If you spot a wild boar from a distance, steer clear of its path. If the animal is nearby, get to higher ground—climb a tree, a car, or a large boulder. If you are charged by a wild boar, which can travel at speeds up to thirty-five miles per hour, outrunning the beast won't be an option. But you can take advantage of the creature's heft and lack of agility by doing last-minute sidesteps.

As a method of last resort, fight back. Aim to shoot or stab the animal in the face, between its shoulder blades, in its belly, or at its axillary nodes, just beneath its front legs. Do not let the animal take the fight to the ground—maintain your height advantage at all costs.

No. 014: Escape a Wild Boar Attack

CONOP: Identify and escape a wild boar attack.

COA 1: Assess your environment. Risk is highest at dusk and dawn. If you cross paths with a wild boar, maintain safe distance. Attacks are highest during winter months.

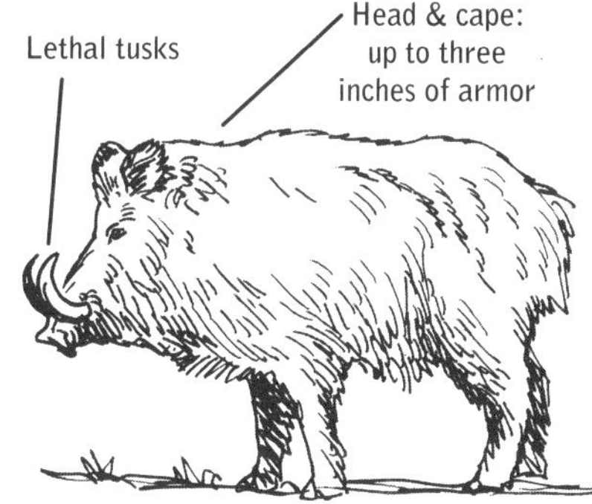

COA 2: Climb a tree, boulder, or car at least six feet off the ground. Larger boars will walk their front hoofs up obstacles.

COA 3: Perform last-minute sidestep when charged. Move at the very last minute, like a matador. Avoid lethal tusks.

COA 4: Fight back. Maintain standing position at all costs. Shoot or stab strategically. A boar's head and cape are heavily armored, stopping some bullets and preventing any damage with a knife.

BLUF: Wild boars are heavily armored, and faster than you.

015 Minimum EDC, Arctic Environment

"Pack light, freeze at night." A common expression among military troops hauling 150-pound packs across frigid terrain, the saying holds true for wintertime campers and arctic adventurers alike. You may be able to maintain your core temperature while traveling through twenty-degree terrain during daytime, but staying warm will prove much harder when temperatures drop far below zero and you've stopped moving for the night.

Better safe than sorry. Pack gear in a slant-bottomed sled in order to be able to carry more of the large, bulky items you'll need for warmth. You'll consume less energy pulling supplies across snow and ice than you will attempting to carry them, which is important because being as efficient as possible about your energy expenditure will help you stay one step ahead of hypothermia (page 52).

Gear and Supplies

Arctic environments are ruthless, matched only by scorching deserts in their hostility toward human life. Assuming there's little chance of finding yourself in an arctic zone by accident, proper preparation for the temperature extremes and food and fuel needs of this environment cannot be overstated. Research is essential. Know the temperature ranges, risks of avalanche, and weather patterns so that you can appropriately pack for and map your itinerary. Navigational aids (not pictured) should include a compass, a GPS device, and maps. If one fails, the others can act as backup. Sunglasses are key, as the reflection of blinding sunlight off white snow can make navigation a challenge. Eye strain and photokeratitis, a painful optical sunburn also known as sun blindness, are also risks.

A snow anchor and a pair of snowshoes act as fail-safes should conditions become impassable by ski. In thick drifts of soft powder, snowshoes displace body weight across the wide, webbed underside

No. 015: Minimum EDC, Arctic Environment

CONOP: Everyday carry requirements for arctic operations.

BLUF: You can never have enough layers.

of the shoe, reducing the amount of sinkage. If snow reaches up to your waist, you could expend hundreds of precious calories in the process of traveling just a few feet.

Should conditions become even dicier, a snow anchor could be the tool that allows you to stop your slide down a steep incline. Learn to use one before you travel. The equivalent of the Kukri knife you'd carry in the jungle (page 24), a snow saw and shovel are the indispensable multi-use tools that could enable you to catch your dinner, build a shelter, or surmount an unexpected obstacle.

In addition to a cold-weather tent and highly insulated sleeping bag, low-temperature sleeping requires a bivy sack, a thin and non-porous external shell layer. Sealing in as much body heat as possible is the only hedge against a night spent tossing and turning—or worse. A thick sleeping pad will help insulate you from the cold ground, which acts as a sponge for the precious heat you're emitting; a folded up "smother" or fire blanket can fulfill the same purpose, while also providing essential insulation anytime you need to warm up quickly. A few lit candles can bump up the temperature inside a tent or snow shelter (page 48) by a few degrees, but must be extinguished before you go to sleep to mitigate the risk of fire.

Food supplies must be extensive. The body burns nearly twice as much fuel in low-temperature environments, requiring food sources that are dense, high in fat, and plentiful. In addition to prepackaged dehydrated meals and energy bars, pack high-fat foods like peanut butter, bacon fat, nuts, and chocolate. There's no such thing as too many calories when your metabolic system is working overtime to burn food into life-sustaining heat. Combine that with the energy expended by hauling a heavy sled and potentially trekking across long distances, and you've got a recipe for tremendous hunger—and rapid weight loss if caloric intake is insufficient. For optimal health, plan to consume five thousand or more calories per day, and pack extra emergency rations just in case.

Water filtration devices are a given. Though in emergencies snow and ice can be consumed without filtering with minimal risk (page 42), filtering is generally recommended, particularly if water is coming from streams or lakes.

Specialized camping retailers offer a great quantity of cold-weather items that will increase your level of comfort, but weigh the inclusion of additional items against the extra weight they'll add to your load.

Clothing

Your primary weapon of defense against the external temperature is a multilayer system that collects body heat and seals out wind and cold. Puffy, porous layers of fleece and down won't perform if they aren't properly sealed off, which is why a high-performance outer shell is key. Choose one in a Gore-Tex-like cold-weather material that locks in heat but remains slightly breathable; unlike with zero-porosity materials, this breathability helps wick sweat off the body.

Keeping not only warm but dry is essential in a cold climate, as a layer of moisture on the skin will quickly freeze when exposed to the elements. Wet socks in particular can rapidly cause tissue die-off as vasoconstriction shuts off blood supply in order to prevent heat loss through wet feet, which syphon off heat twenty-five times faster than dry feet. Even in warm but damp climates (see page 54), cotton kills. Moisture-wicking wool socks are a non-negotiable defense against trench foot.

016 Collect Arctic Drinking Water

When you're trekking through an arctic environment, food and warmth will be hard to come by—but one thing you can be sure of is that you won't be going thirsty. With water all around you in the form of snow and ice, options for hydration will never be far. And they're often very pure. But the principal risk in arctic environments, hypothermia (see page 50), can be compounded by eating snow or ice—cold substances that will bring down your core temperature as they pass through your neck, one of the areas of the body that is most vulnerable to heat loss. The neck's carotid arteries continuously pump a large supply of warm blood directly to the brain, and the jugular vein sends that supply back down to the heart. That's some of your body's most valuable real estate.

Collect Pure Water from the Environment: Though heating water to its boiling point is always the safest course of action as far as purification, fresh snow and ice collected from areas free of standing water or other visible sources of contamination can be consumed with relative confidence. Most bacteria present in the source water won't survive at freezing temperatures.

Choose Ice Over Snow: The former has a greater fluid density, while snow is partly comprised of air.

Melt Ice with Body Heat or Fire: Fuel is precious in glacial environments, so leverage your body heat to melt ice to drinkable water when you can. If you're appropriately layered, you'll release vast amounts of body heat during transit no matter how cold the environment. Avoiding the brachial arteries that travel through the armpit and the femoral arteries of the inner thighs, valuable convoys for a significant portion of the body's blood supply, place ice in a water bottle and allow it to melt between layers of your clothing. When stopped, conserve body heat and switch to melting ice with fire.

No. 016: Collect Arctic Drinking Water

CONOP: Finding filtered drinkable water in arctic conditions.

COA 1: Drink freshwater from lakes, rivers, and streams.

COA 2: Always drink melted ice instead of melted snow.

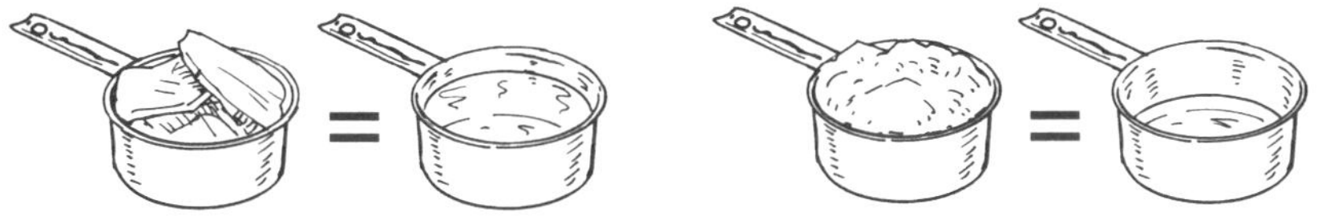

COA 3: Melt ice with body heat instead of fire.

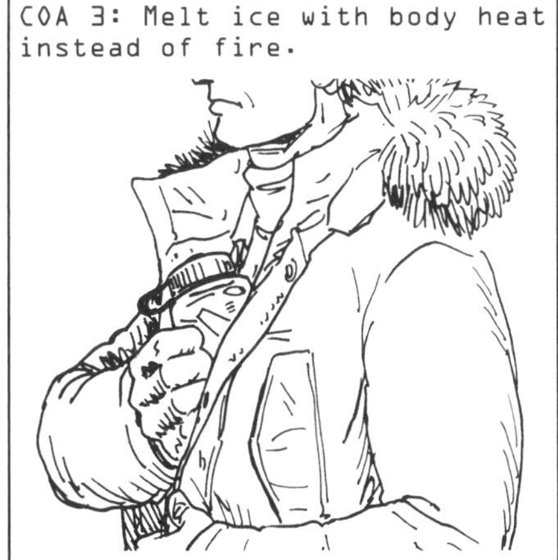

COA 4: When fuel is abundant, melt ice with fire.

BLUF: Always choose water over ice, and ice over snow.

017 Build an Arctic Fire

When snow and ice cover the landscape, locating materials with which to build fire can be a challenge—but given the dire need for a heat source in a subzero environment, expending additional effort to gather materials will be worthwhile.

Despite their appearance, arctic environments may actually be quite rich in dormant and dead plant life. Camp near trees, and you're likely to find fallen branches and dried-out ground cover beneath the snow. Digging in one spot may not yield results, but a treasure trove of kindling and tinder could be buried a foot away. Remove the outer layer of icy or snow-dampened bark, and you'll find dry, usable tinder inside. These endeavors will be time-consuming—but depending on the circumstances, they may also be lifesaving.

With kindling and fuel in hand, harnessing the latent energy of any extra batteries you may be carrying as a fire starter is a potentially dangerous but manageable proposition. Steel wool, an indispensable scouring agent for outdoor dish washing, can be repurposed as a bridging mechanism. As the batteries' charged electrons rapidly course through the wool's fine steel threads (see illustration), they will create a significant amount of heat. The wool's cocoon-like structure, with air pockets distributed throughout its intermeshed threads, creates an ideal environment for combustion.

To assemble, bridge both ends of two AA or AAA batteries stacked positive terminal to negative terminal (anode to cathode) with a length of steel wool, or plunge a single nine-volt battery directly into steel wool. Keep fingers away from the contact points and be prepared to swiftly position the wool beneath your pile of kindling. The wool will quickly turn red and begin to smoke.

To create a black smoke signal that will contrast an all-white environment, add tar-rich pinecones once your kindling is well lit.

No. 017: Build an Arctic Fire

CONOP: Make fire with batteries and steel wool.

COA 1: Collect dead dry grass, branches, and pinecones.

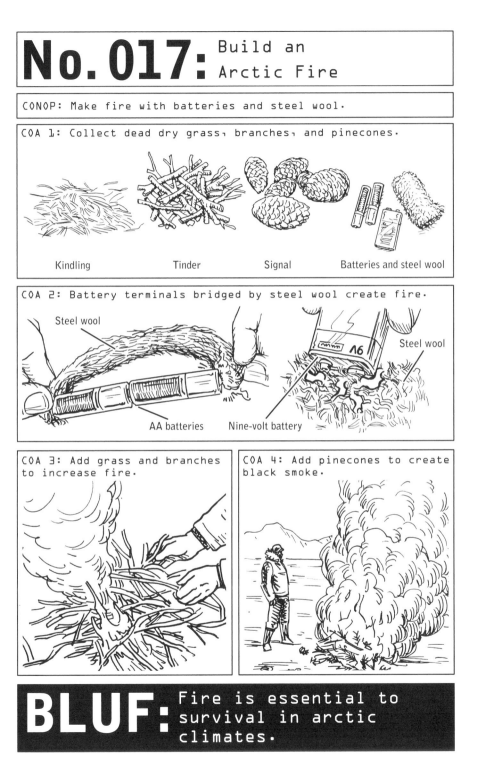

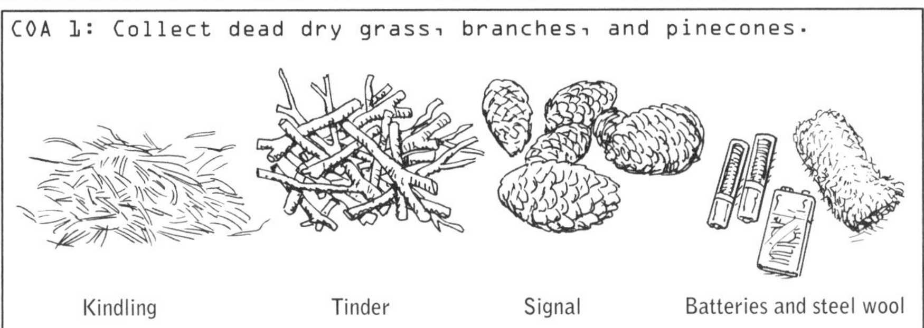

COA 2: Battery terminals bridged by steel wool create fire.

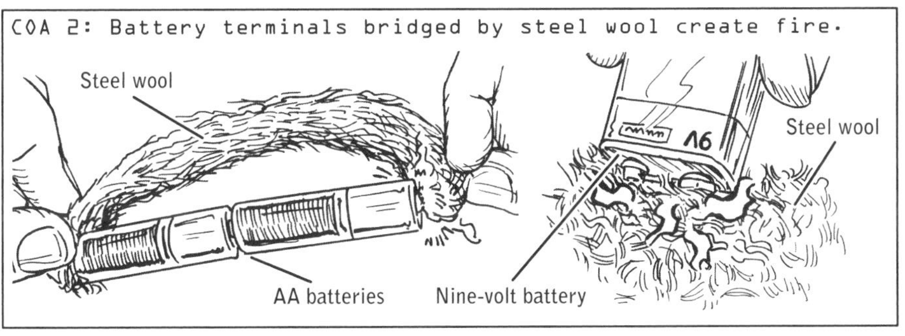

COA 3: Add grass and branches to increase fire.

COA 4: Add pinecones to create black smoke.

BLUF: Fire is essential to survival in arctic climates.

018 Locate Survival Foods in Subzero Conditions

In an arctic survival scenario, maintaining core temperature becomes the human body's number one priority. To that aim, the body will sacrifice fat cells, fingers and toes, and consciousness at the outer limits. And it will burn through any available food at nearly twice the normal rate.

Keeping body temperature fifty or more degrees above external temperature is hard work, requiring a substantial amount of fuel. While you can survive on far less, the optimal number of calories for functioning at full capacity in a low-temperature environment is five thousand. If you're trekking across foot-deep drifts in order to find your way out of a barren wasteland, you're going to need your strength.

Look Along Shorelines: While snow-covered environments may look devoid of sustenance, the shorelines of arctic lakes and rivers are frequently home to nutritional powerhouses like mussels and clams, which can safely be eaten raw and can also double as bait.

Carve Fishing Holes: Finding enough fat to stoke your body's engines will be a challenge, and wading into ice-cold water in search of fatty fish while trying to survive freezing temperatures is inadvisable. If lakes or riverbeds are frozen solid, however, you can use an ice saw to carve fishing holes into the surface. Ensure that the ice layer is at least four inches deep before you walk out onto it by using a knife to test thickness from the shore.

Set and Monitor Multiple Lines: Cut multiple fishing holes to maximize your chances of hauling in a catch, and monitor them with improvised bobbers. Tie lengths of fishing line to pairs of sticks longer than the diameter of your fishing holes and stacked into X shapes. When a fish bites, the sticks will jam across the hole.

No. 018: Locate Survival Foods in Subzero Conditions

CONOP: Hunt and eat safe, high-calorie food in arctic conditions.

COA 1: Clams, mussels, and sea cucumbers are abundant along arctic coastlines.

COA 2: Properly cut multiple ice fishing holes.

COA 3: Set fishing lines, hooks, and improvised bobbers.

BLUF: Consume 5,000 calories per day to survive and thrive in arctic conditions.

019 Build Expedient Arctic Shelters

If you are forced to shelter in a wilderness environment, a preexisting form of natural cover will be a lucky and time-saving find. A cave or rock formation can provide a night's refuge or respite from a storm, as can trees with dense foliage or root systems with deep pockets. But take precautions—a space that looks like it could provide great cover for you may be just as appealing to wildlife. Look for animal tracks, feces, and trampled vegetation before you set up camp. A polar bear or other animal that has staked out a prime location is likely to return.

Insulate a found space by pulling in as much vegetation as you can, lining the floors and walls and creating a makeshift barricade at the opening. Your body heat alone can warm up a well-insulated space by ten to twenty degrees.

When it comes to building a shelter in an arctic environment, the properties of snow and ice can counterintuitively be leveraged to your advantage. Like a properly insulated cave, a shelter made of snow will trap body heat and keep out cold air, because the high concentration of air that makes snow a less than ideal water source also makes it a highly insulating building block.

Digging out a pocket of space below the low-hanging branches of a tree is the quickest way to build a snow shelter, one that leverages the structural fortitude of a natural resource. While it may be tempting to burrow into a deep snowbank, beware of the risk of collapse.

With no sign of cover in sight, a trench shelter can be built into the snowpack in an hour or two with the use of a snow saw and a shovel (see illustration). Build trench and poncho shelters perpendicular to the wind so that the cold air doesn't pass through.

No. 019: Build Expedient Arctic Shelters

CONOP: Construct a field-expedient arctic shelter.

COA 1: Leverage the natural environment by sheltering at base of large trees and caves.

COA 2: Cut snow blocks to create a trench shelter or poncho liner shelter.

BLUF: Get out of frigid winds while trapping body heat in a semi-enclosed shelter.

020 Avoid Hypothermia

Characterized by shivering, a jittery resting heart rate, and a state of mild confusion, the onset of hypothermia can become a medical emergency in a very short period of time. When shivering stops and heart rate decreases, you've moved into dangerous territory. Your core temperature is plummeting, signaling a slowdown in the body's chemical reactions, which can result in death.

There is no set external temperature at which hypothermia will occur. Determining factors include wind conditions, the amount of insulation a person is wearing, the person's level of hydration and fitness, his or her body fat percentage, and his or her exposure to moisture. (Because water is an excellent conductor of heat, moisture on or near your skin will draw heat away from the body.)

If symptoms occur, immediately add layers, or remove wet clothing and replace with dry. Insulate the body from the cold earth with layers of vegetation or available padding materials. If emergency hot packs or other sources of heat are available, place them beneath armpits, around neck, or at groin so they are in direct contact with arteries. Do *not* use them on hands and feet before your core has been warmed back up—warming extremities will cause a rush of blood back to your core that may result in cardiac arrest. The body naturally sacrifices blood flow to extremities in order to conserve resources for essential functions.

Avoid alcohol, caffeine, and nicotine, which cause vasodilation (the dilation of blood vessels) and increase heat loss.

Treatment for more severe hypothermia (a solution of sugar water, the application of mouth-to-mouth or CPR) requires assistance from a second party, so it's essential to remedy the situation before it's too late.

No. 020: Avoid Hypothermia

CONOP: Identify and treat hypothermia.

COA 1: When the body loses heat faster than it can produce heat, mild symptoms begin.

A. Body temperature drops from below 98.6° to 95° F
B. Shivering begins as body attempts to warm itself
C. Increased resting heart rate
D. Increased respirations
E. Slight confusion

COA 2: As the body's temperature drops, moderate to severe symptoms begin.

A. Body temperature drops below 82° F
B. Shivering stops
C. Decreased heart rate
D. Decreased respirations
E. Loss of consciousness

COA 3: Treat mild hypothermia as soon as possible.

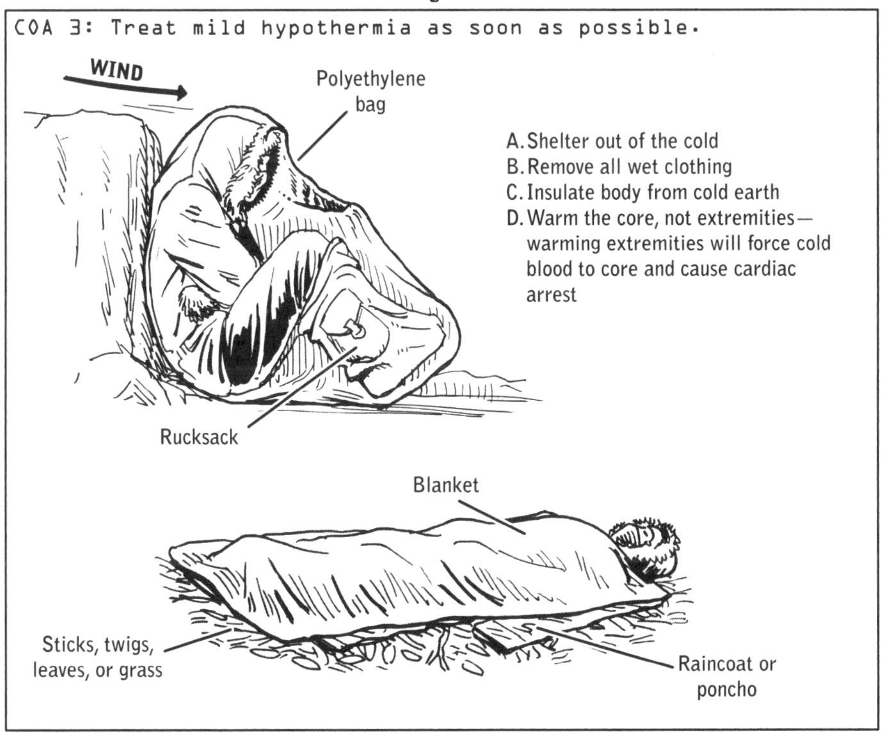

A. Shelter out of the cold
B. Remove all wet clothing
C. Insulate body from cold earth
D. Warm the core, not extremities—warming extremities will force cold blood to core and cause cardiac arrest

BLUF: Stay ahead of hypothermia or it will get ahead of you.

021 Minimum EDC, Desert Environment

Trekking through an arid environment means carrying serious quantities of the number one resource required to sustain life—one gallon of water per person per day, plus emergency rations. But water weighs more than eight pounds per gallon, and the exertion of carrying anything more than a gallon and a half will cause you to lose more fluid through sweat than you'd be able to replenish with the water on your back. You'll also be loaded up with the cold-weather gear that will enable you to survive the desert's radical temperature ranges. All of which adds up to quite a load. Hauling that gear requires only 20 percent of the energy that you'd expend carrying the same load, so a mechanism that allows you to pull rather than carry life-support material becomes essential.

The ideal structure for hauling gear across desert terrain is an expedition racing cart, a simple wagon which can either be purchased or made out of PVC piping and bicycle tires. Double up on wheels as pictured—flat tires are likely on hot surfaces dotted with sharp rocks, and a pre-attached spare means you won't have to stop and waste energy changing a tire.

Navigation

Travel by night and sleep by day to outwit the desert's brutal temperature shifts. When the sun goes down, the day's blazing heat can be displaced by a thirty-degree drop in temperature. Reversing your body clock allows you to conserve on your water and fuel needs by saving your exertion for hours when you'll lose the least amount of fluids through sweat—and ensures that your body won't be wasting valuable kilocalories trying to create warmth as you sleep through a frosty night.

Navigating an unchangingly flat landscape in the absence of vis-

No. 021: Minimum EDC, Desert Environment

CONOP: Everyday carry requirements for desert operations.

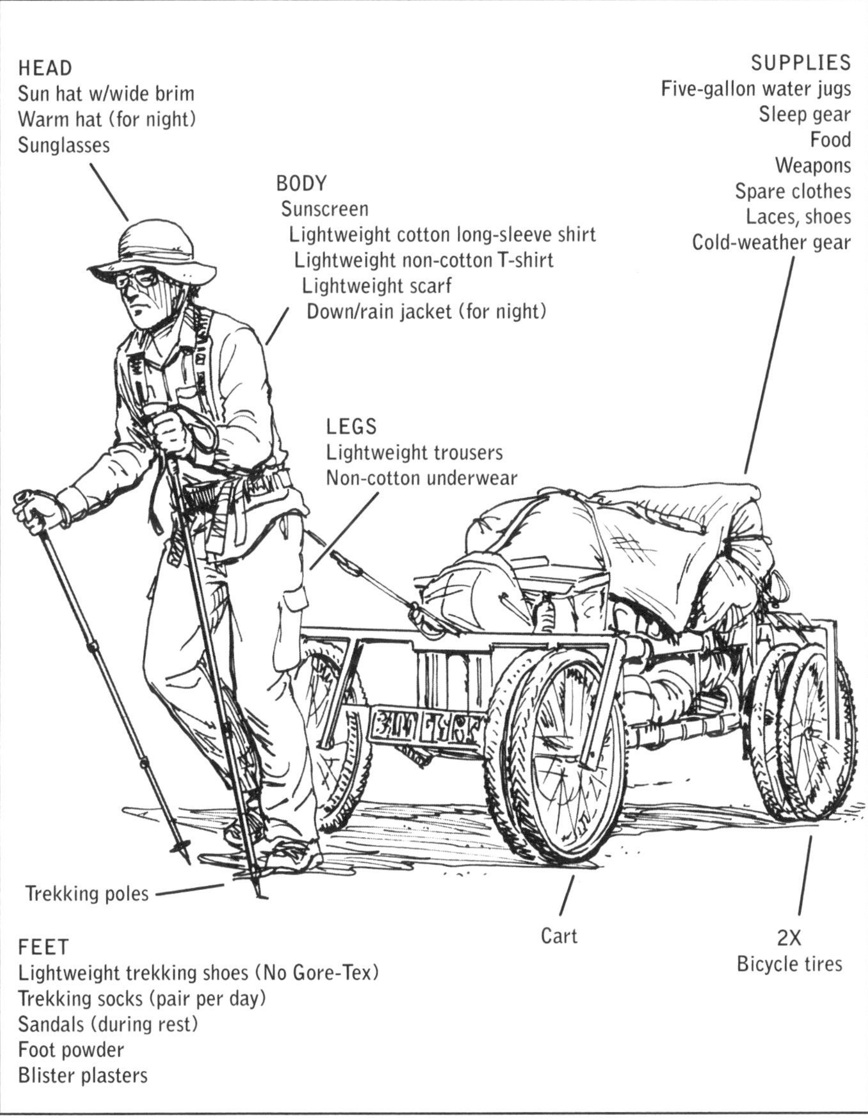

BLUF: Stay covered from head to toe in searing heat.

ible landmarks presents obvious challenges even during the day. While traveling by night certainly magnifies visibility challenges, it also offers one navigational asset: the canopy of bright stars visible in the desert's dark night. (For a short course on using celestial navigation as a backup to GPS devices, see page 18.) The nighttime desert isn't as dark as you think, but depth perception will be compromised after sundown. To compensate, use hiking poles to steady yourself.

When it comes to navigation, it's always safest to assume that one or more of your tools may fail, so bring several forms of backup and start by doing a detailed map study before you set out. The more knowledge you have of the terrain before you start, the better prepared you will be for a potential emergency. In the absence of visible landmarks, use pace counting to keep track of the distance you've traveled in any given direction. Count every other step. A single adult step spans approximately one meter, so one hundred double-steps add up to approximately two hundred meters.

Take advantage of any opportunity to refuel. If you spot cloud cover or rain begins to fall, get to high ground when possible—flash floods can happen quickly in desert landscapes. Be sure to collect water during any downpour.

Gear and Clothing

Proper footwear is essential. Trekking shoes specially designed to withstand high temperatures will prevent hot spots on the undersides of the feet—these occur when the body pushes fluids to contact points that have become irritated, resulting in painful blisters that can impede progress. Pack blister plasters and foot powder along with many changes of socks. Even in desert environments, cotton socks (see page 41) are a liability that can very quickly lead to a dangerous case of trench foot. Lightweight wool socks will keep the feet dry and help prevent tissue death.

On the upper body, cotton *can* be useful in a very hot environment. Though high-performance synthetics claim to achieve cooling and wicking benchmarks that natural fibers cannot, under a baking hot sun, there's no substitute for the breathability of cotton. Layers of synthetic material that *aren't* exposed to direct sunlight can be useful, particularly in the case of non-chafing synthetic underwear. A lightweight scarf can be used to protect your neck and face from wind- and sunburn, and comes in handy in the event of a sandstorm. When in doubt, go native.

Remember: Preparing for the desert's abrupt changes in temperature means you won't be packing light. You'll also need adequate cold-weather layers to pile on as you trek during the night. The saying "Travel light, freeze at night" is just as applicable in the desert as it is in the arctic.

022 Locate Drinking Water in an Arid Desert

Your best hedge against dehydration in an arid environment? Never get lost in a desert without an adequate water supply. But if you do find yourself low on H_2O, take every possible precaution in order to conserve your body's remaining levels of hydration as you seek out new sources of water.

Conserve Your Internal Hydration: Stay covered when moving during the daytime. When the wind blows over your sweat-dampened clothing, you'll benefit from a cooling effect. Better yet, follow the desert protocol of resting during the day and traveling at night, when you're less likely to sweat and release valuable fluid (see page 52). If you are completely out of water, do not eat. Digestion will quickly use up your remaining resources of internal hydration.

Ascend to High Ground: When land formations allow, ascend to high ground before you shelter for the day. As you plot the course that seems most likely to result in rescue, look for clues that potential water sources might be near. From above, track vegetation and animals. Down at ground level, seek out signs of life.

Dig Belowground: Dry riverbeds may yield hidden reserves of hydration in the form of damp sand. If you find nothing after digging at least a foot down, try a few more spots. Even a riverbed that has long been dry might be harboring moisture from a recent rain.

Collect Dew: As a last-ditch effort, sacrifice part of a night's movement to lay out clothes and collect the night and morning's dew. Using a similar technique in drought-stricken regions, researchers have been able to collect as much as half a quart of dew from a single square meter.

No. 022: Locate Drinking Water in an Arid Desert

CONOP: Find water in an impossible desert environment.

COA 1: Conserve your body's water levels.

Stay covered.

Shade during the day. Travel at night.

Do not eat.

COA 2: Get to high ground, carefully observe surroundings. Follow signs of water.

Locate animals and their tracks.

Locate dry stream- and riverbeds: dig for water.

Locate vegetation: water-loving, broad-leaved plants and trees.

Look for swarms of flies, mosquitos, and bees.

COA 3: Dig in dry riverbeds and under vegetation.

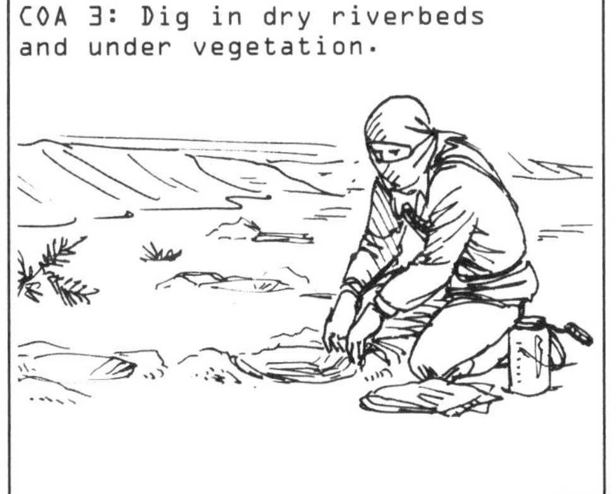

COA 4: Collect morning dew.

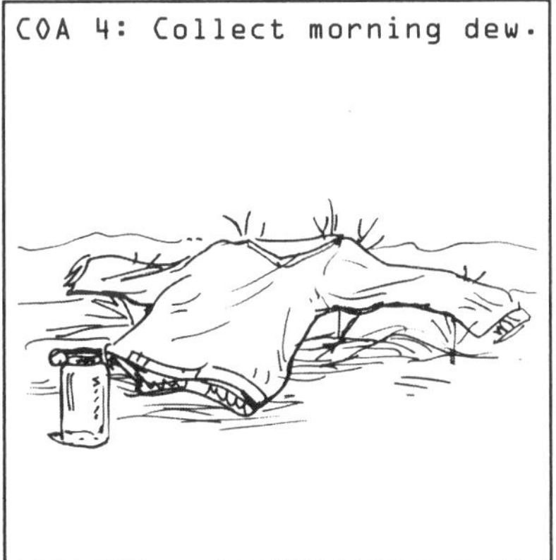

BLUF: Do not get lost in the desert without water!

023 Spark a Fire with Sunlight

Bright sunlight may be the desert's most abundant natural resource—but once the sun sets, a lack of cloud cover means the landscape retains very little of the day's heat. Temperatures can drop very, very quickly in a desert. So if you're not moving through the night (see page 52), you'll need a heat source to keep you warm.

Leverage the daytime's bright sunlight to build a fire while you still can. All you'll need is a clear plastic bottle filled with a bit of water or other liquid and several sheets of newspaper; the ink on the paper will act as an accelerant. In the place of newspaper, dried-out leaves and grass or shavings from a dry branch can also be used as kindling. Most deserts contain plenty of highly flammable brush.

Use the convex end of the water bottle to refract or change the direction of the sun's rays. As the light passes through your makeshift lens, its rays will converge, their heat energy concentrated into a single hot spot. The apparatus should magnify the power of sunlight to such an extent that the newspaper glows red and begins to smoke with heat. Wave the newspaper gently toward the lens, and that smoke will very quickly erupt into flame.

Time of day and season will play a part in determining the intensity of the sun's rays. This technique will be more successful for an adventurer working at high noon on the equator than for an unlucky traveler caught on a Northern Hemisphere desert in the dead of winter.

Note: A glass bottle may also be used, potentially rendering liquid unnecessary if the glass is thick enough to refract sunlight on its own, without the additional magnification provided by water.

No. 023: Spark a Fire with Sunlight

CONOP: Making fire with a water bottle and newspaper.

COA 1: Gather one clear bottle of water and five sheets of newspaper.

COA 2: Magnify sunlight to a small-diameter hot spot.

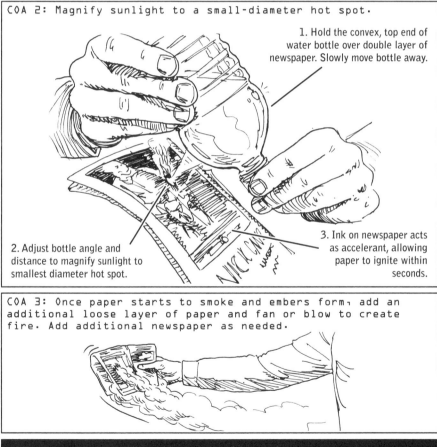

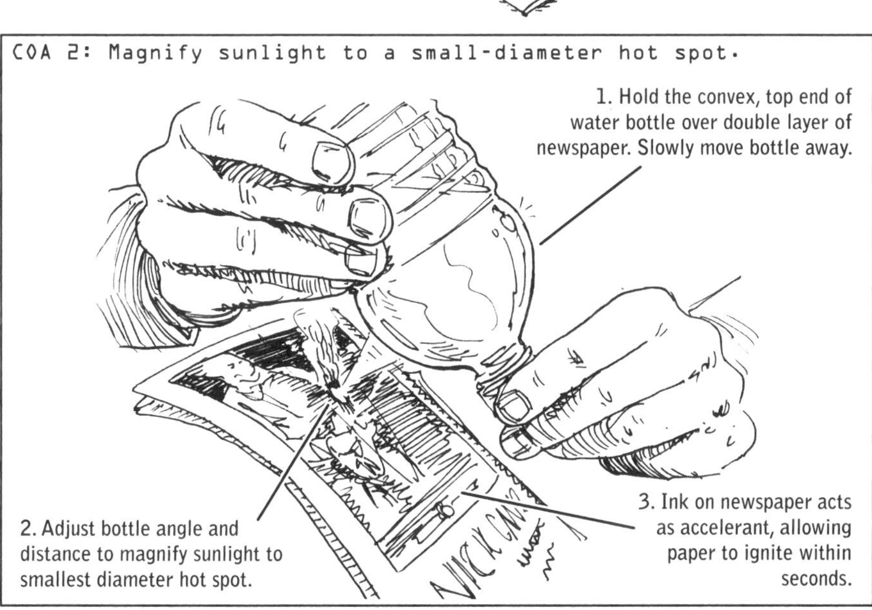

1. Hold the convex, top end of water bottle over double layer of newspaper. Slowly move bottle away.
2. Adjust bottle angle and distance to magnify sunlight to smallest diameter hot spot.
3. Ink on newspaper acts as accelerant, allowing paper to ignite within seconds.

COA 3: Once paper starts to smoke and embers form, add an additional loose layer of paper and fan or blow to create fire. Add additional newspaper as needed.

BLUF: Water is vital—for both survival and starting fires.

024 Hunt and Scavenge Desert Survival Food

Resist the urge to rip into the first form of plant life you come across when trekking through a desert environment. Though vegetation may be sparse, plants such as the candelabras cactus or the flowering datura plant can induce severe vomiting or hallucination. Instead of taking a risk, hold out for some of the safe, edible plants commonly found across the deserts of North America—chia sage, prickly pear cactus, and barrel cactus.

Embraced by the Native Americans and the Aztecs, the chia sage has a long medicinal history. Beat the plant's bright purple flower into a container to release its seeds—nutritional powerhouses that can be eaten raw or soaked in water to form a pudding. Protect hands while shaving spines away from prickly pear cactus pads, also known as *nopalitos* in Latin American cooking, or burn the spines off. And avoid drinking the juice of the cylindrical barrel cactus; its flesh is edible, but its liquid contents can cause diarrhea and dehydration.

To hunt down a snake for food, locate a long, forked stick and have a sharp knife readily accessible. Use the forked end of the stick to pin down the snake's head. Working from behind the snake, slide your hand around its jaw and forcefully clamp it shut. The snake's body may coil around your stick or arm, but focus on controlling the head. Release the stick and, still pinning down the snake's jaw with your other hand, use your knife to decapitate the snake.

Cut three inches below the head to make sure you're getting rid of any poisonous glands, then quickly toss the head away. A snake's strong biting reflex can be set off by electrical charges in its nerve endings for up to an hour after its death.

Though poisonous snakes can generally be identified by their diamond-shaped heads, it's safest to assume that any snake you come across might be dangerous. A snake can lunge a distance equivalent to half its body length, so approach with care.

No. 024: Hunt and Scavenge Desert Survival Food

CONOP: Trap and eat the desert's safest, most common foods.

COA 1: Chia sage, prickly pear cactus, and barrel cactus are the most common edible plants in many deserts.

COA 2: Hunt and trap a snake.

COA 3: Field dress and cook snake.

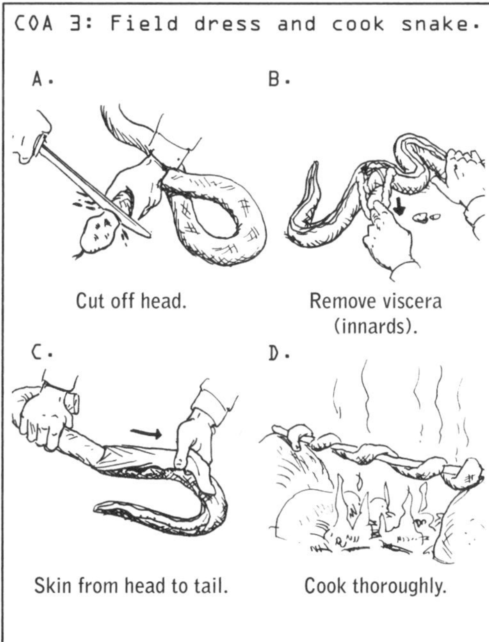
A.
Cut off head.
B.
Remove viscera (innards).
C.
Skin from head to tail.
D.
Cook thoroughly.

BLUF: Lizards follow ants, and snakes follow lizards—all are food for you.

025 Build a Cooling Desert Shelter

When you're in survival mode, you should perpetually be looking to conserve energy, and stumbling upon a preexisting shelter is the kind of lucky break that could help you shore up many precious kilocalories. Your first choices for shelter in any environment should be natural formations.

In a desert environment, protecting yourself from moisture isn't usually a concern, so sources of shade may fit the bill if complete enclosures aren't available. An open rock formation that lets in a cool breeze could easily provide adequate cover. But in a sand desert devoid of nearby land formations, an efficient shelter can be built into the sand using only two poncho liners or tarps and a shovel—or even your bare hands.

The two-layer shelter, pictured opposite, works by counteracting the greenhouse effect that normally accrues in enclosed spaces, most notably exemplified by a parked car on a hot day: The sun's UV rays enter the car through the glass, but then cannot escape, bouncing around until the vehicle eventually becomes far, far hotter than the surrounding environment. Trapping the sun's rays between two tarps, open at both ends, means that even the warmest wind can sweep through and chase the rays away before they have a chance to enter your shelter. On a bone-dry, windless day, the tarps will still trap UV rays and keep your sleeping space considerably cooler than the surrounding environment.

Digging down a couple of feet beneath the layers of sunbaked sand will net you a sleeping space that is many degrees cooler to begin with. Creating a sloped, open entrance for your quarters ensures that air will flow around your body as well. Build the trench parallel to the wind, with the sloped, open end facing into the air current.

No. 025: Build a Cooling Desert Shelter

CONOP: Find or build a shelter to create shade and decrease temperature.

COA 1: Look for caves, caverns, or rock formations that provide shade and protection against wind.

COA 2: Build a belowground two-layer shelter.

1. Dig out a body-height-long, 24- to 36-inch-wide, 18- to 24-inch-deep trench.

2. Cover trench with poncho liner and anchor with large rocks and sand.

3. Place second poncho liner hovering over first, leaving twelve inches of air space in between.

Greenhouse effect will be trapped between liners, and wind will sweep it away.

BLUF: Travel at night. Build shelter at dawn. Rest during the day.

026 Minimum EDC, Wetland Environment

Swamps, bogs, marshes, river flats . . . Though many of the world's wetlands have been lost to logging, sizable examples can still be found on every continent but Antarctica, some of them spanning hundreds of square miles. Often rich sources of fish and plant life, these fecund, low-lying environments are some of the globe's most biodiverse places. But their stagnant waters, rich in decaying organic matter, are also highly effective incubators for parasites, bacteria, and disease-carrying insects.

Water is everywhere in a wetland environment, which is why much of the gear that's specific to the terrain involves keeping you and your belongings as dry as possible. Wetland waters will always be cooler than the temperature of the human body—which means that through convection, prolonged immersion can result in hypothermia even in warm weather.

Use multiple dry bags to keep belongings free of moisture and to disperse weight throughout your watercraft. Even if you're trudging through shallow waters, pulling a well-stocked supply in a kayak is preferable to lugging a partial kit on your back. Do not abandon your gear if you become stranded in a remote area. You may be underestimating how long you'll be forced to depend on the survival tools you've brought with you.

Practice capsizing and reentering your watercraft long before you have to do so during an emergency, and tie down all gear as a precautionary measure. Boost the usefulness of your PFD (personal flotation device) by placing a knife, whistle, and strobe light in its pockets. In the event that you capsize or are separated from your watercraft, you can use the knife to cut yourself free from any weeds or foreign matter you encounter, and your whistle or strobe light to signal for help.

No. 026: Minimum EDC, Wetland Environment

CONOP: Minimum everyday carry for wetland operations.

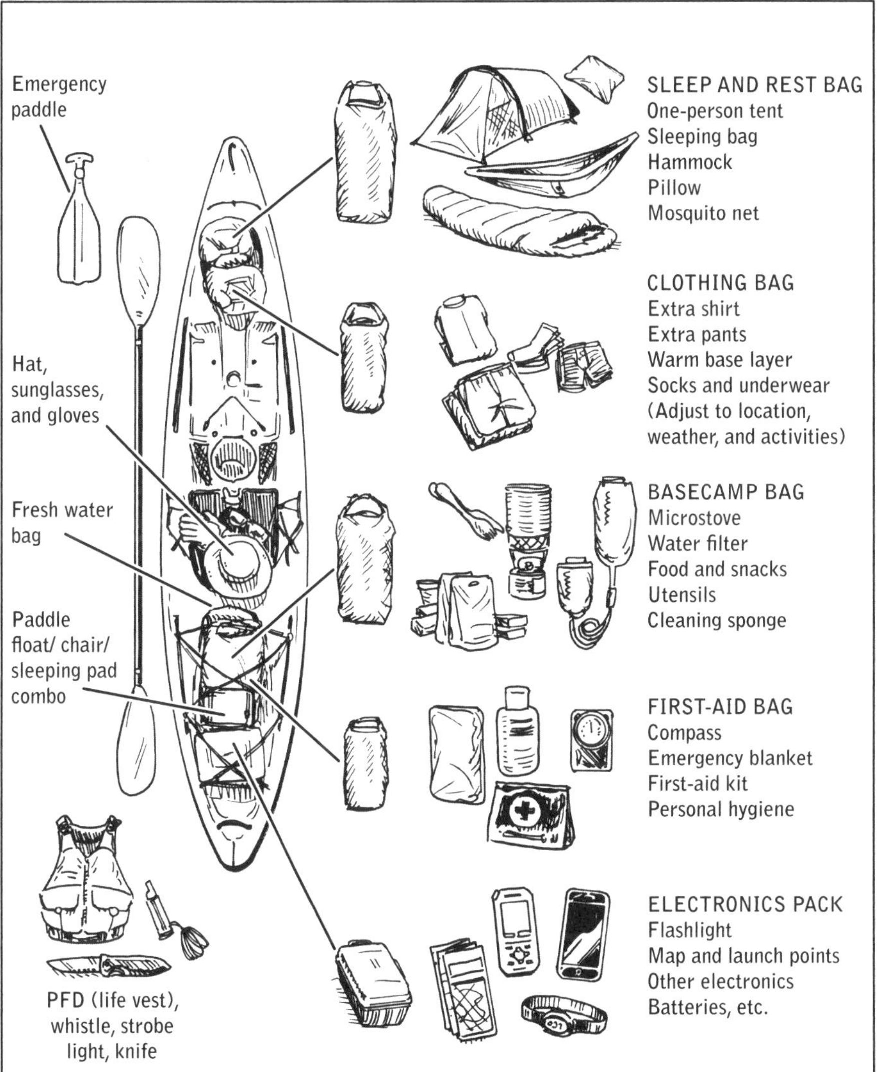

BLUF: Better to paddle than to swim.

027 Filter Water in a Swamp

Water purification is non-negotiable in a wetland environment, where hydration may be plentiful but will almost certainly be laced with harmful parasites and bacteria. "Swamp fever" (a catch-all term for malaria, leptospirosis, and the mumps), the Everglades virus, and cholera are just a few of the waterborne ailments common to swamps around the world. These diseases can have devastating physical and sometimes neurological ramifications.

Though your EDC kit should contain both a water filtration kit and a stove with which to boil water clean, an improvised filtration system can also be made from a collection of found materials: a plastic bottle (often found floating around swamps near urban environments), a sock, charcoal, and an assortment of gravel culled from the shoreline.

The most indispensable layer in this improvised filtration system is the charcoal, well known for its ability to bind to a wide range of toxic substances. In its "activated" form—when it's been treated for optimal absorption—charcoal becomes the main ingredient in most commercially sold filtration systems, and it's also used to tend to ailments from flatulence to poisoning.

To make your own charcoal, build a campfire on shore and let it burn until the logs have burned down into coals. (Store-bought barbecue briquettes are treated with chemicals and thus not suitable for use as a filtration layer.)

Organize your layers so that the largest particles are at the top, catching large pieces of debris, and the finest are at the neck of the bottle. When you pour water through your filtration system, the drip should be slow; a steady stream means your filtration system is too porous.

Boiling water is the safest approach to purification (see page 94), but you should never die of thirst in a swamp.

No. 027: Filter Water in a Swamp

CONOP: How to filter swamp water.

COA 1: Gather required items:

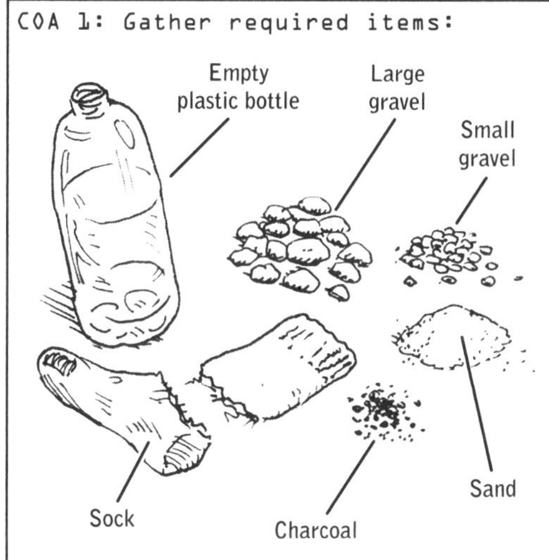

COA 2: Cut bottom off plastic bottle.

COA 3: Load layers of materials in order.

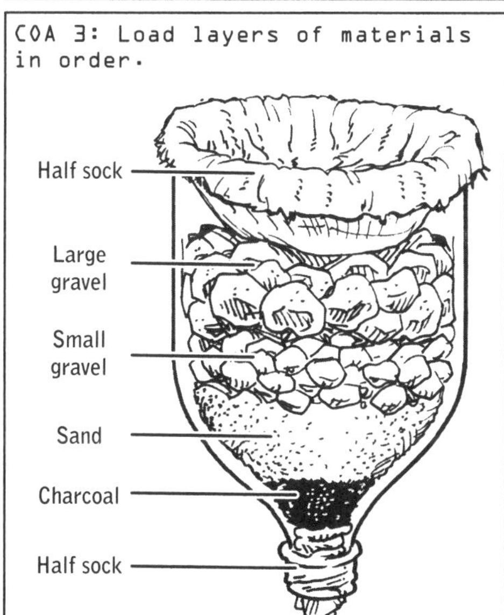

COA 4: Pour dirty water in, drinkable water drips out.

BLUF: Filter water only when you cannot boil it.

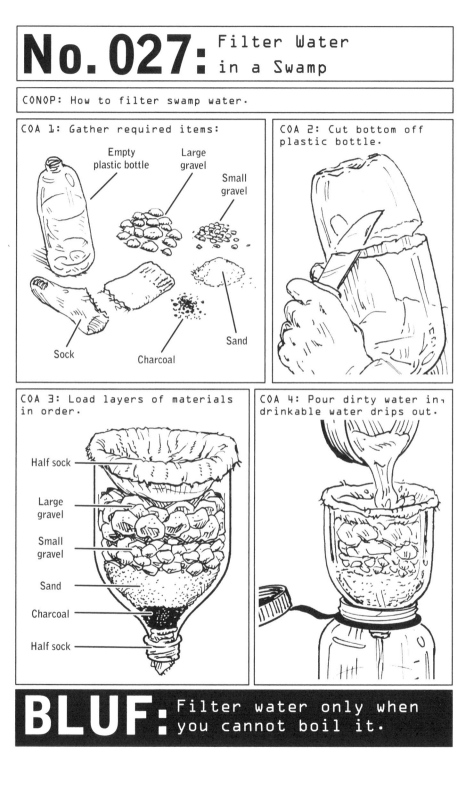

028 Spark a Fire with a Mobile Phone

You've tried to use your phone to call for help, to find your way to safety, to contact loved ones. But after the last remaining sliver of battery fades away and the device goes dead in your hands, that mobile phone can still be used as a lifeline.

Outfitted with powerful batteries packed with valuable chemical components, personal electronic devices like phones, tablets, and navigational systems can be used as fire starters long after they cease to function. Powered by lithium ions, they are so energy-dense that, when shorted, their contents have a tendency to overheat and burst into flame.

The first challenge will be accessing the battery, which manufacturers typically make difficult by design for safety reasons. Once you've pried the battery from your device, try to use any remaining charge by bridging the battery's positive and negative terminals with a knife or other piece of metal with a nonconductive handle or grip. The resulting spark may succeed in getting your tinder to smoke, but a significant shock may be the more unwelcome by-product.

If the first approach doesn't work, set the battery on the ground and rupture the battery cells by spiking the surface with the tip of your knife. The battery will short, releasing a burst of energy as its protective circuit is destroyed. Dousing the battery with water will achieve a similar and potentially even more explosive effect. The liquid will quickly degrade the protective circuit that prevents the battery's cells from mingling and attaining peak voltage.

Stand back quickly. The battery will erupt into flames the size of a small campfire or explosion while releasing toxic compounds.

Note: Lithium-ion fires are dangerous, toxic, and very difficult to suppress. This skill must only be attempted in survival scenarios as an option of last resort. Do not attempt to practice these steps.

No. 028: Spark a Fire with a Mobile Phone

CONOP: Use a cell phone lithium battery to create fire.

COA 1: Disassemble phone to reveal battery. Remove battery from phone.

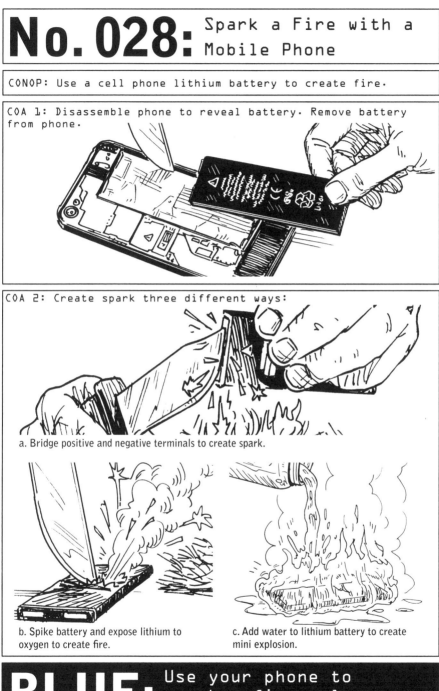

COA 2: Create spark three different ways:

a. Bridge positive and negative terminals to create spark.

b. Spike battery and expose lithium to oxygen to create fire.

c. Add water to lithium battery to create mini explosion.

BLUF: Use your phone to spark a fire only as a last resort.

029 Find Food in a Wetland

Despite their often forbidding look of decay, biodiverse wetland environments tend to be home to an array of plant and animal life, from the reptiles, fish, and amphibians that dwell in their waters to the birds and insects whose calls and humming fill the air. One amphibian that's abundant in many wetlands is the common frog, which favors standing water over currents. Easy to catch, the creature yields a well-known delicacy when relieved of its torso, its legs roasted over a spit.

Beware of the poisonous frogs native to tropical environments. Small and brightly colored, they secrete lethal poisons that can cause adverse reactions like seizures, paralysis, and heart attacks. The golden poison frog is said to secrete enough lethal toxin through its skin glands to send ten adult humans to their graves—which is why native populations historically used those secretions to create lethal poison darts. Today, pharmaceutical companies cull the secretions and use them as the basis for potent painkillers.

Avoid toads, which secrete toxic substances emanating from the parotid glands located on the backs of their heads. Squat and wide, toads are considered less dangerous to humans than poisonous frogs, but they can still sometimes be lethal.

To catch a frog, use a sharpened stick to pin the animal to the ground. Look for frogs on muddy banks close to the shoreline, or buried beneath logs or rocks during colder months. They feed on insects and earthworms, so follow their food trail to suss them out. Frogs tend to be most active at night, though hunting them in the dark without a light source is inadvisable; a bright light will not only protect you from potential injury, but will also cause frogs to freeze in their tracks.

Spear in shallow waters from inside your watercraft, or from a perch on an improvised shelter (see page 72).

No. 029: Find Food in a Wetland

CONOP: Catch, skin, and cook frog legs.

COA 1: Using a stick, trap and kill frogs.

COA 2: Skin by pinching and cutting skin just above back waistline.

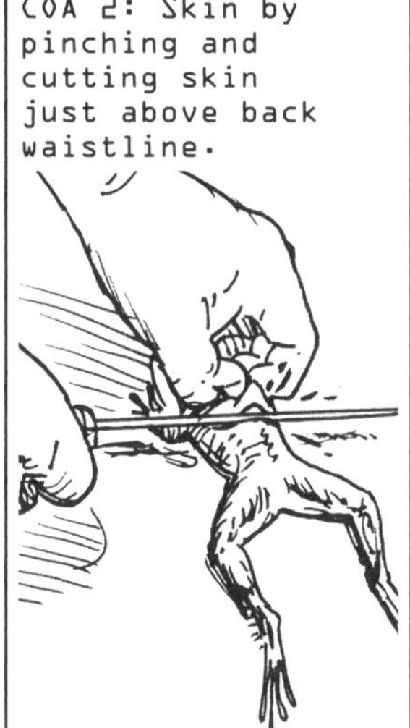

COA 3: Pull skin off like a pair of pants.

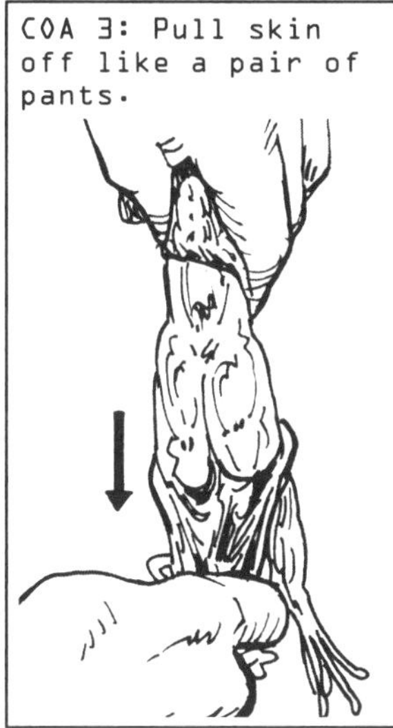

COA 4: Cut at waistline to separate rear legs from trunk. Cut off feet and split legs apart (optional).

COA 5: Rinse in fresh water, then roast over open fire.

BLUF: Fine dining without the price tag.

030 Build an Elevated Swamp Bed

If there's little hope of reaching the shoreline before nightfall, there are many reasons to consider building an elevated temporary shelter, roof, or shelf over standing water in a wetland environment. Sleeping on your watercraft will expose you to cold and damp, and to possible undesirable encounters with water moccasins or alligators.

Assuming you had the forethought to pack a hammock (see page 34), you may want to build a roof over your sleeping quarters to protect you from the elements—or from aerial surveillance. A shelf could be useful as a surface on which to build a fire (in an enclosed container like a cooking pot), a perch from which to fish, or a docking station from which to work on a vessel in need of repair.

To build, look for three trees that create a triangular pattern sizable enough to act as a sleeping or work surface. Collect three straight branches long enough to extend from tree to tree; in this environment, you may need to do some climbing in order to find them. Strip the branches down and lash them to the trees using parachute cord, rapelling line, or vines and bark shavings collected from the environment.

Lash each branch individually from tree to tree to increase the overall strength of your shelter.

Lay a tarp over the frame, wrapping and tightening it around the edges. Or create a taut surface by weaving and lashing vines and large leafy branches over and around the frame.

Leave the structure in place when you transit to your next location if you want to sow a trail of bread crumbs for potential rescuers. If you don't want to be found, dismantle the structure.

No. 030: Build an Elevated Swamp Bed

CONOP: Construct a swamp bed from natural wetland materials.

COA 1: Identify three trees, two at least body height's distance apart, in a triangular pattern.

COA 2: Collect three straight branches and lash a triangular frame from tree to tree at least three feet above swampy ground.

COA 3: Lash and weave vines and large leafy branches from frame to frame to create a sturdy platform.

BLUF: Where it's dry, millions of insects reside—sleep suspended to avoid them.

031 Minimum EDC, Mountain Environment

With specialized equipment becoming more and more streamlined in recent decades, we've condensed our food, camping, and survival needs down to the single pack we can carry on our shoulders. But we often do so at expense to our energy levels, our joint health, and our ability to fully prepare for the vagaries of the environment. Early explorers would never have attempted an expedition without an assortment of pack mules and wagons, and while we don't want to compromise our independence, we can use a modified form of transport to approximate their pioneering ways.

If trail conditions and regulations allow, a mountain bike provides a form of locomotion that broadens your options as it lightens your load. Store camp and survival essentials like cookware, water filtration supplies, water, and navigational tools in one dry bag. Another bag should hold the food appropriate to your expedition (MREs, dehydrated rations, energy bars), and yet another should contain your clothing. Pack for the varying temperatures that are common to mountain environments by bringing light, midweight, heavyweight, and shell layers. Do not skimp on socks. (See page 27 for a reminder of their importance.) Carry bulky, lightweight sleep gear in a pack on your back.

An inflatable personal dinghy that packs down to approximately football size, along with a paddle that breaks down into four lightweight pieces, is a useful hedge against impassable waterways that would otherwise cause lengthy detours. Lay your bike across your lap or the bow of the dinghy as you ford the river or lake.

This methodology, familiar to athletes who've competed in multi-day adventure courses, is an update on the scouting model of mountaineering that allows for maximum mobility and flexibility.

No. 031: Minimum EDC, Mountain Environment

CONOP: Everyday carry requirements for mountain operations.

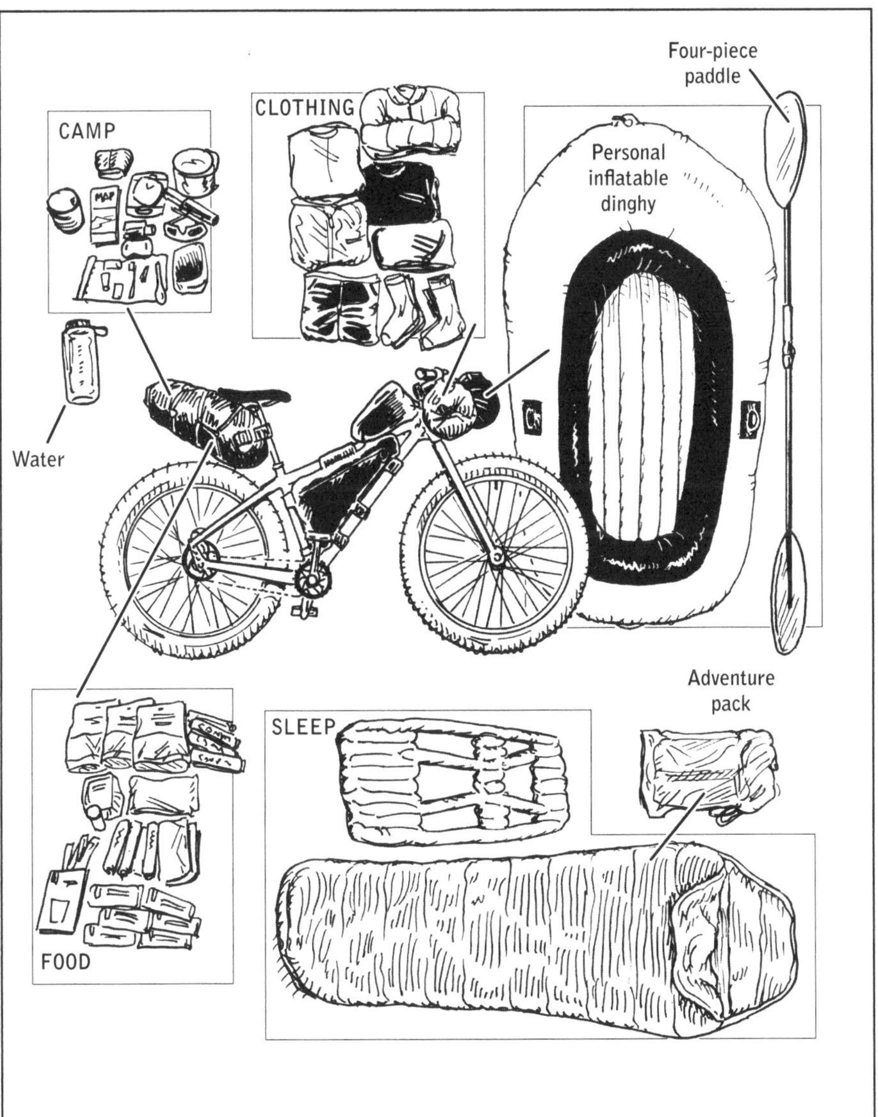

BLUF: One is none, two is one.

032 Purify Mountain Water

Thinking of taking a sip of that crystal-clear mountain springwater without filtering or boiling it? If you're at a high enough elevation, the water will generally be pure, but you never know whether an animal has been bathing or defecating just a few hundred feet upstream. Cryptosporidiosis, giardiasis, shigellosis, and the norovirus are just a few of the bacterial, viral, and parasitic infections that can result, but boiling or filtering water will effectively kill or sequester most impurities. Bring water to a rolling boil to purify, and keep at a boil for one minute, plus one additional minute for each one thousand feet of altitude, just to be safe.

In the absence of a workable pot, you can boil stream water in a plastic bottle filled all the way to the top, making sure no air pocket is left inside. Because plastic melts at a higher temperature than water boils, you'll be able to heat the bottle without melting it. Use a piece of rope or strong string to tie the bottle to a tripod made of sticks. Due to the lack of oxygen, the water will not visibly boil, but tiny bubbles will appear when boiling temperature is reached.

If you're unable to build a fire, employ nature's built-in filtration system by digging a hole near the water's edge and using socks or other pieces of cloth to soak up hydration. The liquid will have been partially filtered through layers of soil and rock.

Avoid standing pools of water. Bacteria thrive in warm, wet environments where they are undisturbed by current.

Keep your hands clean. Some experts believe the transmission of bacteria from hand to mouth to be more of a threat to outdoor enthusiasts than waterborne bacteria.

Note: Plastic bottles will leach carcinogenic contaminants when heated, so the plastic bottle boiling method is to be used only as a last resort.

No. 032: Purify Mountain Water

CONOP: Filter or boil water to eliminate bacteria.

COA 1: The Well Method

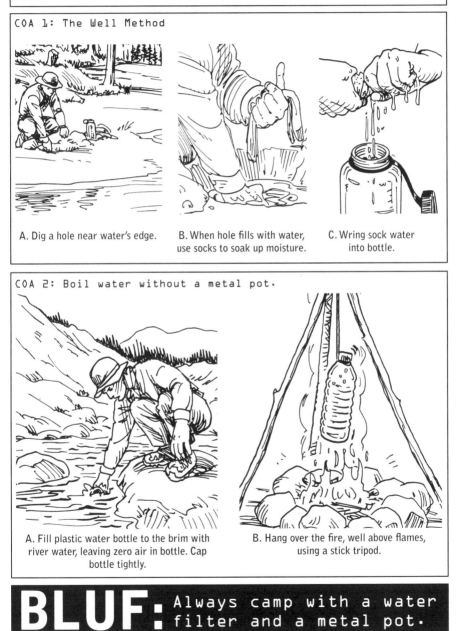

A. Dig a hole near water's edge.

B. When hole fills with water, use socks to soak up moisture.

C. Wring sock water into bottle.

COA 2: Boil water without a metal pot.

A. Fill plastic water bottle to the brim with river water, leaving zero air in bottle. Cap bottle tightly.

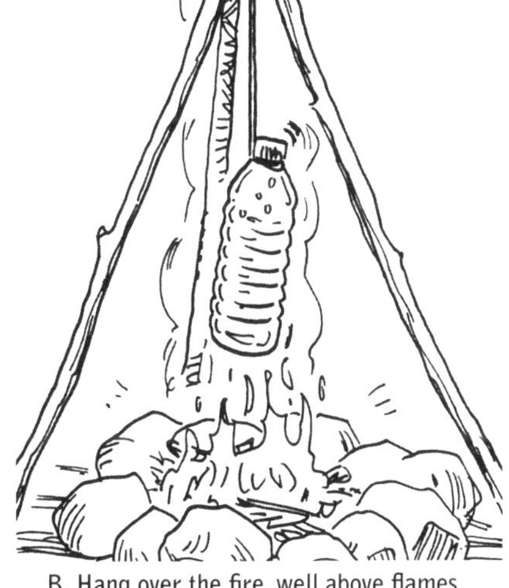

B. Hang over the fire, well above flames, using a stick tripod.

BLUF: Always camp with a water filter and a metal pot.

033 Build a Fire with Damp Wood

Even in a damp environment, if wood is plentiful, a successful fire will be within reach. Follow these fire-making tips, applicable to any setting, to make sure yours burns hot and strong.

1. Seek out pine needles or sticks that are coated in or filled with highly flammable sap.
2. If you find a wet log, peel off a couple of layers of bark to expose dry wood.
3. A smooth log with a large mass won't burn very well. Split larger pieces of wood to expose their ragged internal surfaces.
4. You need fuel, spark, and air to make a fire. To make sure the last element is in bountiful supply, shape logs into a teepee triangle or a lean-to that allows room for air to circulate. A pile of sticks will eventually smother itself.
5. Travel with fire starters like Vaseline, hand sanitizer, or a dedicated store-bought product, or collect lint from your dryer, douse it in lighter fluid, kerosene, or gasoline, and store it in a Baggie.
6. Light the fire from the windward side, blocking the wind with your body so the flames don't blow out before they're burning strong.
7. Light your fire from below. Fire burns upward, and lighting from the lowest point gives the flames every opportunity to climb.
8. A good supply of tinder (pine needles, brush, dry leaves) is the lifeblood of an effective fire.
9. There's no overstating the importance of tinder. Add hefty pieces of wood too early, and your fire will go out. Keep adding tinder until your fire has the strength to burn a bigger log.
10. Unless strong winds are burning down your fire, a fire pit may be isolated from the airflow necessary to keeping a fire burning. Instead, build your fire atop a mound of dirt.

No. 033: Build a Fire with Damp Wood

CONOP: Build and maintain fire in damp mountain environments.

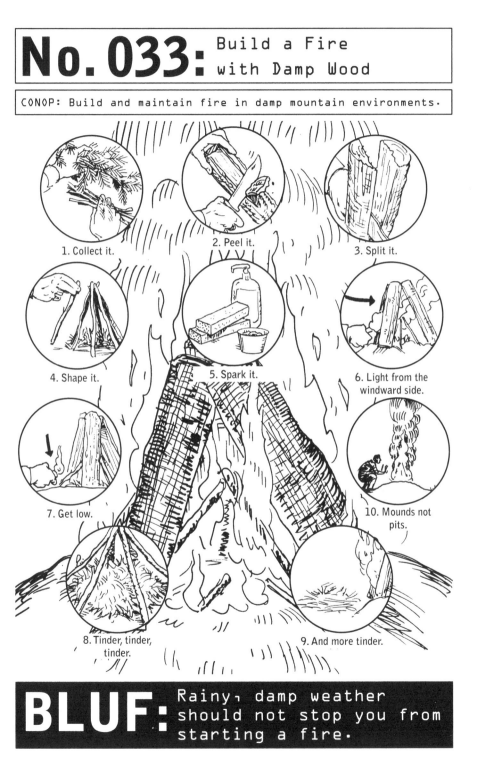

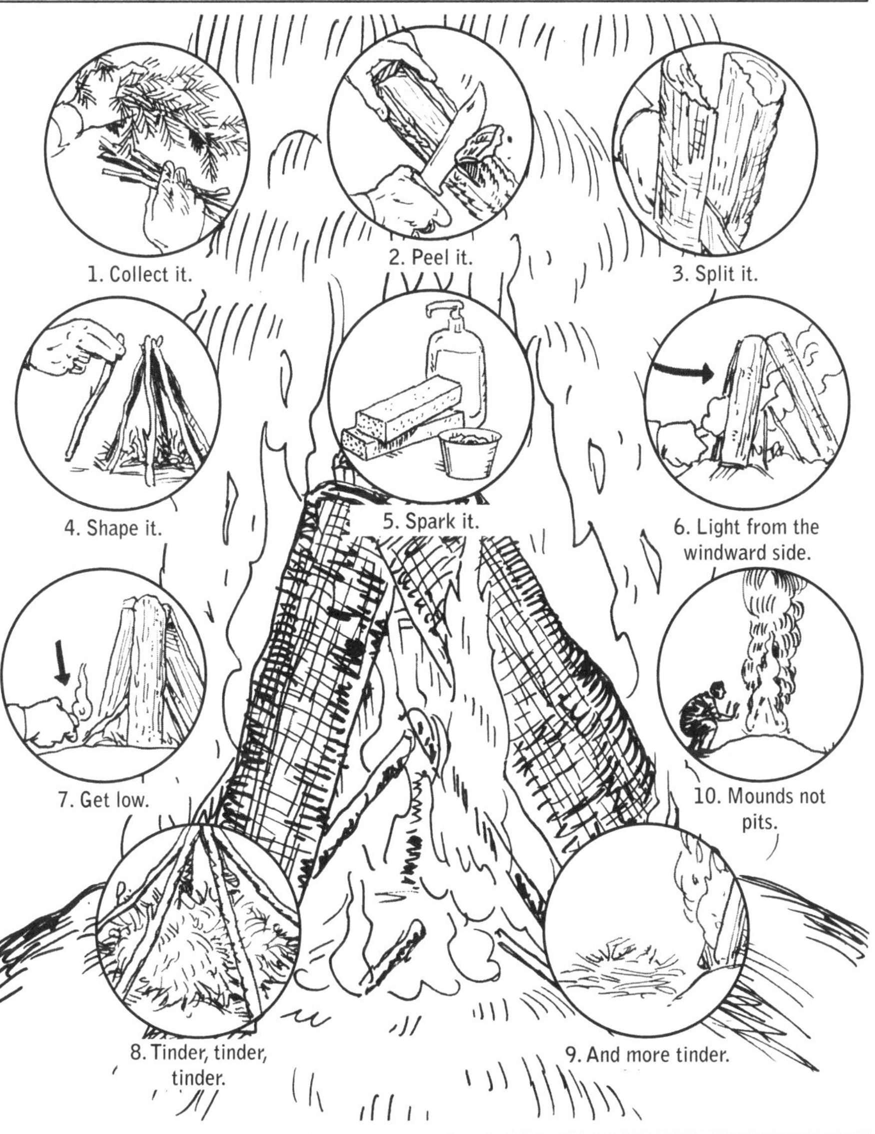

1. Collect it.
2. Peel it.
3. Split it.
4. Shape it.
5. Spark it.
6. Light from the windward side.
7. Get low.
8. Tinder, tinder, tinder.
9. And more tinder.
10. Mounds not pits.

BLUF: Rainy, damp weather should not stop you from starting a fire.

034 Find Food in the Mountains

Game is abundant in many mountainous regions. But if your aim is to transit through the environment and find your way to safety within a few cycles of light and darkness, you don't have time to waste building or setting traps—or potentially contracting a severe digestive ailment from improperly cooked animal flesh. Your goal should be to continue your movements across the landscape, gathering any edible vegetation you come upon and casting a line if you are fortunate enough to find a body of water. Many of the world's lakes and rivers are swarming with fish, so unlike an attempt to catch up a rabbit, casting a line in a survival scenario is an appropriate use of your energy and time.

Setting up a trotline is one way to maximize your chances of catching a fish. Attach multiple segments of fishing line, of varying lengths, to a string of parachute cord or a strong vine. Bait and hook the lengths of fishing line, then anchor the string to a tree, a bush, or a rock on one end, sinking it with a weighted water bottle or large rock on the other. When you see the line move, haul in your catch.

As you're performing a map study in advance of transiting through the environment, familiarize yourself with the edible plants and insects native to the area. Commonly available and safe sources of fats, nutrients, and proteins include pine nuts (the seed of the pine tree), clover, and grubs and earthworms. Select dried-out pinecones whose scales have already opened, smashing them against the ground to release their seeds. Sour root clovers are a particularly tasty member of the clover family, but typically any type of clover is edible and harmless. As a general rule, any plant you see animals eating is likely to be safe for human consumption.

No. 034: Find Food in the Mountains

CONOP: Catch and collect survival food in the mountains.

COA 1: Collect pinenuts, sour root clovers, grub worms.

COA 2: Set a trotline.

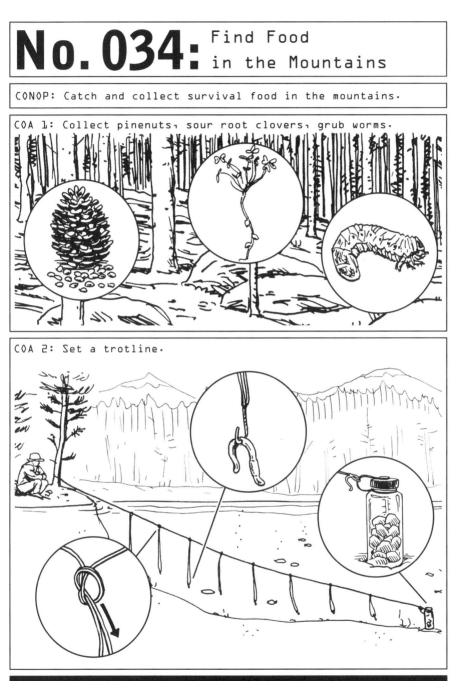

BLUF: Don't waste hours trapping and hunting in a survival scenario.

035 Build Efficient Mountain Shelters

At close range, the optics on a mountain can be extremely deceiving. Viewed from afar, the idyllic trail you climbed belongs to a massive, unforgiving ecosystem with the power to alter wind and weather patterns for hundreds of miles. And come nightfall, or when a cold front suddenly blows in, a sun-drenched rocky outcropping can become an ice-cold, windblown tundra in a matter of minutes.

If you're forced to shelter overnight on a mountain without a tent, insulation will be key. When you're hiking or driving through mountainous terrain, a poncho (stashed in the trunk of your car or a backpack) is a light and useful form of insurance that can be deployed as a tent, rain cover, ground cloth, or insulating layer in the event of an unexpected sleepover. In warmer weather, a sleeping bag and bivy sack may be sufficient to get you through a night spent under the stars, but better safe than sorry.

To prevent a sudden rain from dousing you in feet of rushing water, check to make sure the ground you're sleeping on isn't a dried-up creek- or riverbed. Stake out flat, elevated ground free of scat or large animal tracks, ideally near trees.

If you're traveling with quality tools (see page 74), you should be able to make an insulated shelter out of branches and foliage. Ski poles, hiking poles, or ice axes can be substituted for tree trunks or stumps to create both poncho tents and lean-tos.

Before you set out on any trip through an unpopulated area, do a thorough map study. If you're stranded on a mountaintop, even a basic knowledge of the surrounding area (e.g., knowing that the closest town is due east) may help you find your way to safety. In the absence of topographical knowledge, follow rivers and streams downstream.

No. 035: Build Efficient Mountain Shelters

CONOP: Build a field-expedient mountain shelter.

COA 1: Build a poncho tent.

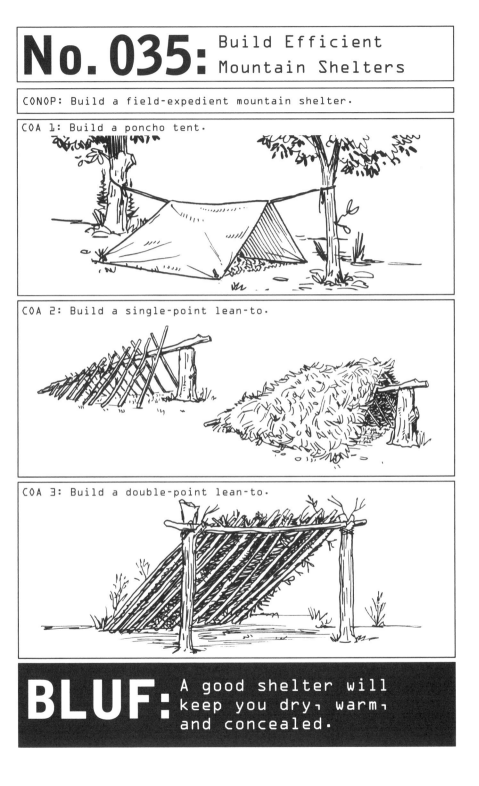

COA 2: Build a single-point lean-to.

COA 3: Build a double-point lean-to.

BLUF: A good shelter will keep you dry, warm, and concealed.

036 Emergency Climbing Techniques

Inexperienced climbers generally make the same mistake: overrelying on arm strength, a bias that quickly results in fatigue for all but the most overbuilt. Whether you're climbing a mountaintop or the side of a building, you're far better off recruiting the powerhouse muscles of your legs and core, spreading the effort throughout the body rather than delegating the work to a single, isolated muscle group. The key to successful climbing is to revert to the natural, full-bodied movements toddlers instinctively use to escape their cribs and playpens—before they gradually unlearn the human body's natural facility for climbing over and around obstacles.

The principle of full-body climbing is easy enough to grasp when it comes to chimneying or stemming up a narrow chute (see illustrations). To chimney, brace back and feet against opposing surfaces and walk up the walls, shifting pressure between opposing hands and feet to ascend. To stem, spread the body in a wide X position, and use a sideways crab walk to gain elevation.

To hoist the body over a ledge, use arms and legs to raise the chest to ledge level—then recruit the legs, hooking a heel on the overhang.

When dangling on a steep incline, your arms shouldn't necessarily always be the highest point. If you can identify a third point of contact within reach, hold your body as close to the wall as possible, then scissor up a leg to hook the heel. Once you're stable, release a handhold and reach for the next contact point.

When using the hands for grip, apply the whole-body principle to the hands themselves. Rather than letting the weight dangle from your fingers, distribute the tension of the grip throughout the hand. And remember: Not all holds are horizontal. A vertical protrusion can be equally useful in a moment of crisis.

No. 036: Emergency Climbing Techniques

CONOP: Understand self-rescue climbing techniques to overcome unforeseen obstacles.

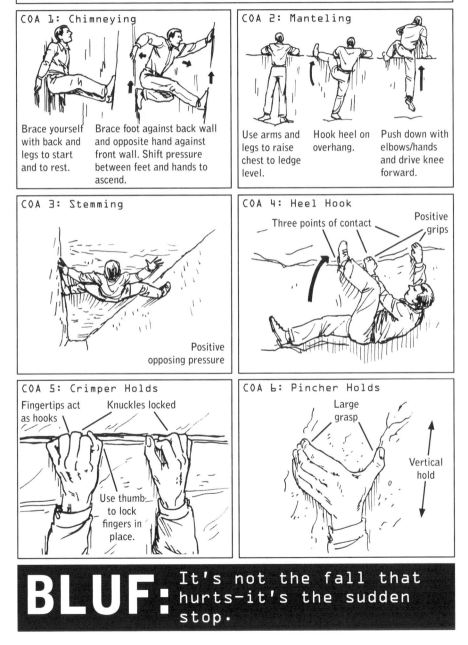

COA 1: Chimneying

Brace yourself with back and legs to start and to rest.

Brace foot against back wall and opposite hand against front wall. Shift pressure between feet and hands to ascend.

COA 2: Manteling

Use arms and legs to raise chest to ledge level.

Hook heel on overhang.

Push down with elbows/hands and drive knee forward.

COA 3: Stemming

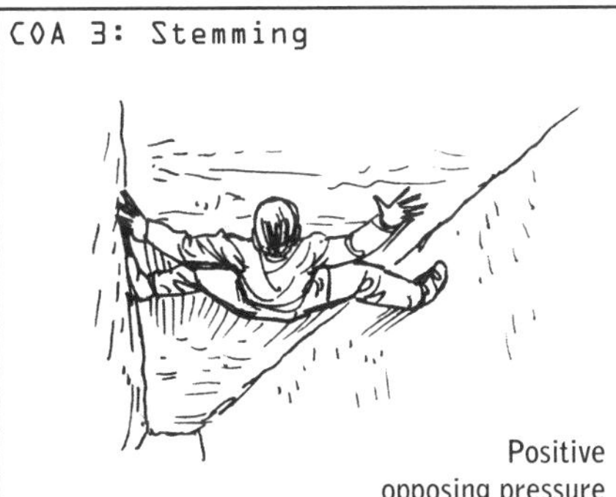

COA 4: Heel Hook

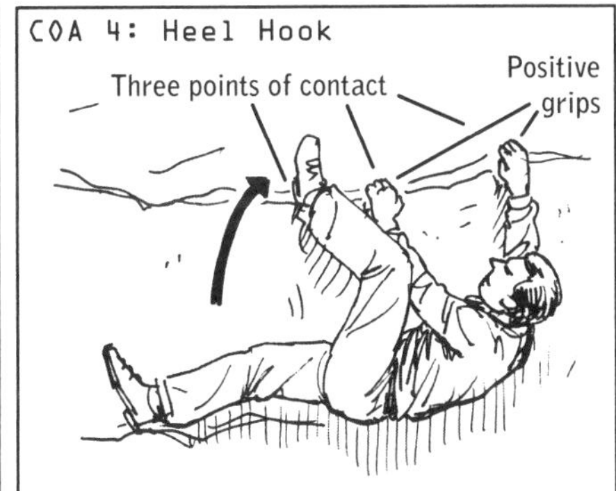

COA 5: Crimper Holds

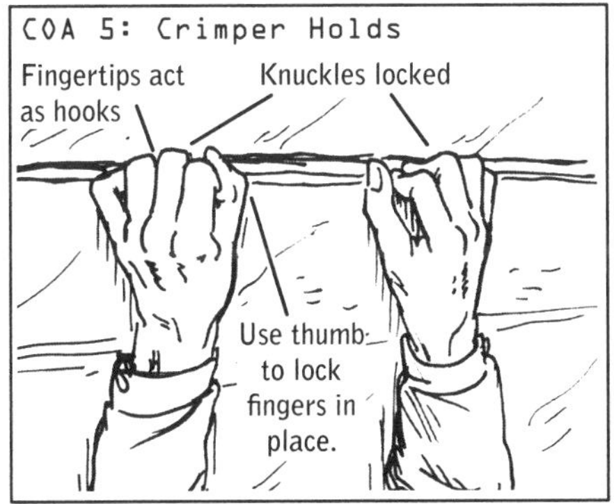

COA 6: Pincher Holds

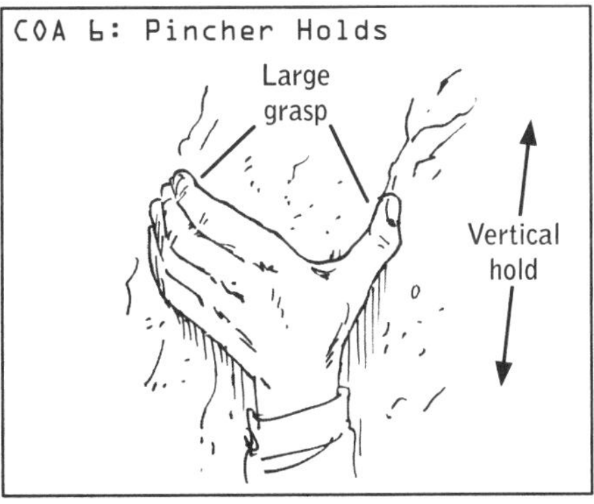

BLUF: It's not the fall that hurts—it's the sudden stop.

037 Survive a Bear Attack

If you run into a black bear on a mountain trail, be grateful for your good fortune. Compared to polar bears and brown bears, black bears are much less likely to attack. Brown bears (sometimes also known as grizzly bears) are the most aggressive species of bear, while polar bears are always hungry—and unlike black and brown bears, polar bears will actively track and hunt down humans across their arctic terrain. Their massive height and heft make them formidable opponents, capable of disemboweling prey with a single swipe of their claws.

Human-bear interactions have become increasingly frequent as various regulations and conservation efforts have swelled the bear population across North America, with black bear sightings particularly on the rise. Fortunately, bear attacks are very rare in general—you have a 1 in 2.1 million chance of being mauled, which means that almost any routine daily activity has a greater chance of killing you. But activities such as bow-hunting for elk in the mountains of Montana or backpacking in the Yellowstone range will significantly increase your risk of a lethal attack. And there's no discounting the occasional suburban visitor who rifles through Dumpsters or even locks himself inside the family sedan.

Commonsense Precautions

The number one reason for bear attacks? Humans getting too close for comfort. Give bears an extremely wide berth, and never get between a female bear and her cubs. If you spot a bear from a distance, change your route. Stay quiet, so as not to pique the bear's interest. Should a change in direction be impossible, do not proceed until the bear has been out of sight for thirty minutes.

If you've spotted bears in the vicinity, clap your hands and use your voice to emit a steady stream of noise as you transit. Bears have a formidable sense of smell, so when you're stopped for the

No. 037: Survive a Bear Attack

CONOP: How to prevent and survive a bear attack.

COA 1: Identify the bear.

COA 2: Distant Contact Tactics (100s of meters)

COA 3: Close Contact Tactics (10s of meters)

BLACK:
Never turn your back.
Prepare bear spray.
Get big.
Make noise.
BROWN:
Never turn your back.
Prepare bear spray.
Prepare to fight.
FIGHT!
Play dead if attacked.
POLAR:
Never turn your back.
Prepare bear spray.
Prepare to fight.

COA 4: Where to strike a bear:

BLUF: Most bear attacks are defensive-very few want you for dinner.

night, follow the commonsense strategies of double-bagging and hanging your food. Place food, cookware, and utensils at least one hundred feet from your tent, and never set up camp near bear scat or tracks. Store any scented products (toothpaste, soap) with food and cooking supplies. Do not sleep in the same clothing you cooked in, as food scents may remain on fibers.

Transit through bear country with two or more companions if possible—bears don't tend to attack groups.

Carry bear spray (a form of pepper spray), which has been shown to be more effective than handguns at deterring bear attacks, and a whistle. Grizzly bears are currently protected as a threatened species in the lower forty-eight states, so killing one will result in a federal investigation complete with forensic analysis.

If the bear is close and has spotted you, get big. Wave your arms around and make noise. Often this strategy will make bears stop in their tracks and run off.

When Bears Attack

If the bear charges you, this is the moment to use bear spray or shoot. Dispense bear spray when the bear is within forty feet, or aim rifle sights at a spot below its chin, or just behind its front legs if shooting broadside. If you are unarmed, stand very still. The bear may be doing a false charge to test your mettle as a potential predator, and could lose interest once it sees that you are not a threat.

If the bear attacks, most experts agree that this is the moment to lie down and play dead. You want to convince the bear that it has done its job and effectively minimized the perceived threat you posed. Lay flat on your stomach to protect your organs, crossing your hands behind your neck to guard your arteries. Or curl into the fetal position, covering the back of your neck with your hands. Playing dead is an effective strategy with a 75 percent success rate; because most bear attacks are defensive in nature, bears will back down once they recognize that you are not a threat. Of course, nothing is predictable in the wild. Bears, though omnivorous, subsist mostly on plants and fish—but they have been known to feast on human flesh.

Never turn your back on a bear, and never try to run. Both of these actions can kick-start a bear's predatory reflexes—and you'll never be able to outrun a bear, as the animals can travel at up to thirty miles per hour. Instead, slowly walk away sideways, keeping an eye on the animal so that you can monitor its movements.

If playing dead does not cause the bear to lose interest, you are the rare victim of a predatory attack. The bear intends to kill and possibly eat you, so fight back with any available weapons—a knife, sticks, rocks, your fists. Aim for the eyes and nose, where the bear is most sensitive.

There's no tried-and-true, written-in-stone protocol for handling a bear attack, in part because attacks are so rare. So it's no surprise to find debate among bear-country dwellers about how to handle a grizzly charge versus an encounter with a black bear. Some say that playing dead is more likely to work with the former, claiming that the latter's less frequent attacks are more likely to be offensive. But all agree that pepper spray is the single best deterrent, one so effective that it has been used successfully by children under the age of ten.

038 Cross Rapids Safely

Look both ways before you cross. Better yet, avoid crossing rivers entirely if you know you are going to be exposed to the elements for any length of time. Wet shoes and socks can lead to serious problems a few miles down the road, and rapids can be stronger than they appear.

If you must cross a river with fast-moving currents, scope out areas upstream or downstream of your position, seeking out a path that will make your crossing as efficient and safe as possible. Crossing straightaways between two bends may allow you to take advantage of a slowdown in current after a curve. Look for shoals or shallow points that may allow you to hop from one dry spot to another. Avoid a visible pileup of debris along an embankment, which could indicate strong currents and may entail a risk of getting trapped. A gathering of ripples is a likely indicator of a mass of rocks, another obstacle that could make a crossing more difficult.

To cross on foot, locate a long stick—adding a third leg to your walking posture will increase your stability. Face the current, and make your crossing slow and steady. Rushing will only increase the likelihood of getting knocked off your feet.

Cross deep, rushing waters only as an option of last resort. If you must swim, strip and place gear in a large garbage bag. Tie off the bag securely, leaving air inside so that the inflated bag functions as a flotation device. Swim diagonally up current to counter the effects of drift.

No. 038: Cross Rapids Safely

CONOP: Cross fast-moving water safely and efficiently.

COA 1: Understand best points to cross.

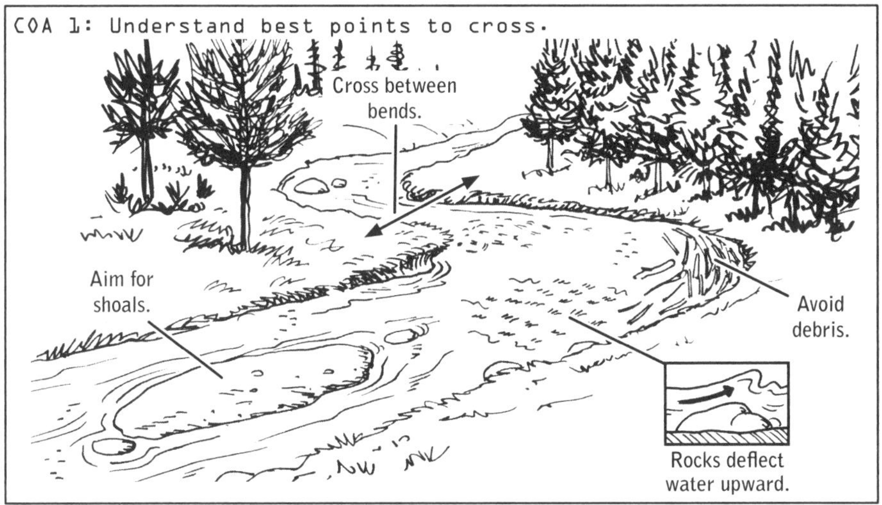
Cross between bends.
Aim for shoals.
Avoid debris.
Rocks deflect water upward.

COA 2: Solo Crossing

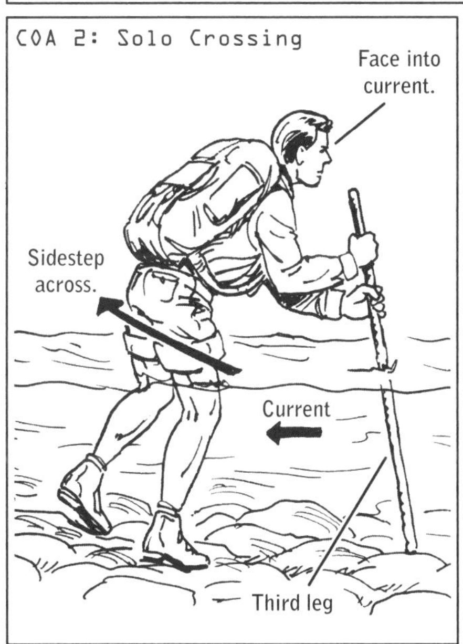
Face into current.
Sidestep across.
Current
Third leg

COA 3: Swimming

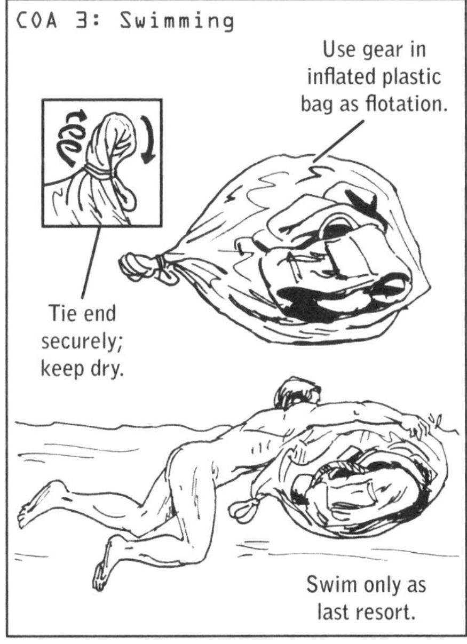
Use gear in inflated plastic bag as flotation.
Tie end securely; keep dry.
Swim only as last resort.

BLUF: The best way to cross any body of water is by boat or bridge.

039 Minimum EDC, Maritime Environment

Though cruise ships carry a supply of emergency survival rafts and require passengers to submit to safety drills, deep sea fishing expeditions or voyages aboard private yachts may take a more casual approach to emergency prep. Familiarize yourself with basic strategies for deep sea survival in order to hedge against the unexpected.

Generally stocked on larger vessels, emergency survival rafts are constructed to automatically inflate upon hitting water. Some older models will require you to unscrew a valve, but generally won't involve inflating the raft while passengers are still onboard the ship.

Shipowners assembling their own maritime EDC kits should stockpile a variety of signaling, navigational, medical, and life-support essentials. Rafts should be outfitted with external lights that will be seen by passing boats in the night, as well as flares, flare guns, and ChemLights that allow passengers to actively signal to get the attention of aircraft and nearby vessels. The earth begins to bend at seven nautical miles at sea level, but a flare gun enables passengers to send signals one thousand feet up into the air, where they can be seen by ships or aircraft many more miles away.

Rafts should be stocked with paddles, but passengers should not make uneducated decisions about navigation unless they can see their way to shore. Their best chance of rescue will be to drop anchor and remain close to the shipwreck, the site of any last-minute transmissions that may have been caught by the coast guard.

If a GPS device indicates that a shoreline is within twelve miles, an attempt to reach the shore may be worthwhile, but activating a personal location beacon (PLB) that beams out your location on rescue frequencies may turn out to be a more useful maneuver. Devices that depend upon satellites function very accurately on open water, where signals won't be interrupted by tall buildings or dense vegetation.

No. 039: Minimum EDC, Maritime Environment

CONOP: Minimum everyday carry items for survival at sea.

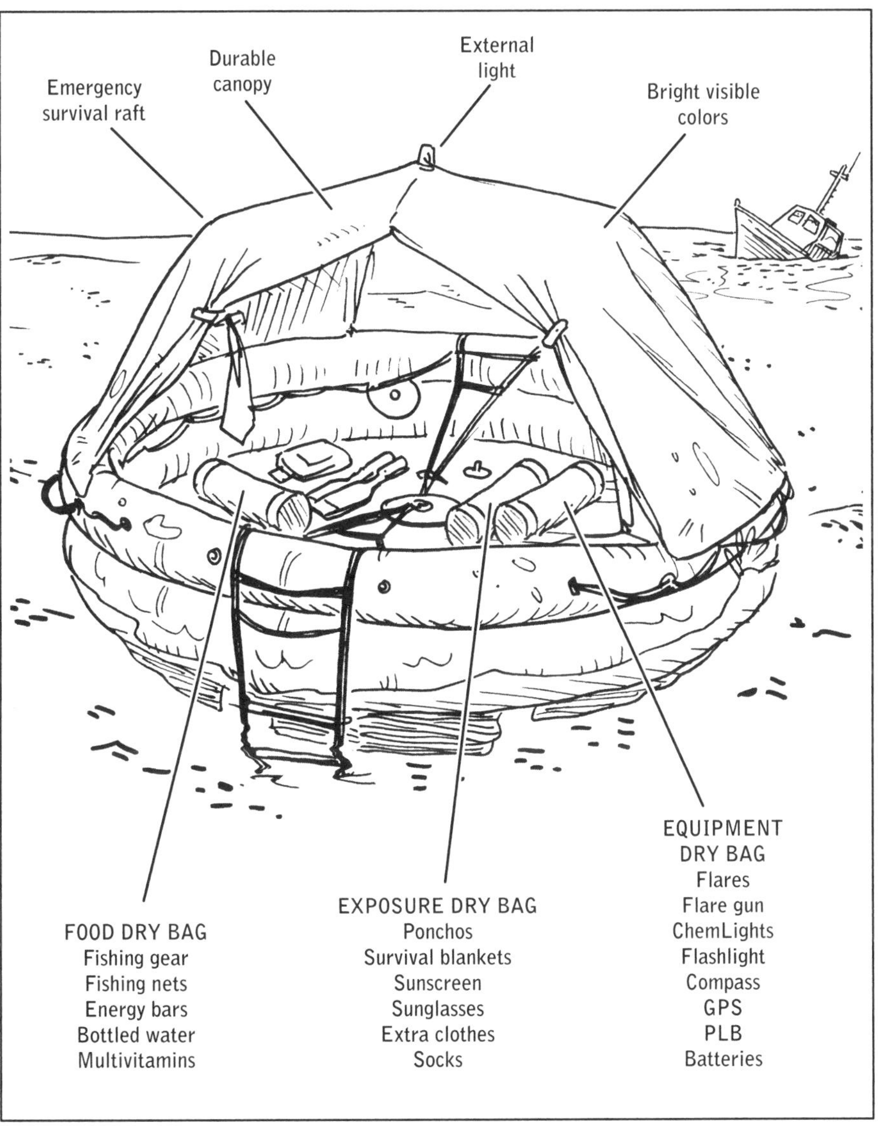

BLUF: The ocean can be a desert if you're not prepared.

040 Convert Seawater to Drinking Water

Water everywhere, but not a drop to drink. No truer words were ever spoken in a maritime environment, where drinking salt water will only hasten your demise. As the kidney begins to work overtime to purge the body of excess salt, the body expels liquid faster than it can be replenished, with fatal dehydration the rapid result. But by using a pocketknife or razor and a couple of found objects, you can create an improvised desalination system that harnesses the single resource most abundant at sea.

Leaving the cap screwed on, cut off the bottom from an empty cylindrical water bottle (the bigger the better) and discard. Cut off and discard the top from an aluminum beverage can. Fold the bottom of the water bottle up into itself, rolling up the plastic to create a gutter of two inches or more. Fill the open can with seawater and place it on a solid surface. Place the bottle over the top of the can. The heat will evaporate the water, which will rise and condense on the interior surface of the bottle while the salt is left behind inside the can. As droplets accumulate on the plastic, they will slide down into the gutter you've created. Let the receptacle sit in the sun until a sufficient amount of drinkable water has accumulated.

Though we rely on the formula of a gallon of water a day for emergency preparedness, under survival conditions human beings can live on a liter—which translates to a quarter of a gallon or one tall bottle of water, less if you're able to find high-moisture foods like fish and seaweed rather than subsisting on emergency food rations. Without any water at all, fatality will result in three to five days, depending on external temperature, genetics, and starting level of hydration.

No. 040: Convert Seawater to Drinking Water

CONOP: Use everyday items to convert salt water to drinking water.

COA 1: Cut the bottom off an empty plastic water bottle, and the top off a beer/soda can.

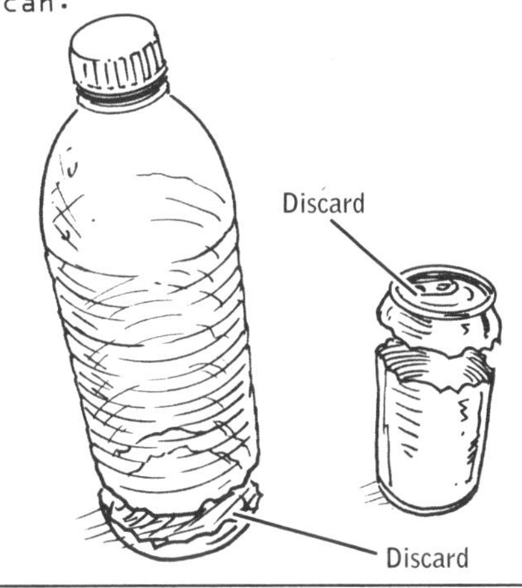

COA 2: Fold bottom of water bottle up into itself, creating a gutter to trap water.

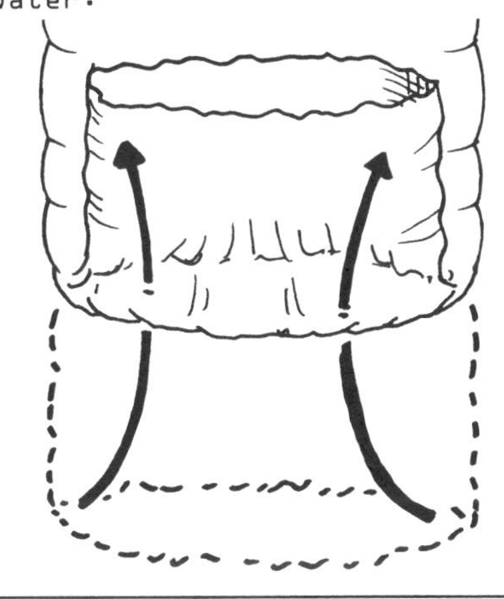

COA 3: Fill can with seawater and place bottle over can with cap in place. Left in the sun, drinkable water will condense and run down into gutter.

COA 4: Remove cap and drink.

BLUF: Never drink salt water—it will rapidly dehydrate you.

041 Reinforce Food Supplies While Drifting at Sea

Though the human body can survive thirty days without food, depending on your personal supply of good luck it may take as long to catch a fish. So in the event of a shipwreck, don't assume you'll be able to coast on your emergency food supply. Begin to ration food immediately, and gather improvised materials in order to construct a net and /or a set of fishing tackle.

Any piece of material can be used as an improvised net, from the shirt off your back to a poncho liner to a pair of pants. Tie shirt arms to a paddle or stick and knot the bottom of the shirt. Submerge the shirt so that fish can swim into the "net" through the neck opening.

Creativity will come in handy in assembling improvised fishing tackle. If emergency food supplies include canned food or beverages outfitted with aluminum pull tabs, these can be used as hooks. Cut or break off the larger of the tab's two rings at the midline to create the hook, and thread your fishing line through the smaller ring. Work with what you have. The needle of a safety pin can be twisted into a hook, but even a pair of scissors lifted from an emergency medical kit could be jammed open and put to good use. A length of fishing line can be fashioned from either dental floss or paracord, the nylon utility cord that's a favorite among both members of the military and serious outdoor enthusiasts. Also referred to as 550 cord for its maximum weight-bearing ability, the cord can be split into six smaller strands, each capable of holding about a hundred pounds.

While a seagull sighting may be a sign that land is nearby, that landmass could be uninhabited—and any animal that enters your orbit should be considered potential food. While the odds of successfully clubbing a seagull may seem low, there have been several instances of shipwreck survivors who have done just that.

No. 041: Reinforce Food Supplies While Drifting at Sea

CONOP: Supplement emergency rations with wildlife while stranded at sea.

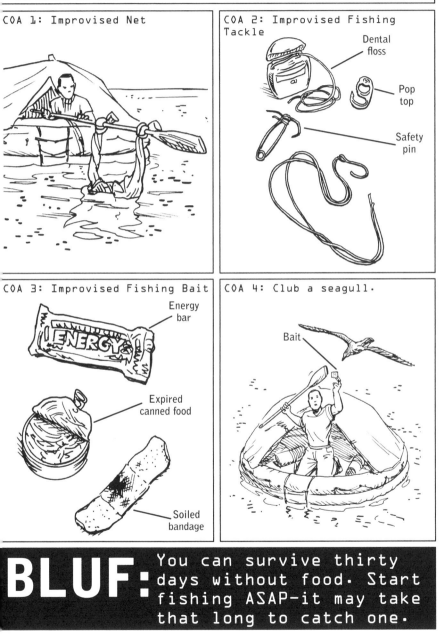

COA 1: Improvised Net

COA 2: Improvised Fishing Tackle

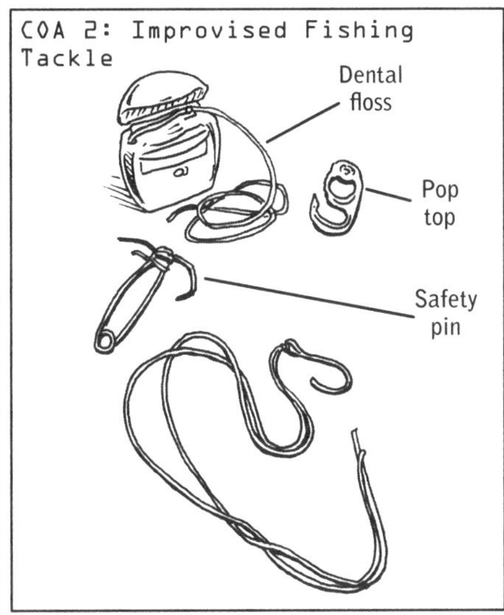

COA 3: Improvised Fishing Bait

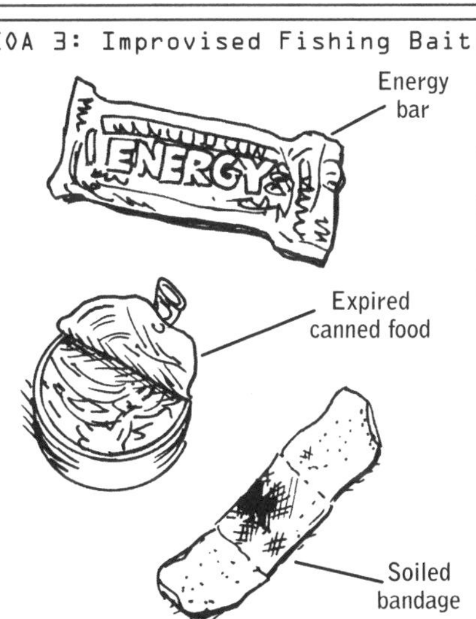

COA 4: Club a seagull.

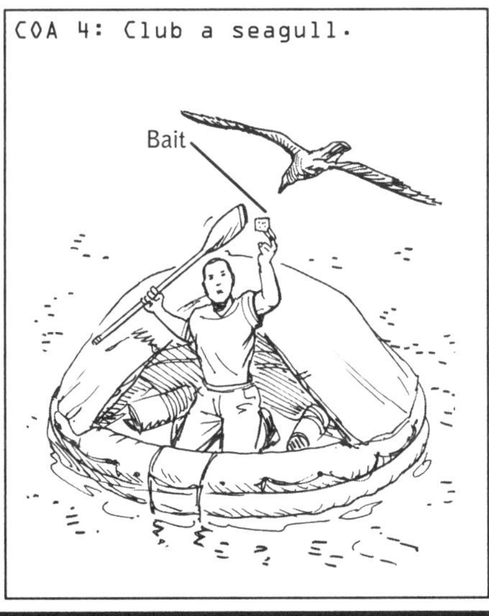

BLUF: You can survive thirty days without food. Start fishing ASAP—it may take that long to catch one.

042 Create Improvised Flotation Devices

Even at temperatures of sixty to seventy degrees, submersion in open waters can quickly cause hypothermia to set in. Long before muscles would ordinarily fatigue from treading water, disorientation and a lack of muscle coordination will result. Securing a flotation device becomes essential as energy wanes.

In the event of shipwreck, the safest course of action is to remain as close as possible to the sunken ship's debris. A Mayday call placed by the ship's crew would have alerted coast guards and nearby boats to the ship's last known position. And if you are stranded without a working raft, the debris will also become part of your survivability plan.

Large cans, barrels, and any other empty containers can be gathered and tied together to create a makeshift buoy. Water bottles can be grasped onto or shoved inside clothing once you've drunk their contents and screwed the cap closed. Trash or other plastic bags can easily be inflated by being swept through the air. Clasp the openings in your fists as you swiftly plunge the bags down into the water to create bobbing balloons with a high level of buoyancy.

Even a pair of pants can be transformed into an improvised flotation device, a survival trick familiar to many young graduates of scouting courses. To execute, tie knots at the bottom of pant legs and zip and button the fly. Grasping the pants at the waistline, fling them forward so that the waistband traps air in the legs before entering the water.

No. 042: Create Improvised Floatation Devices

CONOP: Stay afloat while lost at sea.

COA 1: Large Cans, Barrels, and Other Debris

COA 2: Consolidated Empty Water Bottles

COA 3: Inflated Trash Bags

COA 4: Inflated Pants and Clothing

BLUF: Stay dry! Body temp drops one degree per hour in eighty-four-degree water.

043 Survive a Shark Attack

For all the widespread horror their jaws incite, sharks rarely attack humans—and when they do, they're far more likely to bite once and swim away in search of the high-fat flesh they prefer than they are to strike repeatedly. In the average year, the number of worldwide fatalities from shark attacks won't exceed the single digits, and attacks in total number less than a hundred. But of course, a single shark bite can be fatal if it ravages organs or causes massive internal bleeding, and sometimes sharks latch on and won't let go. In the latter case, punching a shark in the nose or ripping its gills may persuade it to disengage.

If you unexpectedly find yourself in shark-infested waters, stay vertical. Floating horizontally makes you a bigger and more visible target from a shark's deep-sea perspective. One of the reasons surfers are such frequent targets of shark attacks, besides their proclivity for dangerous waters, may be the shape of their boards. Backlit by the sun and crowned by a surfer's outstretched arms, the large oblong boards may give sharks the mistaken impression that they've landed a seal or sea lion.

Despite spending significant amounts of time in deep waters and occasionally being sideswiped by sharks, the SEAL community has proven largely immune to shark attacks. There's no explanation for this phenomenon, but the reigning hypothesis holds that the fish could be repelled by the sound emitted by the Dräger rebreathers worn by SEALs. Though the theory remains untested, clanging metal or glass objects together may be a worthwhile method to explore if sharks are circling and rescue seems unlikely. (Though shiny metal jewelry that reflects sunlight could also attract the curious fish.)

Or you could always borrow from the tongue-in-cheek SEAL mantra: "See a shark? Stab your buddy and swim away."

No. 043: Survive a Shark Attack

CONOP: Know what to do in order to keep a shark at bay.

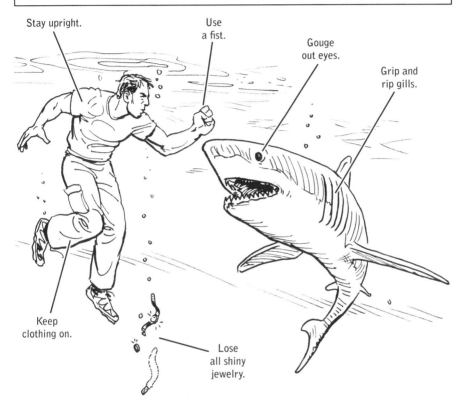

Stay upright.

Use a fist.

Gouge out eyes.

Grip and rip gills.

Keep clothing on.

Lose all shiny jewelry.

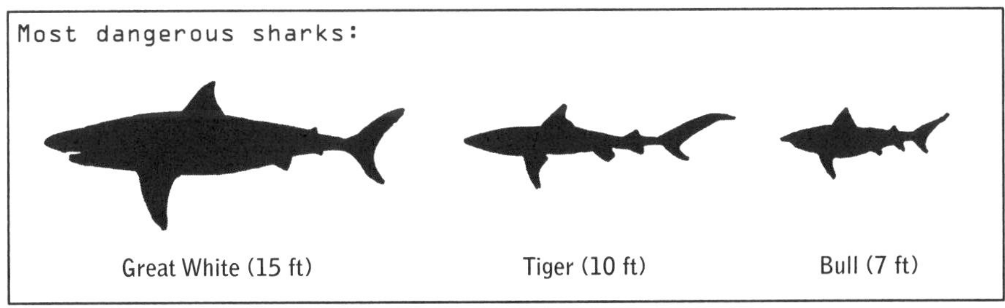

044 Defend a Ship Against Pirates

The Somali pirates who once freely roamed the Horn of Africa have been tamped down by international counterpiracy efforts in recent years, but there's no telling which corner of the world's oceans these and other violent criminals will colonize next. Armed with rocket-propelled grenades, assault rifles, and grappling hooks, the deadly hijackers seek multimillion-dollar ransoms from the shipping companies whose boats they target, along with the occasional cruise ship. Quick to execute their victims when security forces close in, they've also been known to hold hostages for years, refusing to submit until their demands are met.

Despite the typically light security detail present aboard luxury liners, the hijackers' success is not a foregone conclusion, and a number of boats have repelled pirate attacks using the low-tech means pictured here. If your watercraft isn't outfitted with an LRAD, a long-range acoustic device that directs a piercingly high-pitched tone at invading vessels, one of the following methods may come in handy.

Given the susceptibility of ships to devastating fires, every boat comes equipped with a multitude of fire hoses. A ship's captain and crew should freely avail themselves of these as lifesaving defense systems, blasting pirates with powerful jets of water. If they aren't toppled overboard, the resulting chaos will make it difficult for the pirates to take accurate shots. Set to full blast, hoses can also be lowered over the sides of the ship, where they'll turn into violently twisting snakes whose slippery output renders a climb almost impossible.

If the pirates' small vessels are within throwing distance, any available projectile is fair game. Liquor bottles pilfered from the ship's supply can be stoppered with tampons, the string set aflame as they are thrown overboard. The Molotov cocktail will explode on impact, mingling with any gunpowder aboard the pirates' vessel to create a highly repellant blast.

No. 044: Defend a Ship Against Pirates

CONOP: Prevent pirates from boarding a cruise liner.

COA 1: Fire Hoses' Jet Blast

Jet blast pirates with weapons.

Target boat driver, hook points, and ladders.

COA 2: Fire Hose Snakes

Open fire hose nozzle completely.

Lower entire length of hose down side of ship.

Turn on water pressure as high as possible.

COA 3: Molotov Cocktails

Collect bottles of liquor from ship bar. Insert tampon fuses.

Ignite and drop into pirate boats.

BLUF: Pirates generally access ships via ladders they carry with them.

PART IV

DEFENDING YOUR DOMAIN

045 Fortify Your Home Security

Most homeowners think of home security as a simple checklist. Install decent locks, consider an alarm system, make sure window locks are working properly, and you've done your job. But effective home security consists in surrounding your home with active, concentric layers of security, starting with the outermost layer: the eyes and ears next door and across the street.

Create a Sense of Watchful Community

Building rapport with your neighbors is one of the most important things you can do to protect your home. A neighbor who is invested in your relationship and familiar with your routines is less likely to be a complacent bystander to suspicious activity. Choose the right neighbors from the start—most break-ins are perpetrated by bad actors living within two miles of your home.

Control the Information

Always let neighbors know when you're going to be out of town for any prolonged period of time. Have mail and deliveries held while you're away, and check social media settings before posting vacation pics. Do not broadcast to the entire world the fact that your home has been left unattended.

Information gleaned from social media could potentially be used to rob your home while you're away, or to stage a virtual kidnapping that extorts money from your loved ones based on the false pretense that you've been abducted while traveling (see page 162). In general, favor privacy on social media settings. We've learned time and again just how porous the security systems of major tech companies can be, and nimble criminals will continually find new ways of exploiting those very loopholes. Be particularly wary of broadcasting information about your children online.

No. 045: Fortify Your Home Security

CONOP: Implement smarter security to decrease home burglary.

Never broadcast your vacations.

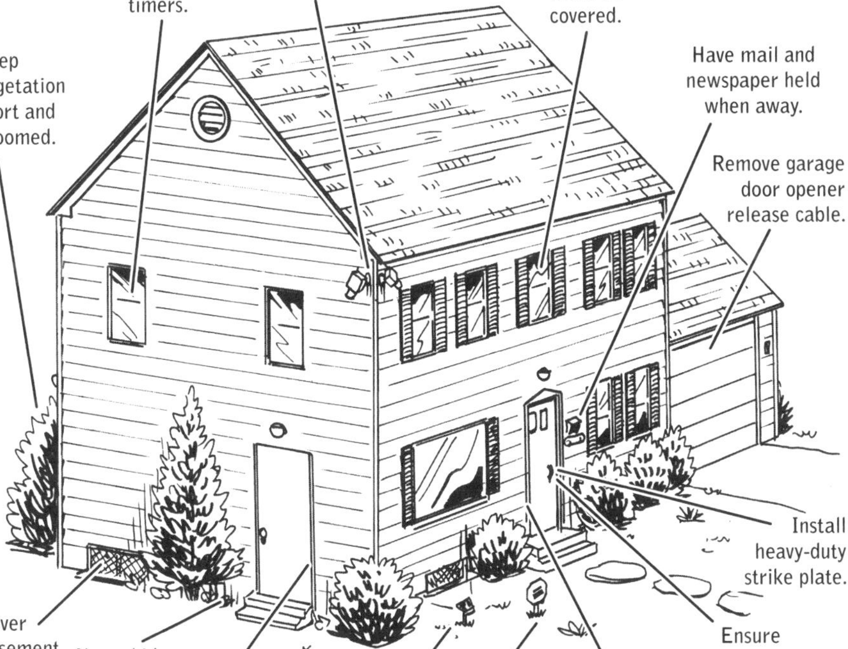

Use light timers.

Install cameras.

Keep windows covered.

Keep vegetation short and groomed.

Have mail and newspaper held when away.

Remove garage door opener release cable.

Install heavy-duty strike plate.

Cover basement windows.

Never hide a key.

Install weatherstripping.

Add perimeter lighting.

Add security sign.

Install two-inch wood screws to door frame.

Ensure deadbolt seats completely.

BLUF: Security signs and perimeter illumination will keep most bad guys away.

Limit Visibility

Working from the outside in, the next set of eyes on your home are those of a malicious perpetrator. Your goal in this respect is to limit a potential intruder's sight lines and access, while increasing *your* visibility of the perimeter of your home. To this end, start by keeping vegetation near your house sparse and neatly trimmed. Don't give criminals a place to hide.

Generously install lighting around the property. Lighting the perimeter of your house at night will tend to scare off the most malevolent class of criminals—for those who strike at night tend to be less interested in your belongings and more interested in harming you.

Tell a Story

Many homeowners know to set interior and exterior lights on timers when they're away overnight or for extended periods, but you can go a step further by using programmable lighting to your advantage, staggering lights to tell a story. A house that is suddenly illuminated at the same time every night lets a watchful intruder know that timers are in play. Scramble the intruder's perceptions by staggering timers, room by room and floor by floor. Early in the night, activate lights in the kitchen and living room areas. As the evening progresses, these lights should gradually be deactivated as bedroom lights come on.

To reduce visibility to outsiders of your home and belongings while keeping them guessing as to your routines, keep windows covered as much as possible, whether you are home or not. Park your car inside your garage and shut and lock the door (see page 110). Using your driveway as a parking spot gives intruders far too much information about your pattern of life.

Collect ID-Quality Footage

Many security cameras are improperly positioned, giving homeowners a false sense of security. To increase the effectiveness of your home security system, be sure camera placement and focal lens length are thoughtfully considered. A camera that spans your entire front yard may create a more dynamic view, but it won't come in handy when it's time to collect ID-quality footage of an intruder. A camera narrowly focused on a walkway or door will have a much better chance of delivering results. On the other hand, a wide-angle lens can be useful in collecting make, model, color, and direction of travel on suspicious vehicles.

Opt for a targeted assortment of lens lengths, combined with proper camera placement.

Though color may seem like the most up-to-date option, black-and-white cameras are better at collecting quality images in low light.

Visible cameras also act as a deterrent, as do security signs and stickers—and there's no law against faking your enrollment in an invented security system. Similarly, women living alone may place large pairs of men's shoes beside their front and back doors to simulate the presence of a male in the household.

046 Profile a Home Intruder

Because protecting your home and its inhabitants starts with an awareness of suspicious activity on the perimeter of your property, a key component of home security is a level of basic knowledge about the profile of the average intruder. The fact that the typical home intruder is 95 percent likely to be a man won't come as a surprise to anyone. But if you're looking out for a wizened professional, think again—the average home intruder is likely to be a kid.

Hot weather is notorious for causing an uptick in violent crime, and the same goes for nonviolent break-ins. Increased traffic to backyard grilling or recreation areas may lead to accidental lapses in security, creating a perfect target for intruders on the prowl. The same goes for open windows on ground floors.

Front and back doors are the preferred methods of entry for 56 percent of home intruders, so be sure to fortify doorways and locks on all exterior access points (see page 106). Securing a deadbolt strike plate and door frame with two-inch wood screws will make it more difficult for intruders to kick down a door. Make sure your deadbolt extends all the way into the strike plate. An improperly installed deadbolt, a common issue in new or haphazard construction, allows an intruder to bypass the lock by shimmying a knife around the bolt.

Though only 37 percent of break-ins occur after nightfall, these have the highest likelihood of being motivated by the will to cause violence—so investing in an inexpensive form of exterior night lighting is essential.

Remove or tie-off the garage door opener cable that allows you to manually release the door from the inside of the garage. Using a tool as simple as a wire hanger, an intruder could easily access the garage—and if that garage is connected to your home, he'll now have an enclosed space from which to work on gaining entry.

No. 046: Profile a Home Intruder

CONOP: Understand the characteristics of a home intruder.

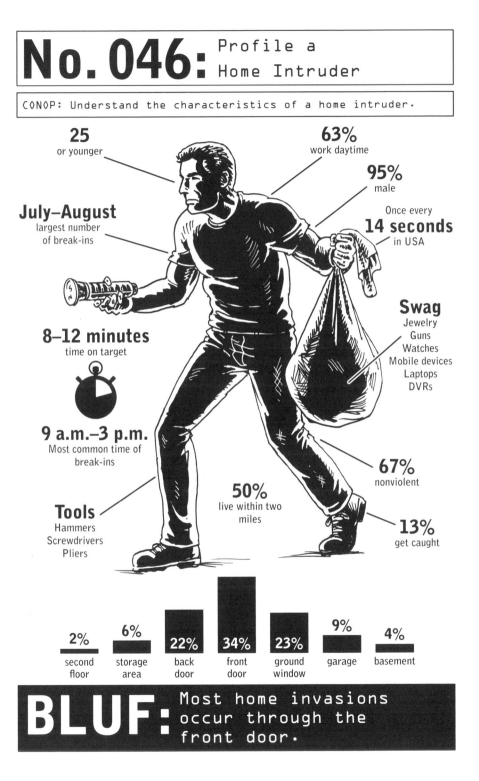

BLUF: Most home invasions occur through the front door.

047 Build a Tactical Nightstand

Why waste the space on a stack of half-read books and periodicals, when you could turn your nightstand into a tactical toolbox? Members of the military and security personnel rarely turn in for a night's sleep without having their kit at the ready—and the principle of constant readiness by which they abide can be adopted by the average civilian with an interest in safeguarding his or her home (and the people and things inside). If the middle of the night is the time when we are most vulnerable to the most dangerous kinds of attack, it stands to reason that we'd want to stash a portable armory within reach of our beds.

The top of your nightstand can be loaded with innocuous-looking items such as a cell phone and/or wearable device with which to place emergency calls and send distress signals. A candle can light a room in the event of a power outage. And a mouthpiece and steel-barreled pen can respectively be deployed as safeguard and weapon during hand-to-hand combat. Given that each of these items is commonly seen on bedside surfaces, the totality will not arouse suspicion. Improvise at will.

Usually an unkempt tangle of rarely used items, the nightstand's drawer can be turned into a well-organized arsenal of weapons, ranging from the very lethal (a gun and/or fixed-blade knife) to the nonlethal (hornet or pepper spray and a heavy-duty flashlight, equally useful for bludgeoning an opponent and searching your home).

In the space between the nightstand and your bed and/or the wall, stash oversize weapons, emergency response tools, and protective gear, such as a baseball bat, a fire extinguisher, and a set of body armor. While the last may seem like overkill, any situation that requires you to draw your weapon is a solid contender for the use of body armor.

No. 047: Build a Tactical Nightstand

CONOP: Load your nightstand with counter-intruder tools.

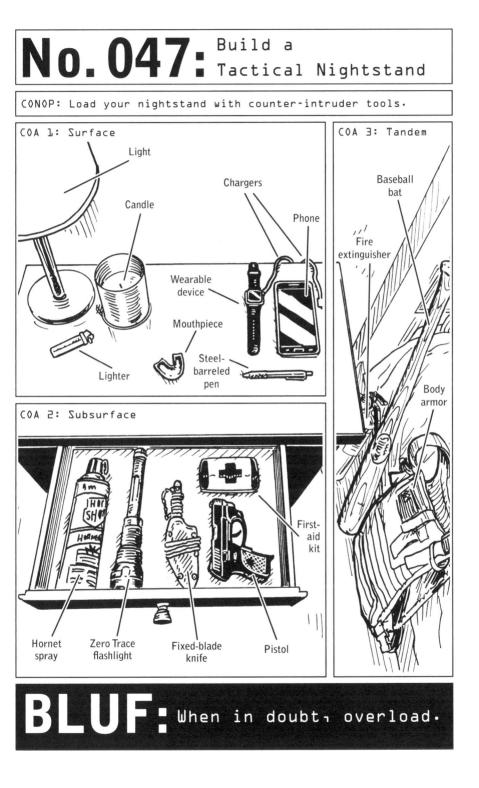

COA 1: Surface

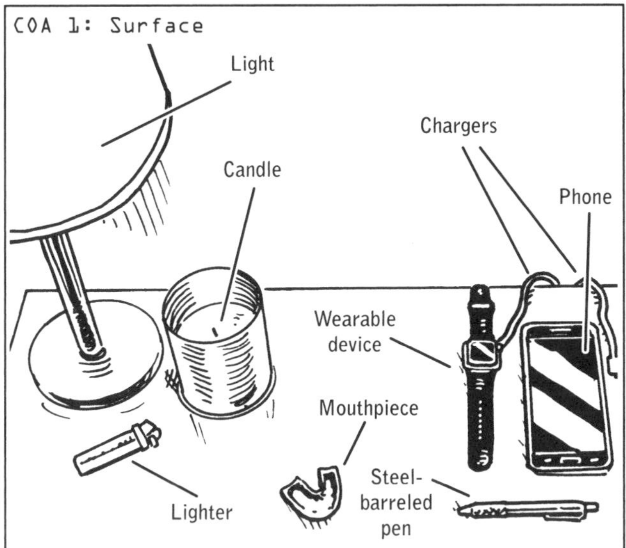

COA 3: Tandem

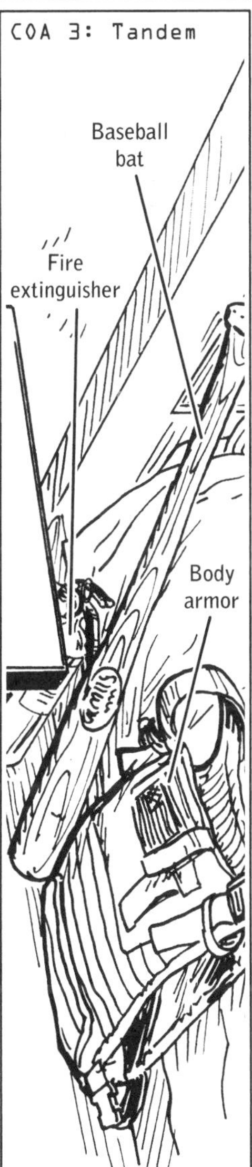

COA 2: Subsurface

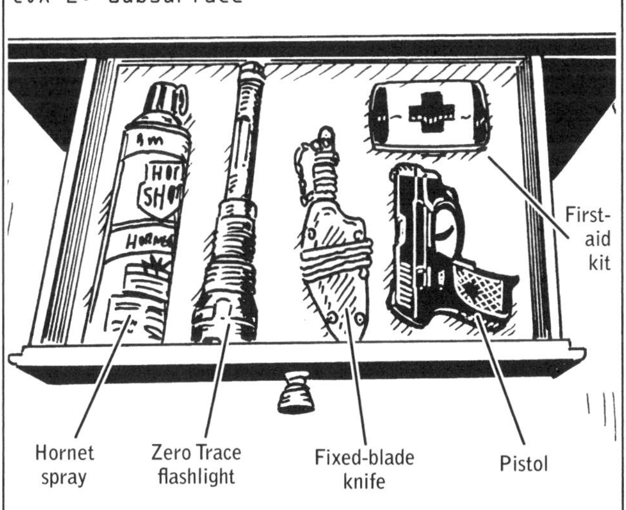

BLUF: When in doubt, overload.

048 Use a Flashlight as a Tactical Tool

It goes without saying that no home or apartment should be without a working flashlight. But many civilians don't realize the possibilities lying latent in the little-used tool they've stashed away in their closets. Beyond its necessity during power outages, a flashlight can also come in handy during nighttime home invasions, as a means of searching the premises, signaling for help, and distracting or disabling an opponent, particularly if it is a heavy model made of steel and aluminum.

Perform a Tactical Search: Hear an unfamiliar sound go bump in the night? A flashlight becomes the optimal illumination tool during a tactical search of your home (see page 122). Shine a beam up at the ceiling to illuminate a room, and use the cover of darkness and your knowledge of your home's blueprint to your advantage in order to deceive your opponent.

Signal for Help: If you are trapped inside your home with an intruder and no means of escape, illuminate neighbors' bedrooms and passing cars to signal for help. Got a dog lying out in the yard? Shining a light in his eyes may cause him to wake up and bark, turning your friendly canine into a safety whistle.

Blind or Strike an Opponent: In a direct confrontation with an intruder, use the flashlight to temporarily blind your opponent. The photoreceptors the human eye uses in low light take longer to adapt to changes in brightness than do those used for day vision. If the eye is suddenly and momentarily exposed to an unnaturally bright light source, temporary blindness is the result. Use that window to escape—or to strike. A heavy-duty flashlight can also be used to physically disable your opponent.

No. 048: Use a Flashlight as a Tactical Tool

CONOP: Leverage a flashlight to search, blind, and fight.

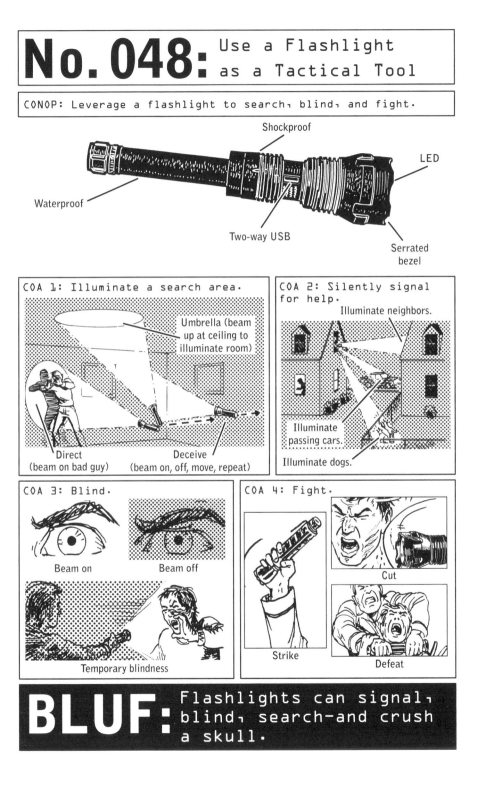

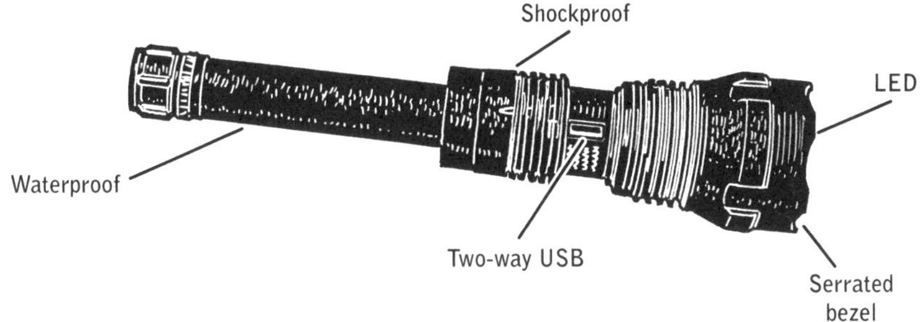

COA 1: Illuminate a search area.

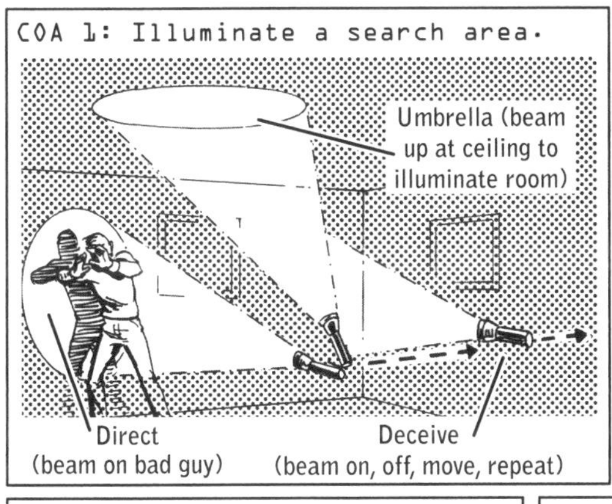

COA 2: Silently signal for help.

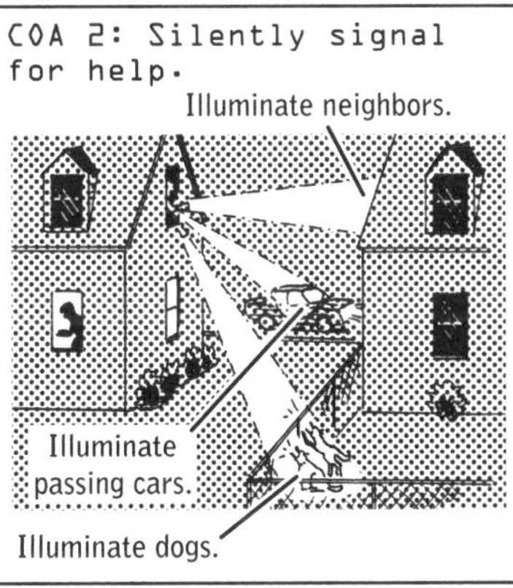

COA 3: Blind.

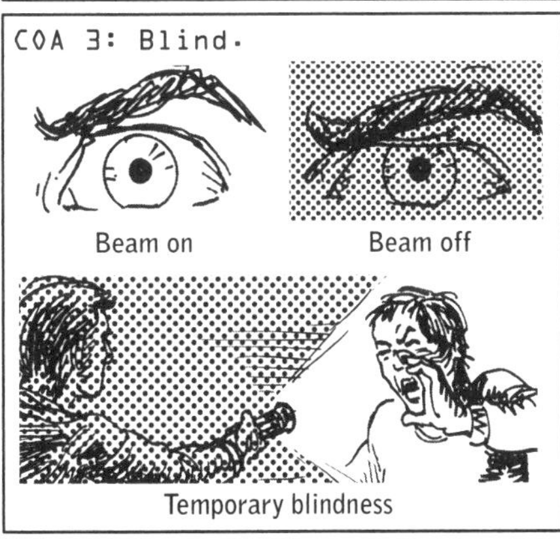

COA 4: Fight.

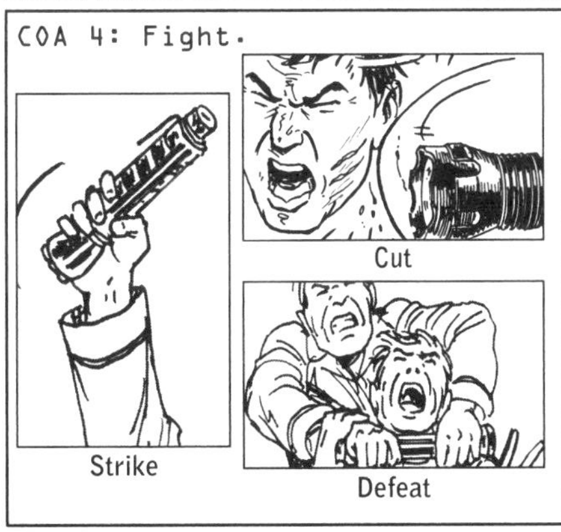

BLUF: Flashlights can signal, blind, search—and crush a skull.

049 Build an Improvised Concealable Rifle Rack

Handy storage solutions for long, unwieldy weapons, wall-mounted rifle racks provide ease of access and create eye-catching displays. They're also visible to anyone who enters your home or peers in through a window, and given that many weapons used in acts of workplace violence and homegrown terror are stolen, weapon theft is a real concern. But hide your weapon too far away, and you're compromising your own ease-of-access in a home invasion scenario.

The standard hacks used by civilians wary of home intrusion—placing a rifle under the bed or mattress, or behind a headboard—may place the weapon in close proximity to sleeping heads of household, but do not facilitate a quick draw. Fortunately, a quick-to-assemble but surprisingly dependable solution can be jerry-rigged from two ordinary hangers jammed beneath a mattress, making an assault or hunting rifle as accessible as a shotgun. (Shotguns do, however, remain the preferable choice for home safety. Unlike bullets, buckshot won't rip through Sheetrock—but it *will* take out a home intruder. Because each shot fired releases a round of lead pellets, buckshot also creates a larger blast site and requires less accuracy than a single bullet.)

To construct this improvised concealable rack, use wooden or plastic hangers with swiveling hooks. Cheap wire hangers will not hold the weight of the weapon. Position the hooks according to the length of your weapon and, if necessary, bend the hooks to create a custom grip. The weight of the mattress will hold down the rack even if you roll around at night. Drape a blanket over the construction for concealment.

Note: Weapons should always be securely locked away when children are present, and weapon storage must follow regional laws applicable to your area.

No. 049: Build an Improvised Concealable Rifle Rack

CONOP: Create an improvised gun rack using coat hangers.

COA 1: Collect two suit or coat hangers.

COA 2: Slip body of hangers in between mattress and box spring.

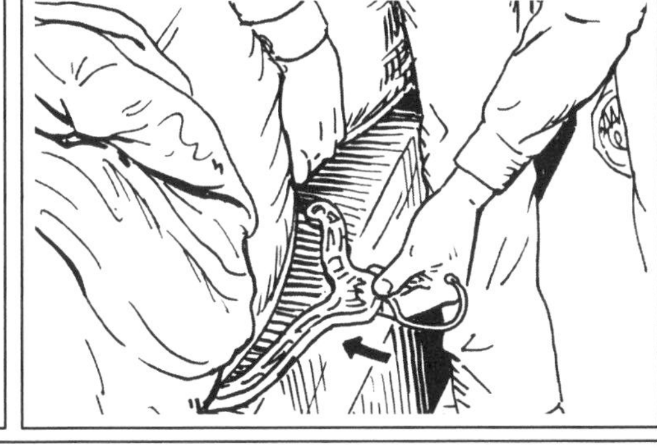

COA 3: Leave only the hanger hooks exposed.

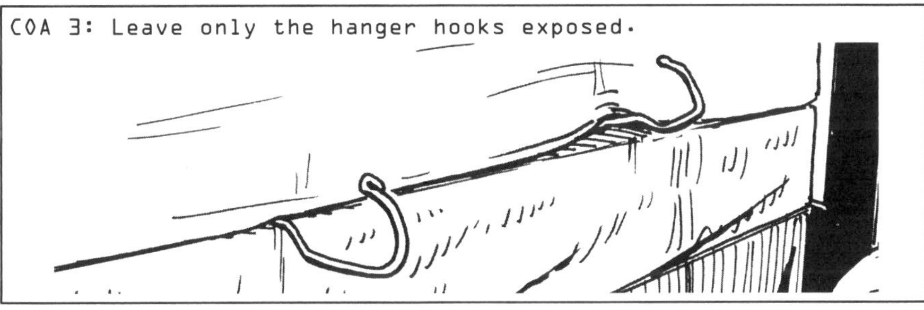

COA 4: Adjust spacing to fit weapon length.

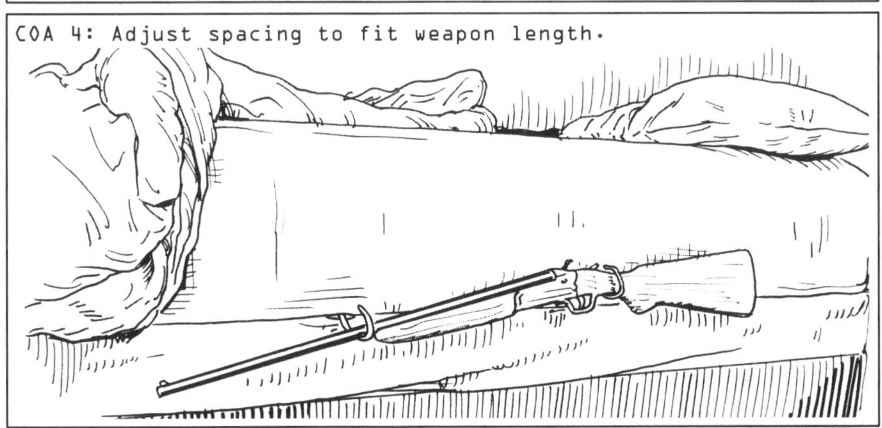

BLUF: Readiness isn't just a state of mind.

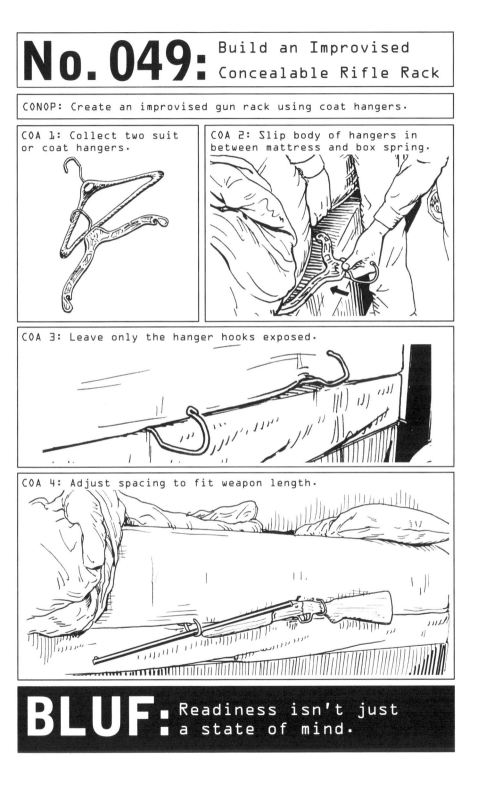

050 Survive Home Invasions

Homeowners are frequently under the mistaken impression that if an intruder breaches the premises in the middle of the night, their only options—after calling for help—are to either await rescue or say their prayers. In fact, there are a multitude of actions that may diminish your risk of injury, abduction, or worse, the overriding key being preparation.

Create an Action Plan

The last thing you want to do is be forced to make decisions *during* a crisis. Plan out your decision-making process ahead of time so that instinct can take over in the midst of uncertainty, and you'll already be one step ahead of a potential intruder who is counting on the element of surprise. Have a plan, and enact that plan to increase your odds of survival. It's a simple proposition, but one by which not enough households abide. Make sure all members of the household are well versed in the plan and have practiced appropriate elements. We're accustomed to the idea of emergency fire, earthquake, and tornado drills in businesses and schools. It stands to reason that we should enact such drills in the home, the focal point for everything and everyone we hold most precious.

Identify and walk escape routes and rally points as a family, running through various potential scenarios. Will you congregate at a neighbor's house or at the park around the corner? If someone is trying to kick in the front door, will parents come down to the children's room and exit through the back door or a second-story window? Store portable emergency ladders in second-floor rooms, and have all members of the family practice using them. Create a plan for getting off the property's perimeter as soon as possible—a backyard could easily become a contained area in which family members are held hostage.

While firearm storage must follow legal safety standards, improvised weapons such as baseball bats or spray bottles filled with

No. 050: Survive Home Invasions

CONOP: Prepare for, respond to, and survive home invasions.

COA 1: Prepare (include entire family, make it fun).

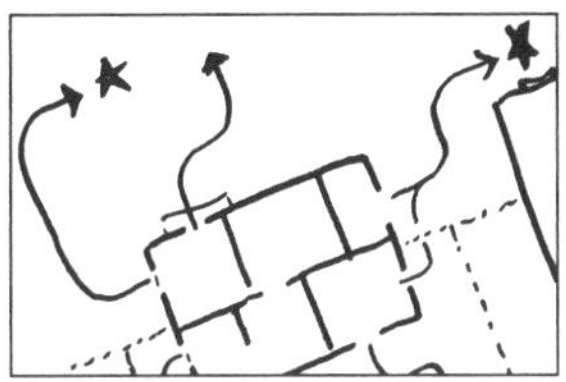
Identify and walk escape routes with rally points.

Identify and conceal weapons.

Have a communication plan (cell phone, car keys, safe word).

Conceal escape tools in every room.

Identify barricades and placement plan.

Identify safe rooms (closets, basements).

COA 2: Respond (stay quiet and calm).

Keep lights off (you know your house better than they do).

Call 911 (whisper).

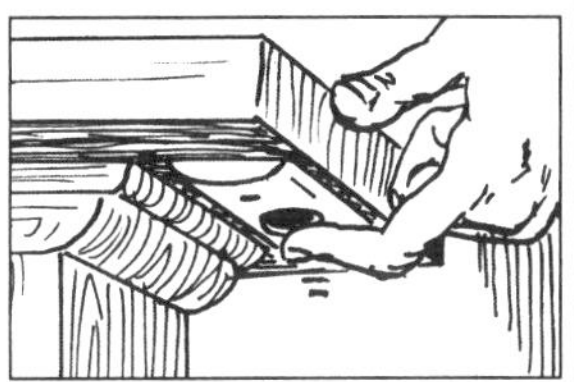
Hit alarm buttons (home alarm, vehicle key panic button).

Grab weapons, flashlight.

Escape to rally point.

BLUF: Always attempt to escape—but be ready to fight.

bleach can be stored around the house, along with escape tools such as Swiss army knives or razor blades. You never know which room could become the site of a potential hostage situation.

Keep cell phones charged and reachable in the middle of the night. Better yet, create a full tactical nightstand in order to prepare for emergencies (see page 112). Always sleep with car keys within reach. These will come in handy in the event that you need to make a quick exit—and you can also use them to set off your car's panic button in order to alert the neighbors or spook an intruder. If you have an up-to-date home security system, be sure you've loaded the appropriate apps onto your phone so that you can set off the alarm without roaming the house to reach the security console. Establish a whispered safe word so family members can quickly and quietly alert each other to emergencies in the dark—as well as signal in advance that you (and not the bad guy) are the person creeping down the hallway.

In each room, identify couches, dressers, and bookshelves that can potentially be used as barricades. These will buy you time as you await rescue or attempt escape.

Store food, water, and concealed weapons in safe rooms outfitted with deadbolts and reachable by only one means of entry. To fortify doorways and locks in these rooms, see page 106.

Run through the drill with family members once a year to ensure that the action plan is not forgotten.

Respond to Crisis

In the moment of crisis, keep lights off. Turning on lights at the first sign that something is awry, a common reflex, will only help an intruder track and find you faster. You and your family know the blueprint of your home better than the intruder. Leaving the lights off keeps him at a disadvantage. If necessary, use a flashlight to illuminate and sweep individual rooms to make sure you are safe (see page 122).

Call 911 and hit alarm buttons as soon as possible. Enact your plan, availing yourself of weapons along the way. A flashlight has a multitude of uses, from temporarily blinding an opponent (see page 114) to hitting him over the head. Be alert to the latent defensive potential of common household objects. An electrical cord can be used to detain and or subdue (see pages 126 and 172). Kitchen knives are fair game for slashing and dashing, and any glass bottle can be brought down with force over an opponent's head. Even empty-handed, you may still find an opportunity to bring down an armed opponent. Particularly if you are able to team up, you may be able to use the element of surprise to disarm an intruder (see page 154). But again, in the case of a home invasion, your primary concern should be getting yourself and loved ones to safety. Inflict enough pain to stun the intruder, and then escape as quickly as possible. Unless you are cornered and forced to fight, your aim should be to leave the dirty work to law enforcement officials and get yourself and your family members to safety as soon as possible.

051 Combat Clear Your Home

Most civilians respond to an unfamiliar nighttime sound by flooding their homes with light. But learn to combat clear your home following professional military and security protocol, and you'll know that leaving the lights *off* preserves your advantage. Because you know the blueprint of your home far better than the intruder does, you'll be able to move about quickly and quietly while he loudly stumbles around in the dark.

If you do not have a weapon and suspect there is an intruder in your home, call 911 and leave the premises. Only search your home with a weapon in hand. Keep lights off as you search, using ambient light or a flashlight to illuminate rooms, flipping lights on, room by room, only as needed.

Slowly and quietly approach corners by skimming walls with your weapon drawn. Clear corners by "slicing the pie," a military technique that enables you to quickly and safely scan a room through a series of sidesteps, following a semicircular pattern that minimizes your profile. Keeping your eyes and the barrel of your weapon moving in the same direction, clear each slice of the pie, moving your eyes and the gun's sights from low to high.

To clear a doorway, pie as much of the room as possible before entering. Move through the doorway quickly, then immediately veer sideways, flattening yourself against the wall as you clear the blind corners directly left and right of the door. Known as "fatal funnels," doorways should be cleared as quickly as possible—the logical place for a gunman to aim, they are frequently the site of an innocent person's demise.

Once you've cleared each room, don't forget to clear any obstacles, checking the far side of couches and beds and the underside of tables and countertops.

No. 051: Combat Clear Your Home

CONOP: Search and clear your home and ensure it is secure.

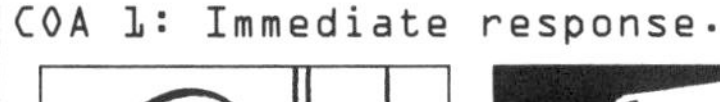

COA 1: Immediate response.

Lock doors.

Keep lights off.

Get weapon.

Call 911.

COA 2: Safely clear corners.

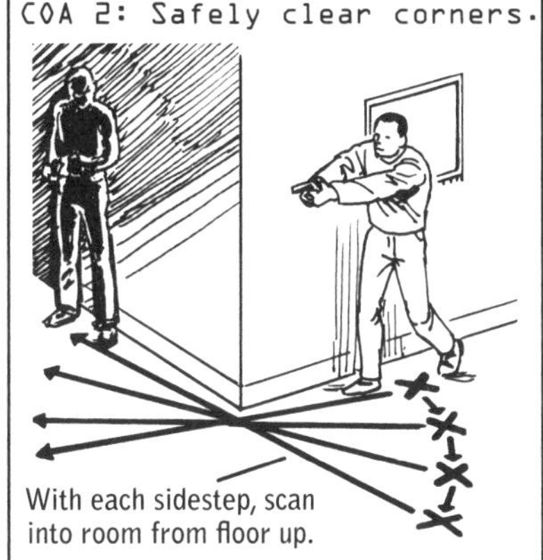

COA 3: Safely clear rooms.

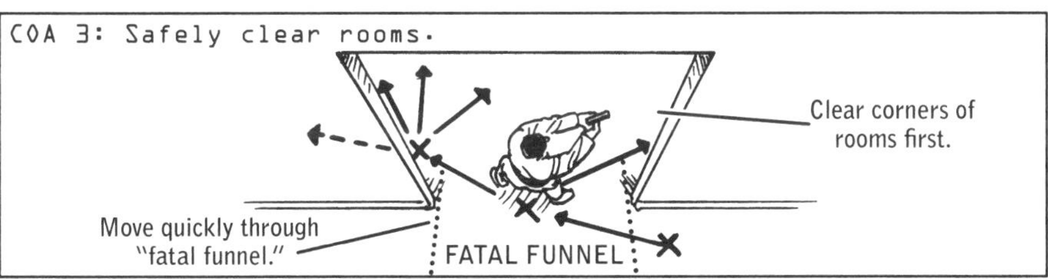

COA 4: Safely clear doorways.

COA 5: Safely clear obstacles.

BLUF: Stay quiet, move slowly, pie corners, and check your six.

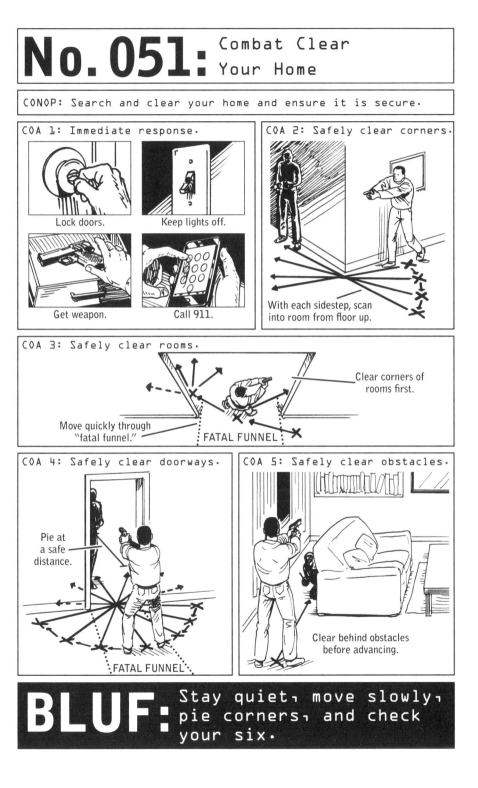

052 Command and Control a Home Invader

Many gun-owning homeowners don't think past the act of brandishing their weapon in the event that they catch an intruder on their property. But what happens next is critical. Your goal should be not only to avoid injury to yourself and your loved ones, but also to avoid getting into a situation in which you need to pull the trigger. You want to command and control the intruder until the authorities arrive. To do that, you'll need more than just a gun.

If your body language or tone of voice betrays insecurity or weakness, the intruder may seize upon a perceived opportunity to turn the tables in his favor. Whether or not you are an aggressive individual in everyday circumstances, in this moment you must act the part. Your verbal commands should be violent and forceful, delivered at a high volume and in simple, direct language. Your tone and language should communicate confidence, seriousness, and a will to do harm if the intruder does not submit to your commands.

Do not simply hold the intruder at gunpoint. A standing posture, with eyes on you, gives him far too much leverage. Use commands to force intruder into a prone or kneeling wall position with his eyes away from you as pictured. Both of these positions will create a significant handicap, causing a serious delay in the event that the intruder attempts to charge you. Keeping his head turned away from you allows you to place a 911 call or have loved ones cross the room and exit the premises, without giving the intruder the opportunity to catch you in a moment of inattention.

Note: Do not attempt to search an intruder and strip him of his weapons alone. Only restrain an intruder if you have others to support you (see page 126). Unless you have prior experience, wait for law enforcement.

No. 052: Command and Control a Home Invader

CONOP: Utilize verbal commands to control a suspect until police arrive.

COA 1: Always maintain safe distance.

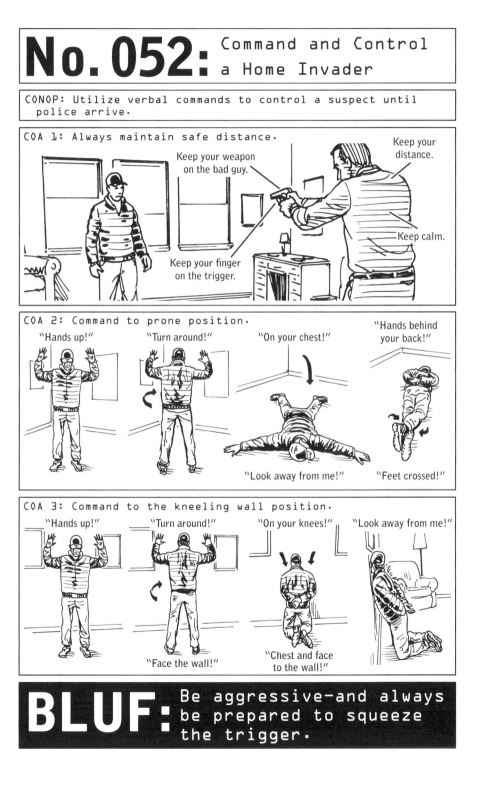

Keep your weapon on the bad guy.
Keep your distance.
Keep calm.
Keep your finger on the trigger.

COA 2: Command to prone position.

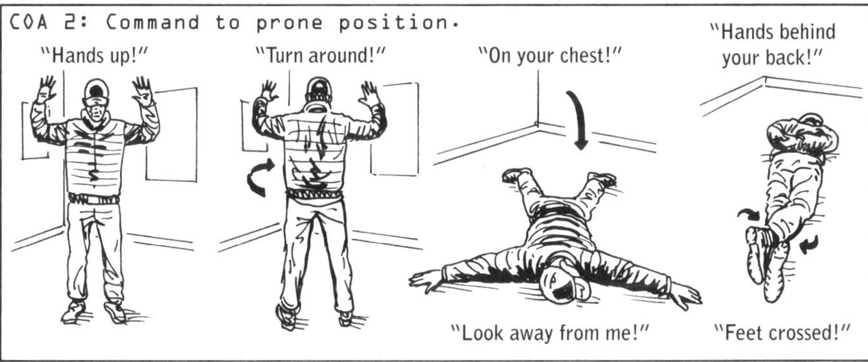
"Hands up!"
"Turn around!"
"On your chest!"
"Hands behind your back!"
"Look away from me!"
"Feet crossed!"

COA 3: Command to the kneeling wall position.

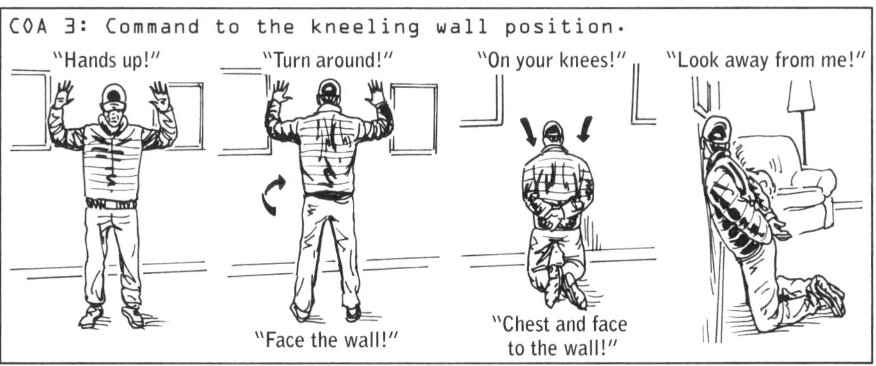
"Hands up!"
"Turn around!"
"On your knees!"
"Look away from me!"
"Face the wall!"
"Chest and face to the wall!"

BLUF: Be aggressive—and always be prepared to squeeze the trigger.

053 Create and Apply Improvised Restraints

If you have successfully apprehended a violent criminal or home intruder (see page 124), call 911 and wait for help to arrive. Do *not* attempt to restrain a potentially violent criminal unless you are unable to call for help or help isn't coming anytime soon. Unless you are a trained security professional or have rendered the intruder completely unconscious, you don't want to be in the position of restraining an intruder on your own. Ideally, you'll want one person to hold a weapon and another to apply the restraints.

If the situation requires the application of restraints, always tie an intruder's hands behind his back, knuckle to knuckle, a position that will make it exponentially harder for him to escape from his bonds. Tie restraints as tightly as possible. The intruder's comfort is not your concern! Give him the smallest window of opportunity for escape, and he will take it—potentially harming you and your loved ones in the process.

As far as the type of restraints, you have a variety of options, from handcuffs and zip ties to paracord or electrical wire. Two to four pairs of zip ties can be used to create interlocking sets of cuffs and elbow restraints, a preferential method of temporary restraint among many law enforcement officials. (See illustrations, pages 128–29.)

Create Adjustable Cuffs

Don't have a pair of handcuffs or zip ties at the ready? If you have a length of twine or paracord nearby, you can use it to create a set of self-locking cuffs as pictured. Start by tying a two-turn Prusik knot around your index finger. Remove your finger, and insert the ends of the cord into the knot. Slip the loops around the intruder's wrists and pull the ends to tighten.

For an even quicker, if more brutal, way to restrain an opponent using a length of cord, tie his wrists together using a girth hitch, pictured on pages 128–30. Gather both ends of the cord together and loop them around your opponent's neck. Pull the ends until your opponent's hands are raised behind his back and movement has become impossible. Hold on to the ends as you're moving the intruder around, or tie them off to the wrist hold down below. Adapted from a restraint technique used in highly sensitive military operations, this method places torque on the restrained party's hands, shoulders, and neck.

If you don't have cord or zip ties, you can still gain the upper hand over an intruder through the use of belts or duct tape, items commonly found in many homes. In both cases, after you've securely wrapped the wrists, loop the end of the belt or an additional pull of tape vertically between the wrists, tightening and lashing the structure together so that escape becomes impossible.

Note: Do not attempt the girth hitch unless you've been properly supervised by a trained self-defense instructor, as the maneuver can result in accidental choking.

No. 053: Create and Apply Improvised Restraints

CONOP: Restrain a bad guy with everyday items.

COA 1: Adjustable Twine/Paracord Cuffs

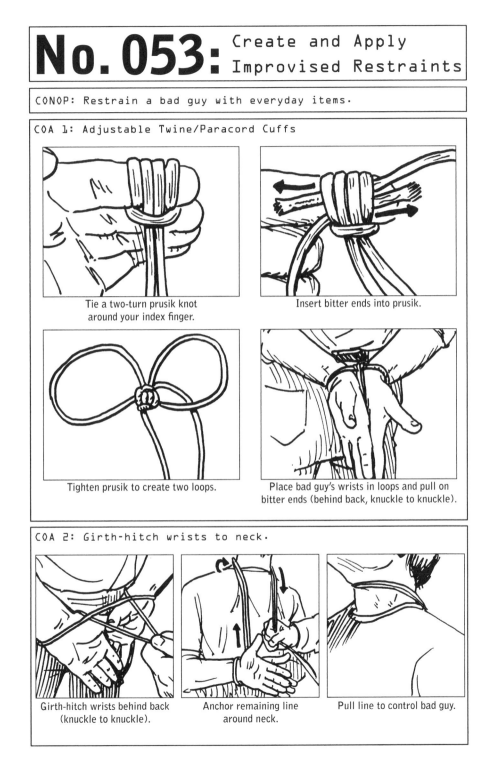

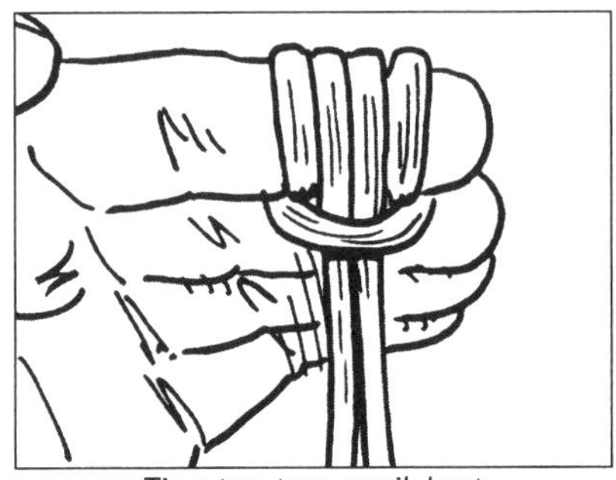
Tie a two-turn prusik knot around your index finger.

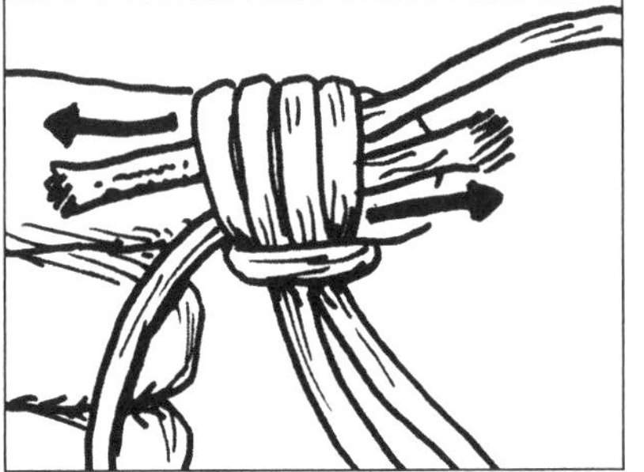
Insert bitter ends into prusik.

Tighten prusik to create two loops.

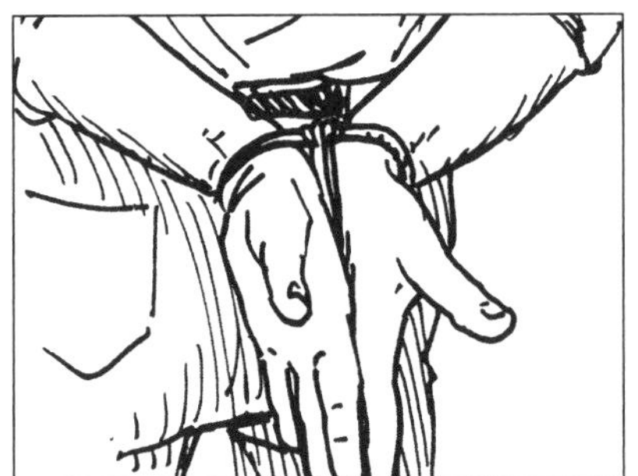
Place bad guy's wrists in loops and pull on bitter ends (behind back, knuckle to knuckle).

COA 2: Girth-hitch wrists to neck.

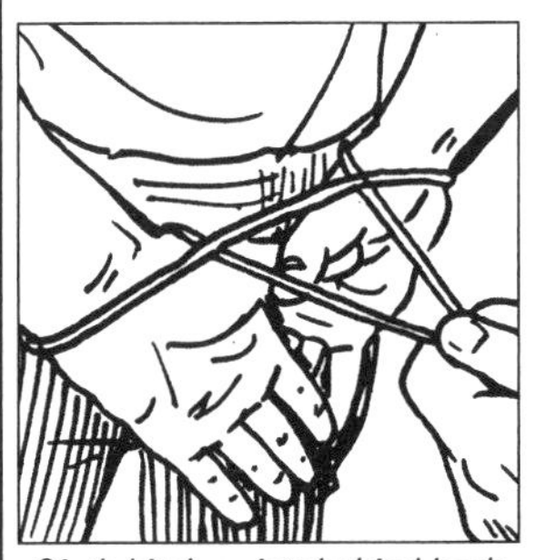
Girth-hitch wrists behind back (knuckle to knuckle).

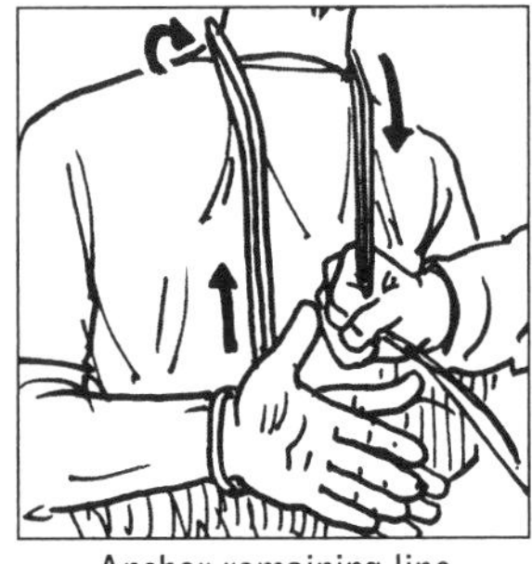
Anchor remaining line around neck.

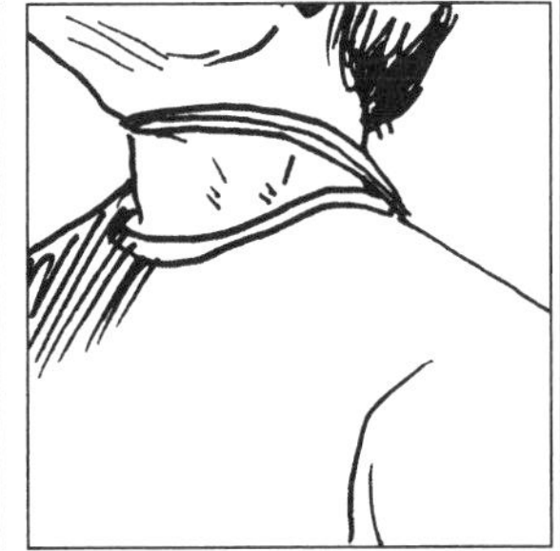
Pull line to control bad guy.

COA 3: Zip Ties

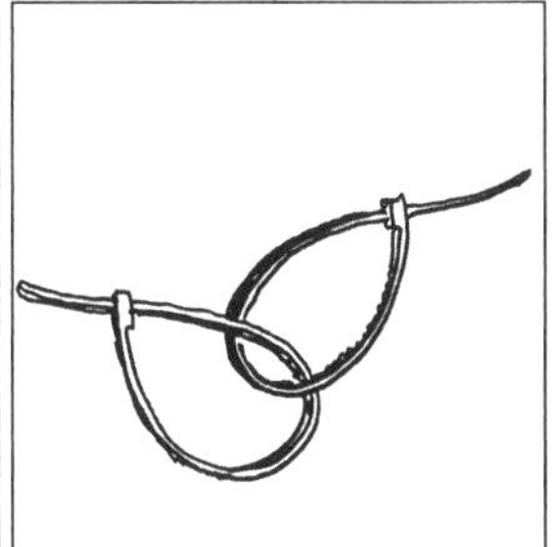

Loosely chain two zip ties together, creating two closed interconnected loops.

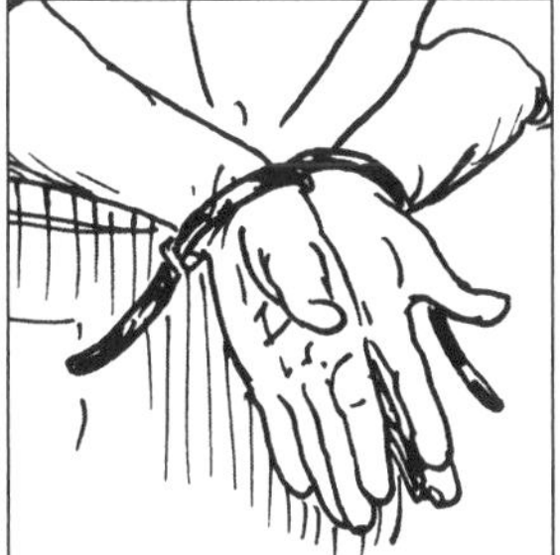

Place on wrists and tighten each zip tie (behind back, knuckle to knuckle).

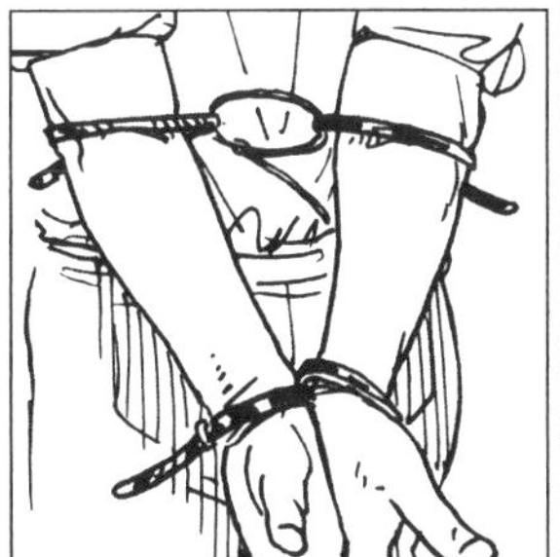

Loop three to four interconnected zip ties from elbow to elbow.

COA 4: Belts and Straps

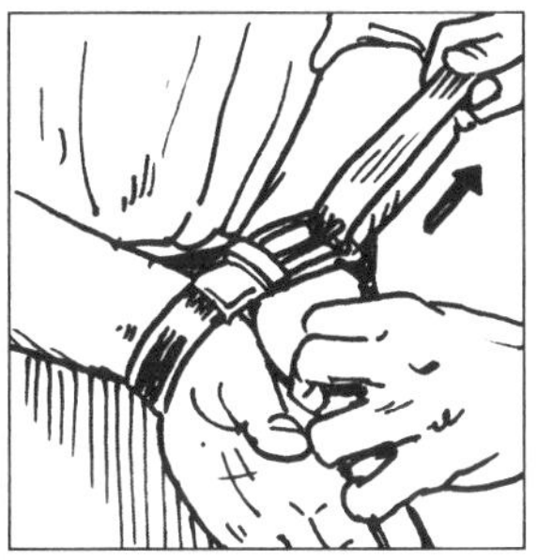

Girth-hitch wrists together with belt looped through buckle.

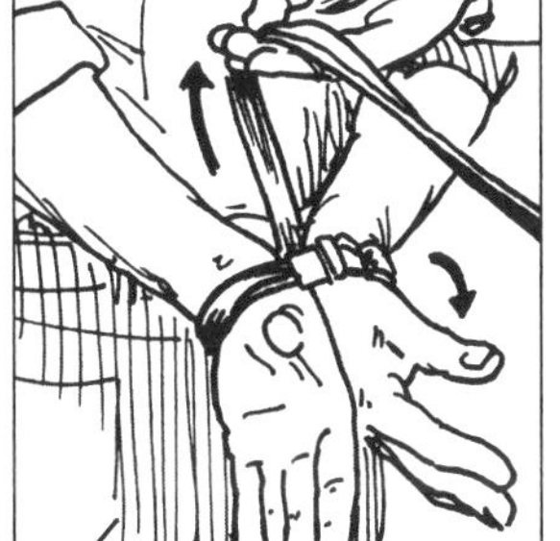

Lash bitter end tightly between both wrists.

Girth-hitch a second strap from elbow to elbow.

COA 5: Duct Tape

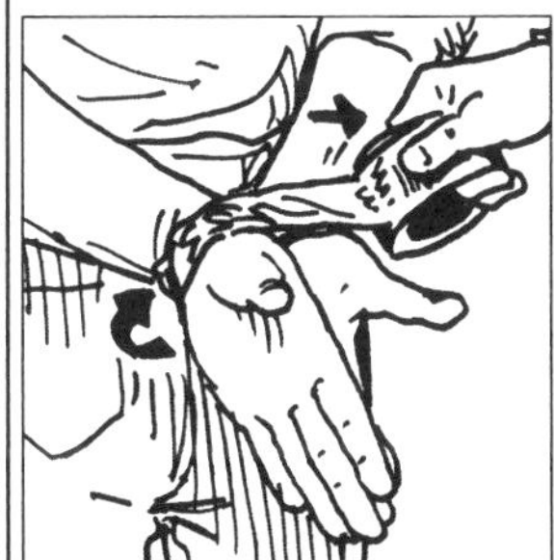

Tightly wrap wrists with tape multiple times (behind back, knuckle to knuckle).

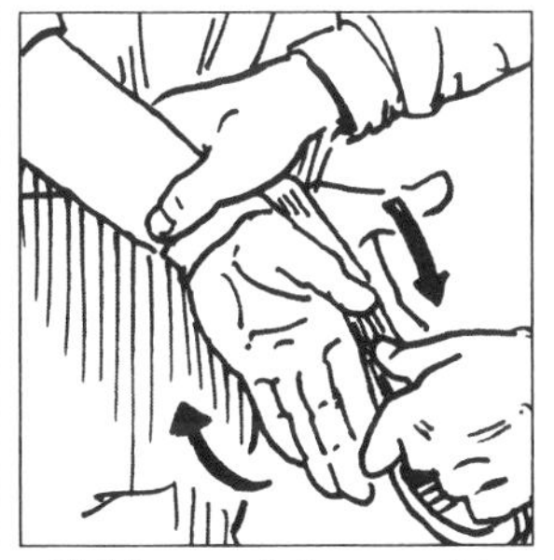

Tightly wrap between wrists several times.

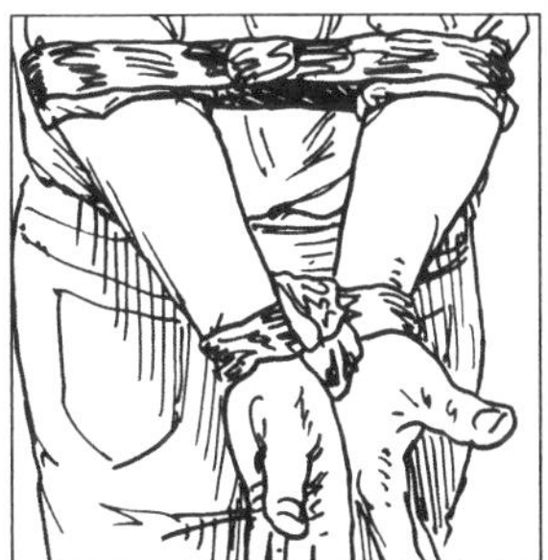

Tape elbow to elbow.

BLUF: Never restrain a bad guy by yourself unless he's completely unconscious.

054 Prisoner Handling

Once you've apprehended an intruder and successfully commanded him to a prone position (see page 124), the safest course of action is to await the arrival of law enforcement officials. But if responders are delayed or you need to move to another room to make the call, you may be in the unfortunate position of needing to apply restraints—a task best undertaken with a partner who can cover the intruder while you make your approach (see pages 126–27). Should you have to handle a captive on your own, the following protocol will maximize your chances of safely restraining your charge.

Again, to start, the captive should be lying chest-down in the prone position with his head turned away and his hands crossed behind his back (see illustrations). Approach quietly with restraints at the ready, using his lack of awareness about your movements to your advantage.

Crouch down, digging a knee and shin into his neck and upper back as you grasp his wrists. Put weight into your knee—controlling his head and upper body will make it very difficult for him to get up. Creating minimum vulnerability for you and maximum discomfort for him, the position allows you to quickly rise to your feet and grab your weapon in the event that he puts up a struggle.

If you need to move the intruder to another room or location after he's been restrained, use the arm bar technique (see illustrations) to control his movements while restraining his head. Hooking your forearm up through his elbow and toward the back of his neck, grasp him by the collar and pull him up to a standing position, ordering him to cooperate. Use your arm as a leverage point to guide the prisoner in the direction you want him to go. This one-handed control technique leaves your other hand free to open doors or hold a weapon.

No. 054: Prisoner Handling

CONOP: Safely approach, restrain, and move a bad guy.

COA 1: Approach and apply restraints.

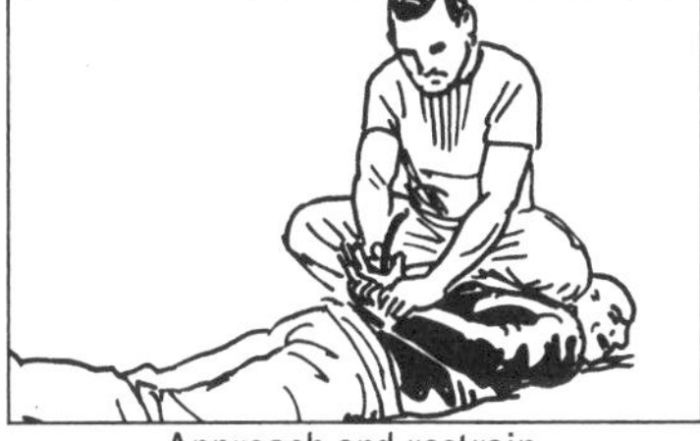

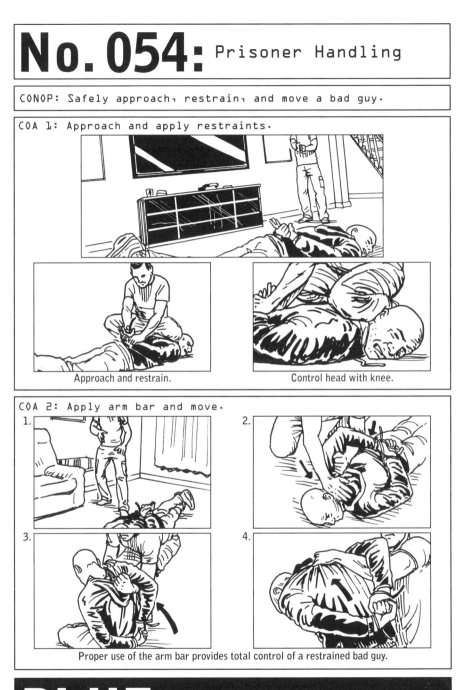

Approach and restrain.

Control head with knee.

COA 2: Apply arm bar and move.

1.

2.

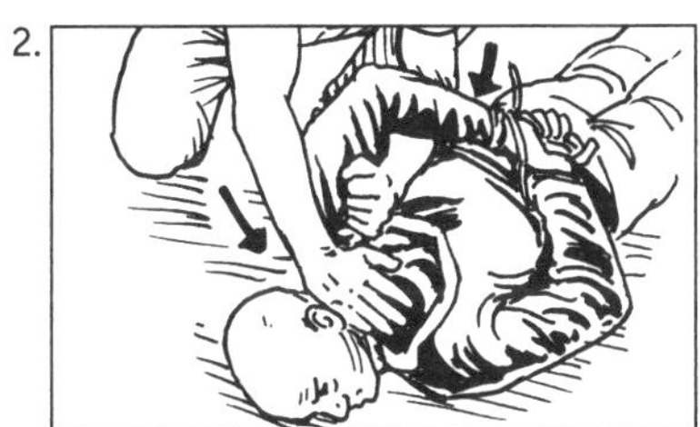

3.

4.

Proper use of the arm bar provides total control of a restrained bad guy.

BLUF: Gunpoint is always the best form of restraint.

055 Escape a Carjacking

Often the province of desperate individuals on the run, carjackings can also be a starting point for express kidnappings (see page 164), a form of temporary abduction in which the perpetrator may force you to drive from ATM to ATM, performing multiple withdrawals as a means of immediate ransom. Whatever the perpetrator's ultimate aim, being taken hostage in your own car is a worst-case scenario—so give up the car or attempt escape before allowing a hostile, armed abductor to enter your vehicle. Better yet, decrease your vulnerability to carjackings from the outset by practicing personal and situational awareness.

Use personal awareness to avoid standing out on the road. Beware of renting flashy cars while traveling. Select the vehicle most likely to blend in with the cars already on the road in the environment.

Employ situational awareness at all times by remaining alert to potential threats in the vicinity. Be particularly aware of your surroundings as you transit through volatile areas.

Be a Safe Driver

Whether you're moving through traffic or stopped at a light, always maintain a car's length between your car and the vehicle in front of you, leaving yourself room to make a quick getaway in case of emergency. Do not fall prey to the common trap of burying your nose in your mobile device while waiting for a red light. You risk rendering yourself even more vulnerable during the most critical moment of your route—a driver zoned out at a light is a perfect target for a carjacker lying in wait. Pay attention to your surroundings, particularly when you come to a stop, and always keep doors locked during transit.

Keep your car in drive and your doors locked while using drive-through ATMs. Drive away as soon as you receive your withdrawal, rather than sitting in your vehicle and counting bills. Using an ATM puts you at a disadvantage to begin with. The several prompts

No. 055: Escape a Carjacking

CONOP: Implement a plan to survive a hostile carjacking.

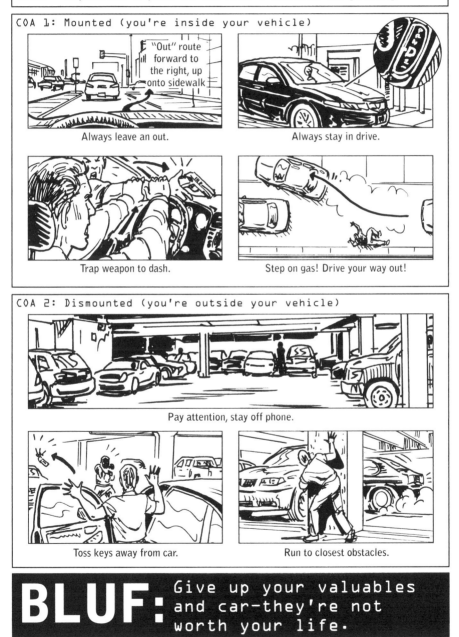

COA 1: Mounted (you're inside your vehicle)

Always leave an out.

Always stay in drive.

Trap weapon to dash.

Step on gas! Drive your way out!

COA 2: Dismounted (you're outside your vehicle)

Pay attention, stay off phone.

Toss keys away from car.

Run to closest obstacles.

BLUF: Give up your valuables and car–they're not worth your life.

required by the machine will absorb your attention for an extended period of time, making you catnip for the seasoned criminal who prowls this fertile ground. Reorient yourself to your surroundings by performing rapid situational awareness checks between prompts of the machine. Has the man loitering on the edge of the lot moved toward you and your car? What is going on behind you?

Fight Back

Should a carjacker manage to take you by surprise, surrender the vehicle if you can. But if the perpetrator orders you to slide over into the passenger seat or you have children in the backseat, giving up your vehicle may put you or your loved ones at risk.

You may feel powerless in such a scenario, but keep in mind that the hostile carjacker currently confronting you isn't the only one armed with a deadly weapon—within moments, the car you're driving could be transformed into a four-thousand-pound weapon of self-defense. Most drivers don't consider the fact that the very object of a violent perpetrator's desires could become both the getaway car that ferries you to safety and the deadly tool that takes that perp out of commission.

If the perpetrator's weapon has breached the inside of the car, the best option may be to raise your hands in a motion of false surrender, then violently push and trap the weapon against the dashboard as you floor the gas. The perpetrator isn't likely to expect such a response, and may either drop the weapon or retract both hand and weapon to avoid being dragged.

Drive away quickly, without concern for the usual rules of the road. Drivers are conditioned to think that they can't cross yellow lines or drive onto curbs or medians, but in an emergency (whether a perpetrator has already breached the vehicle or is rapidly approaching) all terrain becomes drivable.

Practice Pedestrian Awareness

When you're returning to your vehicle in garages or dark parking lots, stay off your phone and double down on your situational awareness. Garages and parking lots are frequent settings for both carjackings and violent crimes. If you see anyone suspicious prowling around the premises or sitting in a parked car, make a U-turn and briskly walk back to wherever you came from.

If you are caught unawares by a carjacker who demands your keys, do not simply hand them over. Doing so will put you within arm's reach of a potentially violent criminal. Instead, toss keys away from the nearest exit. Ideally, the perpetrator will head toward the keys, allowing you to run for escape.

Run to the nearest obstacle or form of cover, concrete pillars being preferable due to their bullet-stopping density.

Keep your eye on the perpetrator as you run from cover to cover on your way to safety.

If the perpetrator heads toward you instead of going for the keys, he may have been intending to harm you regardless of whether or not you surrendered your vehicle. See pages 154, 166, and 172 for self-defense techniques.

056 Access Your Locked Vehicle

Accidentally locking your keys inside your car may not rise beyond the level of a frustrating mishap. But if you've locked a child or pet into the vehicle, the stakes will be considerably higher.

Fortunately, particularly on older-model vehicles, shimmying past a door frame to reach an old-fashioned thumb puller–style lock is easily achievable. All you need is a single piece of string, worked into the car through the opening between the top of the window and the car door frame. The most difficult part of the process will be wedging the string past the rubberized weather seal around the top of the frame. The older the car, the looser the seal.

On newer vehicles, the seal will be tighter, and the unlock mechanisms less forgiving. A wire antenna or hanger curved into a hook can be used as a long-reach tool with the dexterity required to pick up keys, open door handles from the inside, or flip locks to the unlock position. But before you can feed a tool into the vehicle, you'll probably need to use a wedge to create an opening between the door and the frame.

Farthest away from both hinges and the door-lock mechanism, the upper-right corner of a car door is its most vulnerable spot. Use a wooden door stop or a similarly shaped solid wedge to breach the door frame, forcefully pressing the thin end of the wedge down between the door and the frame. If you still find it difficult to gain purchase, shimmy a soft object, such as a shoe, into the opening to create another gap in the rubber weather seal.

No. 056: Access Your Locked Vehicle

CONOP: Utilize everyday items to gain access to a locked vehicle.

COA 1: Use a shoelace.

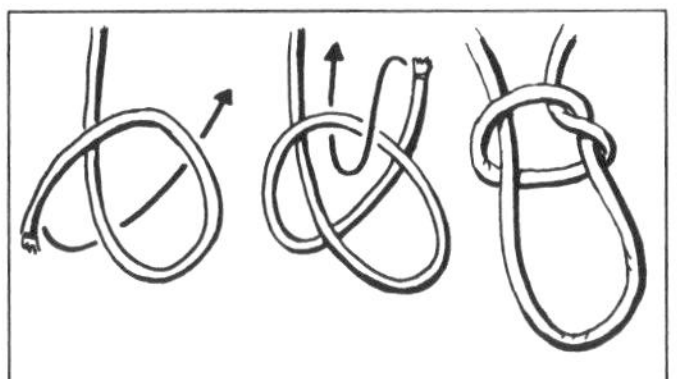

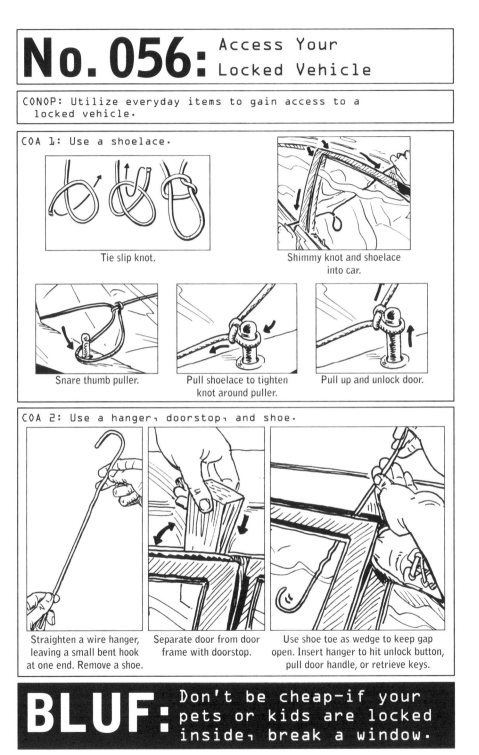

Tie slip knot.

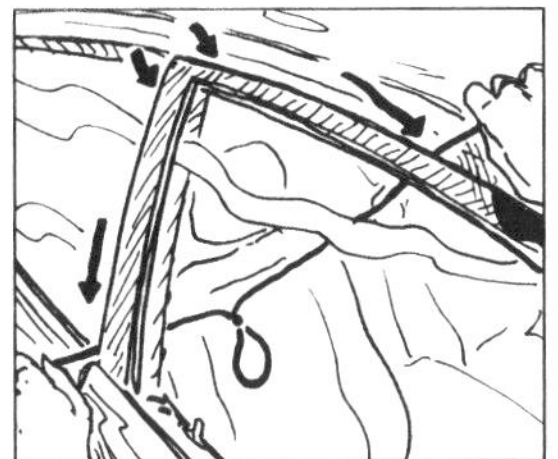

Shimmy knot and shoelace into car.

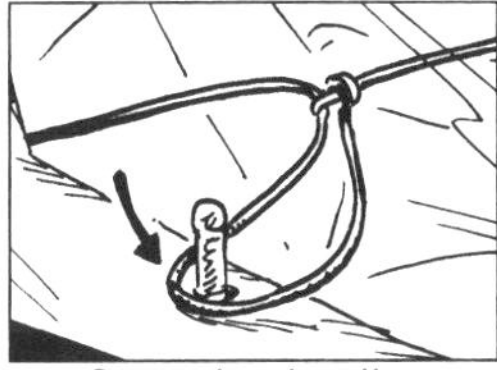

Snare thumb puller.

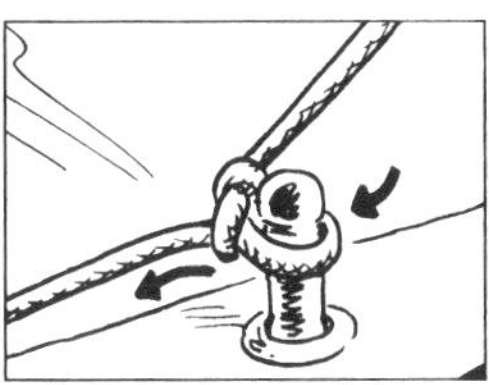

Pull shoelace to tighten knot around puller.

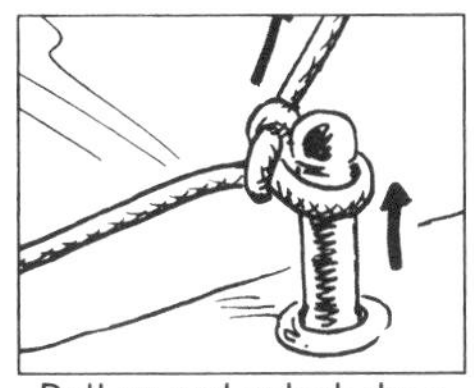

Pull up and unlock door.

COA 2: Use a hanger, doorstop, and shoe.

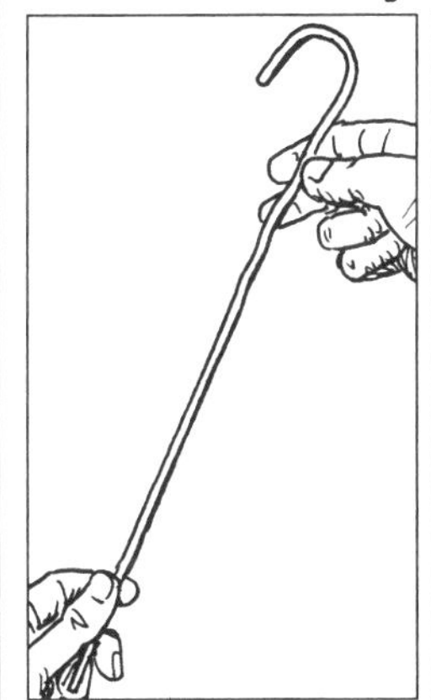

Straighten a wire hanger, leaving a small bent hook at one end. Remove a shoe.

Separate door from door frame with doorstop.

Use shoe toe as wedge to keep gap open. Insert hanger to hit unlock button, pull door handle, or retrieve keys.

BLUF: Don't be cheap—if your pets or kids are locked inside, break a window.

PART V

SECURING PUBLIC SPACES

057 Create an Improvised Door-Closer Lock

Commonly found in schools, offices, hospitals, restaurants, movie theaters, and most forms of commercial real estate, outward opening doors allow for rapid mass exit in the case of emergency. But if the emergency takes the form of a hostile, armed intruder attempting to force his way *into* the building, outward opening doors present a downside in that they cannot be barricaded. They can, however, be jammed shut through the use of a belt, purse strap, or length of rope or twine.

To slow or halt a violent intruder's progress, collect available straps and belts from the crowd. Belts or straps with buckles should be your first choices, as buckles can be used to create torque and increase constriction. Wrap belts or straps around door-closer arms on closed doors, at the wide end of the triangle, closest to the door. Increase tensile strength by wrapping straps around multiple times. Secure the lock by wrapping straps back through their buckles or folding ends of straps back underneath themselves.

Such a contraption may not present intruders with a permanent obstacle, but it will slow their progress, bridging the gap between the moment of crisis and the arrival of emergency services.

As you secure doors, move from cover to cover until you are out of harm's way or out of sight. In selecting hiding places, try not to corner yourself. Leave yourself with multiple outs if you can. Do not splinter off from the group. Break up into teams of two or three or shelter as a herd. There is strength in numbers, as you'll see on pages 154 and 174.

No. 057: Create an Improvised Door-Closer Lock

CONOP: Use straps or belts to immobilize a door-closer arm.

COA 1: Collect purse and messenger bag shoulder straps or belts for the number of doors to be secured.

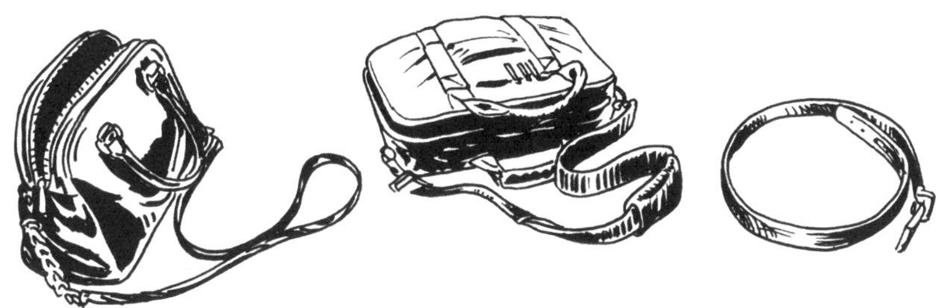

COA 2: Wrap belt or strap around end of door-closer arm closest to the door. Use the buckle to create torque and increase constriction.

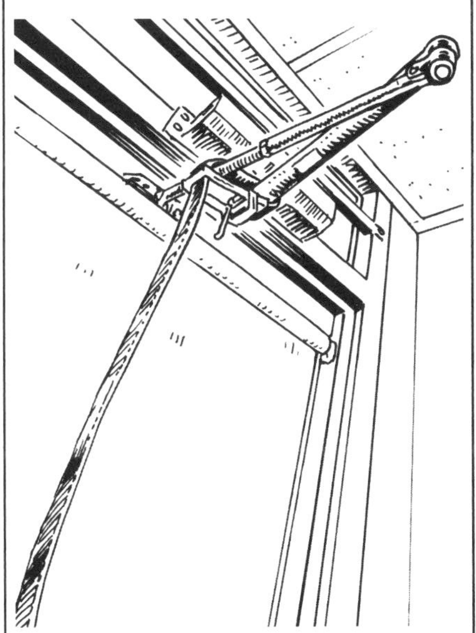

COA 3: Loop tightly, then secure the lock by folding strap or belt back underneath itself.

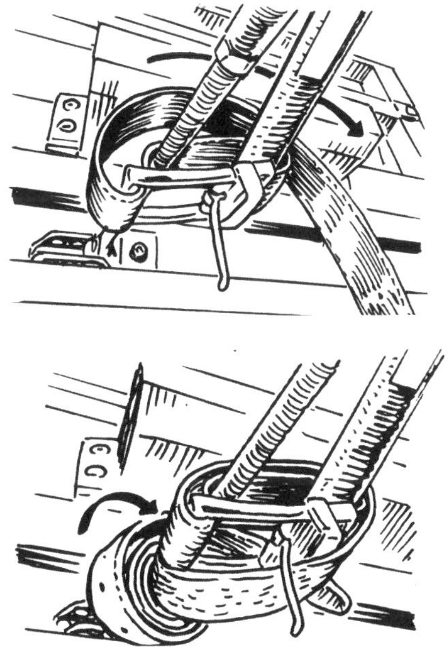

BLUF: Lock down commercial door-closer arms to prevent intruder entry.

058 Barricade Inward-Opening Doors

When an armed and violent intruder breaches the premises of your home or workplace, the first course of action is to attempt escape. But if a timely exit isn't possible, proceed to a lockdown. Do not rely on locks alone—locks and hinges can be shot out, and doors can be broken down. Fortify doors and place obstacles in the intruder's way in order to create a potentially lifesaving delay.

Bolt or Bar a Door: Following a trip to your local hardware store, two simple types of lock fortification can quickly and easily be jerry-rigged in advance. The first consists of four single-cylinder thumb-turner deadbolts, screwed into a doorway in unexpected spots. Affix bolts in a square pattern, just below the top and middle set of hinges on both sides of the door, in order to multiply the power of a door lock. Or barricade a door and spread the weight of a potential blow across the door frame by barring it with two steel round rods, affixed to the doorway, or beside it, with large eyelet screws. Neither method will leave a visible footprint on the outside of the door. Both should help maintain the structural integrity of the door even if the assailant shoots out the hinges and the visible locks. Though their effectiveness will depend on the quality of the door, door frame, and hardware, as well as the integrity of the surrounding walls, these interior locks will make kicking down the door a much more difficult proposition.

Wedge or Block a Door: If you didn't think ahead, you still have the last-minute options of wedging or blocking a door. Beyond doorstops, any thin object that gradually thickens, from a dustpan to a pair of extended scissors, could be put to use as a wedge—so that the harder the intruder presses against the door, the tighter the wedges will become. Moving heavy furniture against doors can be equally effective as a delay tactic.

No. 058: Barricade Inward-Opening Doors

CONOP: Fortify inward-opening doors to prevent hostile entry.

COA 1: Bolt it (preemptive) (two per side).

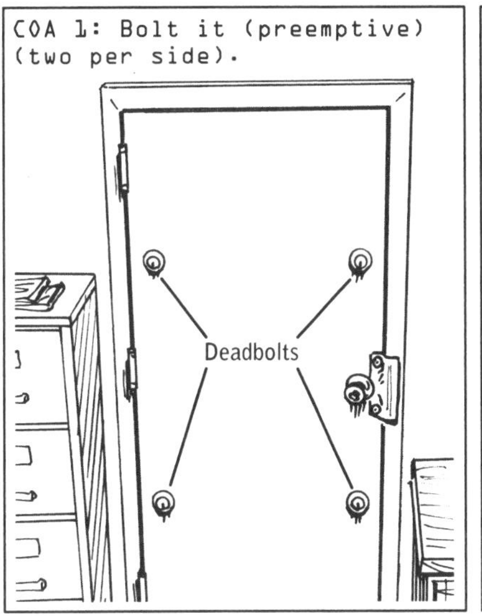

COA 2: Bar it (preemptive).

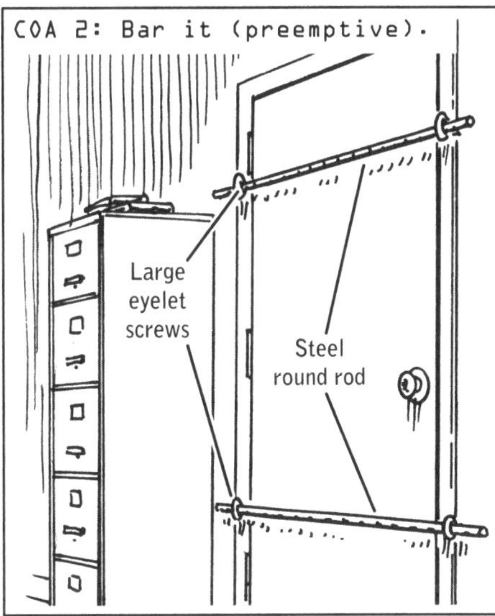

COA 3: Wedge it (hasty).

COA 4: Block it (hasty).

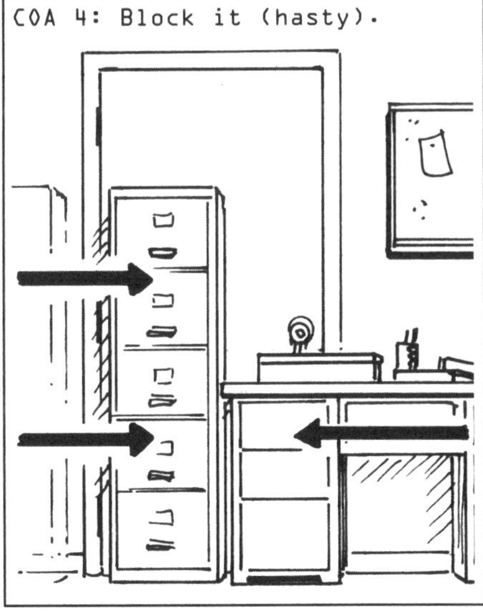

BLUF: Bad guys *will* breach locks and hinges.

059 Barricade Outward-Opening Doors

Not all outward-opening doors are outfitted with door-closer arms, which can easily be jammed shut through the use of belts and straps (see page 140). But despite appearances, any outward-opening door *can* be reverse-barricaded with heavy furniture, strategically positioned and prepped for quick response in the event of an armed assault.

As a precautionary measure, the large bookcases or file cabinets common to many classrooms and offices can be moved to the side of doorways farthest away from hinges. Create an attachment system by looping a sturdy cable around the cabinet or bookcase (see illustration). Securely attach the cable to a secondary cable or power cord, which in the event of emergency will be knotted around the doorknob to prevent entry.

Doors may also be tied to sturdy pieces of fixed equipment such as radiators. If a door is within reach of another internal door (also outward-opening), tie the doors together, handle-to-handle, to secure them both.

If no furniture is available, scour the premises for long-handled brooms, mops, or other sticks. Combine two or three handles together with zip ties or duct tape, and tightly secure them to the doorknob using several more zip ties. Duct tape the ends of the sticks to walls, and you've created an improvised security bar that will present an intruder with a serious impediment to progress.

Go one step further by installing a prefabricated barricading mechanism, most effective when used with a lever-style handle. Anchor an eyelet screw onto a foundational stud in the wall opposite the handle, then connect to handle using a bicycle cable. When not in use, the cable can dangle from its carabiner.

Test all contraptions to ensure an intruder won't be able to create even a small gap of space in the doorway.

No. 059: Barricade Outward-Opening Doors

CONOP: Barricade outward-opening doors, if running is not an option.

COA 1: Anchor doorknob to hard point.

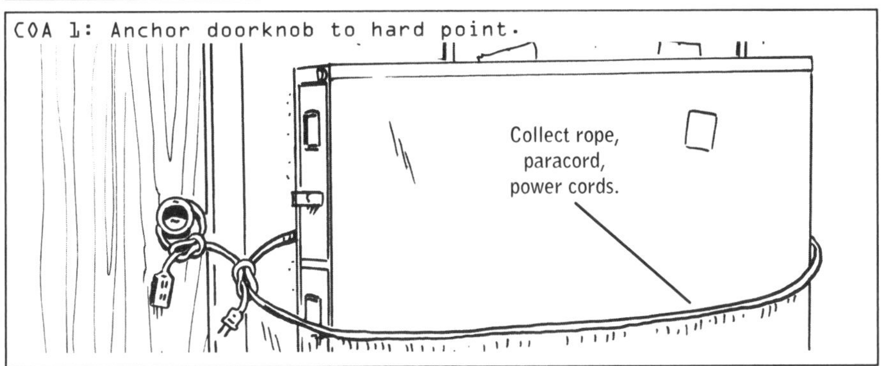
Collect rope, paracord, power cords.

COA 2: Anchor doorknob to obstacle.

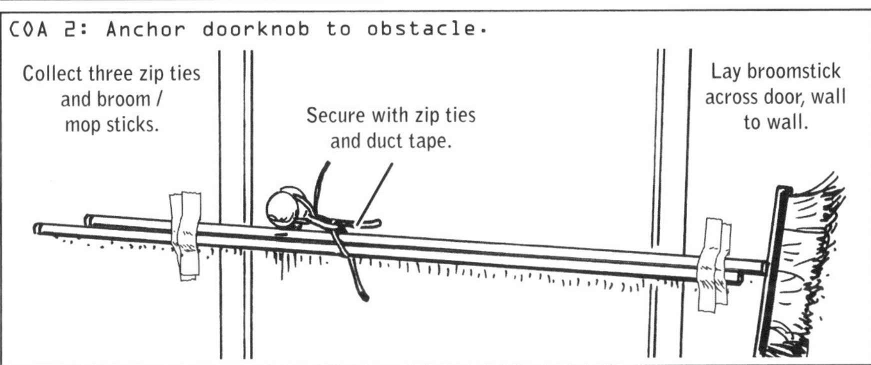
Collect three zip ties and broom / mop sticks.
Secure with zip ties and duct tape.
Lay broomstick across door, wall to wall.

COA 3: Anchor doorknob to preset eyelet screw.

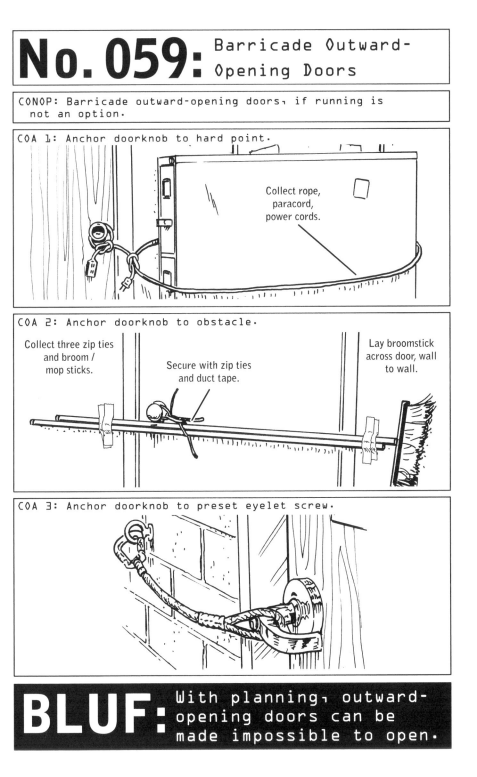

BLUF: With planning, outward-opening doors can be made impossible to open.

060 Handle a Bomb Threat

Though the majority of bomb threats called in to businesses and schools are hoaxes designed to cost companies money or simply create a sense of mayhem, any such threat should be taken seriously and acted on immediately.

Threats that arrive via email or snail mail can easily be bumped up the chain of command and sent to law enforcement authorities, but many threats arrive by phone. If you are the recipient of a phoned-in threat, remain calm.

Pre-establish distress signals in the workplace so that you can silently alert nearby colleagues of an emergency via simple gestures like patting your head or holding up two fingers. This will let your colleagues know to call 911—while listening to your end of the conversation in order to pick up as many clues as possible.

Repeating and/or writing down everything the caller says will give the people around you access to the information in real time. Ask questions in order to extract as much information as possible while stalling for extra time until law enforcement arrives: *Where is the bomb? When will the bomb explode? How big of a blast will the bomb cause? Will it be initiated on a timer, or triggered remotely? What kind of a bomb is it? What can we do to prevent you from initiating the blast?* Pretend not to hear the caller, and ask the caller to repeat him- or herself in order to further the delay. Listen for background noises such as honking or other voices. Make note of the caller's gender, accent, voice, and any other information that might help law enforcement.

The caller may not be willing to give up additional information, but the architects of terror are frequently driven by an egomania that may result in their sharing details of their trade as a result of pride of authorship.

No. 060: Handle a Bomb Threat

CONOP: Report bomb threats and indicators of suspicious packages.

COA 1: Response to a Bomb Threat Received by Phone

1. Remain calm.
2. Signal coworker to call 911.
3. Keep caller on the line.
4. Record caller ID number.
5. Ask caller to repeat message.
6. Ask when, where, and how.
7. Pay attention to voice, language, gender, and approximate age.

COA 2: Questions to Ask

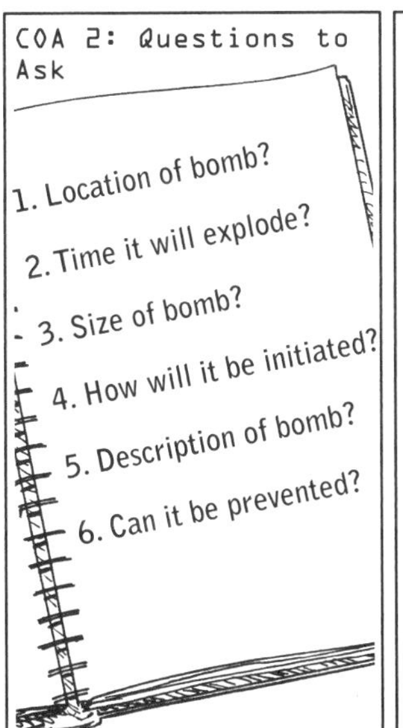

1. Location of bomb?
2. Time it will explode?
3. Size of bomb?
4. How will it be initiated?
5. Description of bomb?
6. Can it be prevented?

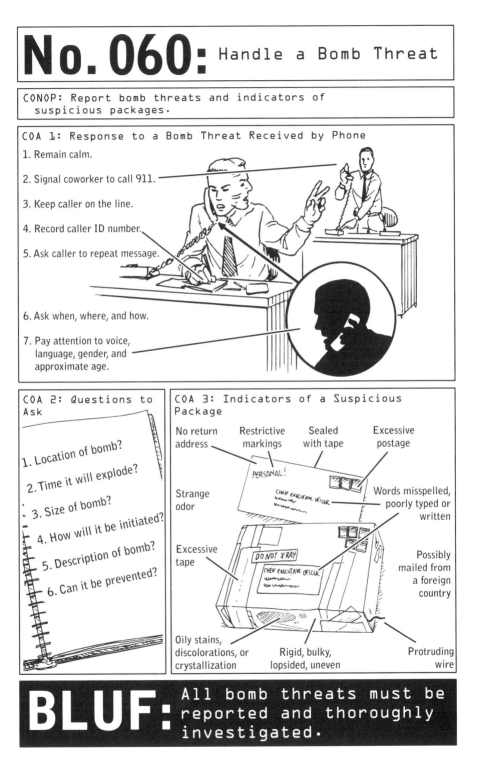

COA 3: Indicators of a Suspicious Package

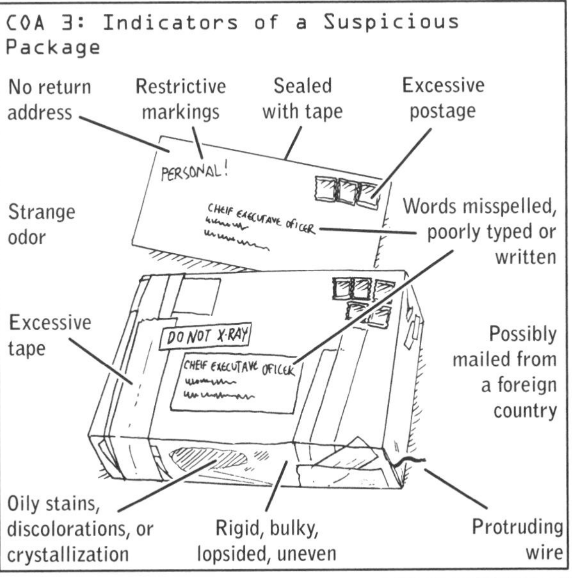

BLUF: All bomb threats must be reported and thoroughly investigated.

061 Elude Ransomware Attacks

Once the province of lone hackers working to disrupt the status quo, cybercrime has become a lucrative bastion of criminal activity, ranging from acts of cyberterrorism that threaten infrastructure and communications to petty crimes used to extort small sums of money from innocent civilians.

The security of an organization's firewalls offer scant protection, as most viral attacks are detonated by a harmless gesture: the click of an employee.

Ransomware attacks prey on this click, spreading a virus that freezes up a computer and encrypts its data. The attackers hold your emails, documents, and data hostage, demanding a fee for their decryption and release. The fee may be small when targeted at individual office workers, or large, in the case of data breaches that compromise the work flow of an entire organization.

Prevent ransomware attacks before you get into a situation where you're left no choice but to pay. Update programs regularly to ensure all security loopholes are closed, and employ a 3-2-1 backup strategy, saving information locally, to an external hard drive, and to a cloud-based data storage system. Do not open suspicious emails or click on unfamiliar links. Be vigilant, and create bona fides such as shared wallpaper or a standardized signature block to use with family and coworkers. Spammers often infiltrate an organization by approximating employees' email addresses. If an email does not refer to a known project or thread or sounds unlike the sender, check the address. Misspelling a username or approximating a domain name (e.g., substituting a .net or .co suffix) are common ruses.

If you do click on a suspicious link or open a phony attachment, immediately disconnect your computer from Wi-Fi and unplug any Ethernet cables, then power down. The odds are against you, but you may be able to halt the malware's spread.

No. 061: Elude Ransomware Attacks

CONOP: Save your data and money from ransomware attacks.

COA 1: Ransomware Defined

A click-activated malicious virus that encrypts your data until you pay to have it decrypted.

COA 2: Prevention

Do not open unknown emails.
Do not click on unknown links.
Update regularly.
3-2-1 backup strategy

COA 3: Response

Off

Disconnect!

Power down!

Use backup!

OR

pay here

Pay ransom!

BLUF: Do not be the one who clicks.

062 Detect an Inspired Terrorist

In times of global instability, a watchful citizenry can make the difference between a heroic tackle and a train car that bursts into fiery flames. And a hero's work may start with a glance at a coworker's monitor.

Where mass shootings are sometimes unplanned, emotionally driven events, acts of inspired terrorism are always the result of careful advance planning and a potentially lengthy period of ideological indoctrination. Which means they may stand a better chance of being detected and halted by observant friends, family members, and colleagues.

In the aftermath of modern acts of mass violence, investigators frequently uncover chilling trails of evidence—not by employing sophisticated forensic technologies, but by combing through social media posts and speaking to the perpetrator's friends, family, and coworkers. The evidence of impending catastrophe is generally hiding in plain sight, and too often overlooked. "It seemed strange at the time, but we didn't think much of it" has become an overly familiar refrain.

Online Behavior

Online behavior can be a powerful indicator of potential radicalization. Religious and ideological propagandists have briskly adapted to changing times by mounting sophisticated campaigns online, and while inspired terrorists-in-training may experience personal recruitment and/or build bonds with local actors, the seeds of their burgeoning ideologies are often sown and harvested on the internet. Indoctrination may begin with innocent curiosity about the wide swath of propaganda that is easily viewable on the web, and then turn into a more sinister brand of research as the subject enters into direct communication with terrorists, becoming more and more consumed by news of distant combat zones.

No. 062: Detect an Inspired Terrorist

CONOP: Identify behavior traits of a possible inspired terrorist.

COA 1: Online Behavior

Deletion of true-name social media and email accounts

Use of encrypted communication apps

I want to be a terrorist
i want to be a terrorist
Google Search
Internet searches of violent extremist sites

Username
fakenameinsupportofterrorism
Password
•••••••••
LOG IN
orgot your password?
Creation of fake or avatar social media accounts

COA 2: Verbal Communication

Voices support of violence as a necessary means to an end
Voices support for violent extremist groups
Verbal desire to travel to war zones
Praising violent attacks

COA 3: Nonverbal Communication

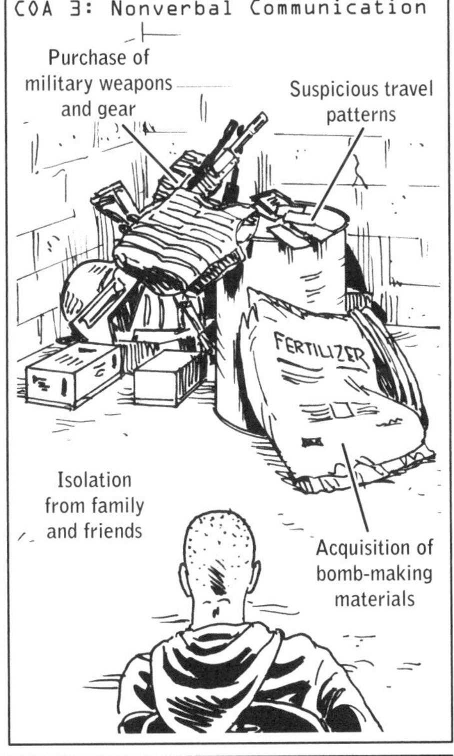
Purchase of military weapons and gear
Suspicious travel patterns
FERTILIZER
Isolation from family and friends
Acquisition of bomb-making materials

BLUF: Not all behavioral changes are benign.

An interest in getting deeper into news accounts of terrorism by viewing available source materials isn't an indicator on its own, but when combined with certain changes in online behavior it could signify that something more complex is in play. Along with the use of encrypted communication apps, the deletion of true-name social media accounts may be a clue that a colleague or friend is attempting to go dark or camouflage conversations that could alert the suspicions of law enforcement.

Verbal and Nonverbal Cues

Ideological conversions don't happen overnight. And they're not necessarily silent. Perpetrators of violent attacks tend to leave behind a trail of evidence about their evolving patterns of thought, and civilians undergoing a sea change in their personal beliefs may actually exhibit an interest in discussing those changes. They may even betray an interest in trying to mobilize or radicalize those around them. Listen to the clues they're providing. The voicing of violent fantasies, support for violent extremism, or praise for successful terrorist attacks should never be taken lightly. Switching from one extreme ideology to another may provide evidence of a potentially dangerous mental instability and susceptibility to influence.

Any sudden interest in or acquisition of military weapons and gear should be cause for concern, particularly if accompanied by antisocial behavior and increasing isolation from family and friends. Any unexplained acquisition of fertilizer, other high-nitrate or nitrogen products, or gunpowder should be regarded with extreme suspicion. The adoption of military-style training regimens and shooting drills may signal a sinister pattern of preparation. Exhibiting a desire to travel to hot spots, as well as a tendency toward unexplained or suspicious patterns of travel, is another indicator of a potential connection to terror organizations overseas.

Interpreting the Signs

None of these signs may be meaningful on their own. But in the aggregate, a profusion of signals should indeed be cause for concern. Counterterrorism experts often refer to "the fighting age," the emotionally volatile period of adolescence and young adulthood during which individuals ages fifteen to twenty-five are extremely susceptible to recruitment into violent extremism. Because behavioral extremes are normal during the teenage years, worrisome preoccupations may be difficult to detect. What distinguishes an alienated youth from an alienated youth who picks up a gun? The answer is much more difficult to discern than it may seem. Watch for abrupt and radical changes in behavior. Withdrawal on its own may be a typical teenage phase. Withdrawal and a sudden interest in explosives should most definitely not be swept under the rug. Alienated youths are more easily manipulated by extremist groups and ideologies that funnel their alienation into orderly worldviews.

063 Ambush an Active Shooter

There's a misconception among the general public that says you need firepower to fight firepower. The notion that even a large group of unarmed civilians is defenseless against a lone shooter tends to go unchallenged. But recent events have shown that one or two motivated bystanders *do* have the power to halt a potentially deadly event before it devolves into a mass casualty scenario. And as the scores of convenience-store owners who've resisted armed robberies can attest, you don't have to be a former member of the military to save lives. Remember, an armed shooter is counting on your fear and passivity. The last thing he's expecting to encounter is a brave and violent act of resistance.

Tackling a Shooter from Behind

A body mass equal to or greater than the shooter's can only be helpful when it comes to an aggressive self-defense maneuver, but it isn't essential. Using the elements of speed, surprise, and technique, any adult, male or female, can take a violent aggressor to the ground. Similarly, outnumbering the shooter or shooters by organizing into teams of two or three is ideal, for a gun can only be shot in a single direction at once. But even a lone resistor can neutralize an armed assailant.

If you're on your own and have the opportunity to tackle a shooter from behind, use momentum and proper form to take him to the ground (see illustration). You don't need a running start, but you absolutely do want to be aggressive in your approach. Put your shoulder into the small of his back and thrust your weight forward, simultaneously encircling your arms around his pelvis and violently pulling back. Bring your back leg forward and use it to trip the shooter so that you both fall forward. Once you've got him on the ground, trap the weapon and use the weight of your pelvis to pin the shooter down. If you've got a free hand, throw an elbow at the back of his head, or just apply pressure to prevent him from regain-

No. 063: Ambush an Active Shooter

CONOP: Tactically employ violent action to dominate and restrain a shooter.

COA 1: From Behind

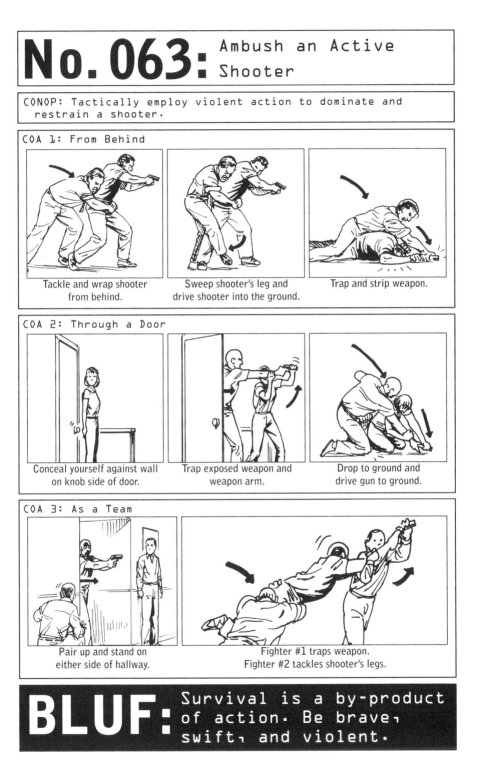

Tackle and wrap shooter from behind.

Sweep shooter's leg and drive shooter into the ground.

Trap and strip weapon.

COA 2: Through a Door

Conceal yourself against wall on knob side of door.

Trap exposed weapon and weapon arm.

Drop to ground and drive gun to ground.

COA 3: As a Team

Pair up and stand on either side of hallway.

Fighter #1 traps weapon.
Fighter #2 tackles shooter's legs.

BLUF: Survival is a by-product of action. Be brave, swift, and violent.

ing control. Flattened out and pinned to the earth, even the strongest assailants will find themselves surprisingly helpless.

Tackling a Shooter Coming Through a Doorway

If you're behind a door or around the bend of a hallway and can hear the shooter coming your way, be ready to act. Combining the elements of surprise and swift, violent action, your aim is to tackle him and strip him of his weapon before he can get victims in his sights. Stand at the ready with your back flat against the wall, to the side of the hallway or on the doorknob side of the door. The moment the shooter's weapon breaches the room or rounds the corner, use both hands to grab onto the weapon and the shooter's arm, then violently drive the weapon to the ground while dropping your body weight into a fall. Ideally, you'll want to wind up with one hand on the weapon and one hand on the shooter's arm, dropped to your knees and leaning over with the weapon pointed to the ground. But violent action is an inexact science. No matter the hold, if you grab the weapon and drop, the likelihood is that the shooter will fall off balance and go to the ground with you in an attempt not to relinquish the weapon. This moment also clears the way for others to get involved in fully stripping the shooter of his weapon and restraining him.

If you're able to work as a team, assign one person to trap the weapon and another to take the shooter's legs off balance. A third could go for the head. Stand with one person on either side of a doorway as the shooter is approaching. If the shooter spots one of you, the other will still be able to take him by surprise. Do not assign too many people to the initial act of taking down the shooter, or you may get in each other's way.

Any number of improvised weapons may be incorporated into these maneuvers. With an improvised garrote at the ready (page 172), one person could be ready to choke out the assailant while another goes for his gun.

Take proper steps toward barricading and fortifying doors (page 110) so that taking down a shooter becomes a method of last resort. If you've successfully ambushed an active shooter, use aggressive commands (page 124) and immobilizing restraints (page 126) to control him until law enforcement arrives on the scene.

PART VI:

NEUTRALIZING PUBLIC SAFETY THREATS

064 Outwit a Pickpocket

While American cities have seen radical downturns in pickpocketing in the past few decades, smartphone theft is still a thriving industry, slowed but not eradicated by the introduction of user-operated remote kill switches. Globally, both wallet and smartphone theft continue to flourish so exercise caution by traveling light and carrying as few valuables as possible. Be particularly cautious in and around crowded areas, known tourist attractions, airports, and public transportation hubs. Pickpockets and smartphone snatchers specifically target travelers, who tend to wander about in a disoriented state and are likely to be carrying some amount of currency. Crowded areas also provide pickpockets with plenty of opportunities for brushing up against targets who've become desensitized to fleeting moments of physical contact in dense crowds.

Be extremely cautious leaving cash machines and retail checkout lines. Both provide pickpockets with evidence that you're carrying cash or credit cards, along with information about where you stash your wallet.

Be alert to distracting ruses such as swarms of begging children, overly aggressive street vendors, and "accidental" spills that allow pickpockets an opportunity to get close as they helpfully offer to clean you up. Assume the worst upon the return of a "found" wallet, potentially a ruse designed to prevent you from canceling cards whose account numbers the thief has already pilfered.

Back pockets and purses are notoriously easy to exploit (see page 160). In high-risk areas, women should transfer their money, cards, and smartphone to a front pants pocket. Die-hard back-pocket carriers can construct a theft-deterrent device by slipping a comb into their wallet (see illustration). In the event that a thief attempts to lift the wallet, the comb will create a telltale snag.

Beware of unconsciously telegraphing the location of your valuables by palpating your pockets. Thieves are on the lookout for this kind of highly informative body language.

No. 064: Outwit a Pickpocket

CONOP: Use simple tactics to protect your valuables from being lifted.

COA 1: Be cautious in crowded areas.

COA 2: Be cautious leaving money machines.

COA 3: Be aware of creative distracting ruses.

COA 4: Pocket Selection

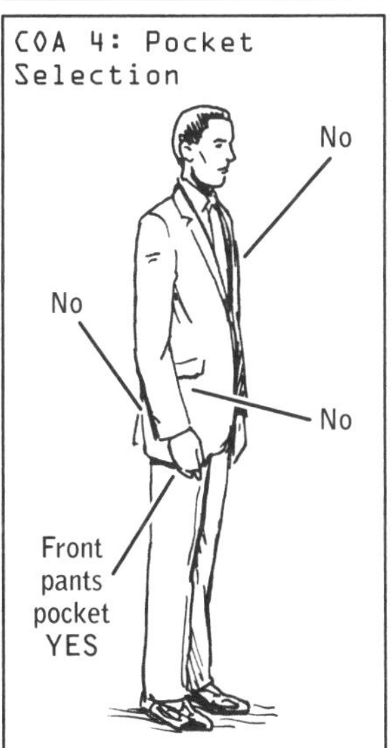

COA 5: Anchor it.

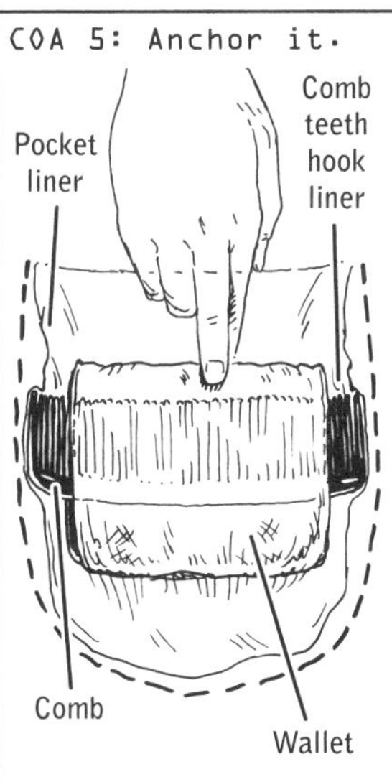

COA 6: Stop checking it.

BLUF: A pickpocket cannot steal what you do not carry.

065 Counter a Purse Snatcher

Women love their purses. And so do petty thieves, who see them as one-stop shops for wallets, smartphones, and other valuables.

Which is why the best form of purse-snatching prevention is not to carry a purse at all. If you must, choose a small, nondescript model with short straps in a common, unobtrusive shade. A luxury bag is a particularly strong enticement for thieves, who see it as assurance that their heist will be worthwhile. (Even the bag itself may be of value.) Long straps are vulnerable to the cut-and-snatch technique. A large bag also makes an easy target, and increases the probability that you'll spend time rummaging around in search of what you need. Losing awareness of your surroundings for prolonged periods of time can make you catnip to watchful predators.

Carry your purse away from the street, and skim building facades as you transit. A common heist has thieves riding by on a moped and disappearing with your purse before you can react, or snatching a purse and running away on foot. Make it more difficult for these brazen criminals to operate.

Tuck your purse under your arm and in front of your body when transiting through high-risk or densely trafficked areas. Wear longer-strapped bags across your body—unless you're walking on a dark street or through a desolate garage where your bag could be used as a leash in an abduction scenario (see page 166).

Place your purse on your lap, and not on the back of a chair or on the ground, when dining outdoors. Wandering bands of thieves commonly target the terraces of European cafés.

Don't make yourself an easy target. Walking while talking on the phone or texting, studying maps, or eating and drinking can all make you both more vulnerable to and less able to react to surprise attacks.

No. 065: Counter a Purse Snatcher

CONOP: Employ tactics that decrease purse snatching and theft of valuables.

Leave it at home.
Use short straps.
Keep close to body in crowded areas.
Sling it.
Carry away from street.
Walk on building side of sidewalks.

BLUF: If at all possible, leave your purse at home.

066 Outsmart a Virtual Kidnapper

There's a new scam in town, one that preys on social media to extort cold, hard cash. The perpetrators use details gleaned on public posts (names, patterns of life, relationships) to fake a kidnapping, calling up victims with enough information about loved ones to sow fear in their hearts. At times they have young actors screaming in the background, a ploy that quickly distorts the perceptions of already panicked parents.

Any kidnapping claim should be taken seriously, but several indicators may help you determine whether a particular threat is real or faked. Real kidnappers worry about their cell phones being triangulated or their landlines being traced. They tend to brusquely make demands and hang up, perhaps delivering details over a series of calls. Virtual kidnappers *want* you to stay on the line as long as possible, in order to prevent you from making contact with your loved one and uncovering the hoax. Real kidnappers may call from a loved one's phone—a chilling sign that something has gone very wrong indeed. They generally ask for large sums of money, then give you some time to gather the funds. Virtual kidnappers ask for smaller sums and want their payment right away, before their scam falls apart.

To determine which one you're dealing with, attempt to reach your loved one while on the phone with the supposed kidnapper. Ask for proof of life. A ream of excuses about why the kidnapper *cannot* supply proof of life is not conclusive evidence of a virtual kidnapping, but when combined with other signs it may be a strong indicator.

Prevent virtual kidnappings from the outset by refraining from posting travel plans or tagging your locations on social media. Deny virtual kidnappers access to any information they may exploit, from the names of your children to the location of their schools.

No. 066: Outsmart a Virtual Kidnapper

CONOP: Avoid becoming a victim of a virtual kidnapping.

COA 1: Virtual Kidnapping Defined

A customized scam to extort money by falsely admitting to kidnapping a loved one.

COA 2: Real Kidnapping vs. Virtual Kidnapping

Note Call Time

Real: Short (don't want to be traced)

Virtual: Long (don't want you to reach out to loved one)

Note Caller ID

Real: Call will come from loved one's phone

Virtual: Call will come from private, blocked, or spoofed number

Note Demands

Real: Large amounts of money

Virtual: Small amounts of money

Ask for proof of life and specific details.

"Can I talk to my loved one? What is he/she wearing?"

Real: Proof of life provided

Virtual: No proof of life because it never happened

Attempt to reach loved one.

Real: No response from loved one

Virtual: Response from loved one

COA 3: Prevention

Do not post travel plans.

Do not post locations.

Turn off location services.

Check in with loved ones regularly.

BLUF: Virtual kidnappers use social media to extort money without ever kidnapping anyone.

067 Prevent and Survive an Express Kidnapping

A category of crime that was once mostly directed at the very rich and their offspring, kidnapping has diversified its stock. Ordinary travelers with working debit cards are now prime targets, their ordeals lasting anywhere from minutes to hours or days. Common to South America, Central America, and parts of Southeast Asia, the crime often starts at ATMs or in cars. Usually uninterested in commandeering your vehicle, its perpetrators are after something far easier to handle—cold, hard cash.

Avoid falling into their clutches by keeping your doors locked and your windows closed when driving in high-risk countries. Do not roll down windows to speak to street vendors or strangers who approach. Speak loudly and you'll be heard through glass. Only use taxi services recommended by local embassies and the State Department, or use hotel shuttles or mass transit. Exercise caution at ATMs and avoid street-side machines.

Practice the same safety measures any smart traveler should employ—travel light, blend in with the local population, and refrain from wearing flashy and/or expensive clothing or jewelry. In areas prone to express kidnappings, consider carrying a dummy wallet as an extra layer of security. Stash a small amount of cash, a single form of identification, and a single credit card in this wallet, leaving your passport and other debit cards at home or concealing them elsewhere on your body. Express kidnappers frequently drive their victims from ATM to ATM, holding them at gunpoint as they max out the machines' daily limits on all debit cards. A dummy wallet will allow you to give the appearance of surrendering while still protecting your valuables.

Express kidnappings are becoming more and more violent, so the appearance of cooperation may not be enough to appease your attackers. If you sense that your life is in danger, attempt escape.

No. 067: Prevent and Survive an Express Kidnapping

CONOP: Understand and survive short-term financially motivated kidnappings.

COA 1: What is an express kidnapping?

Type 1: Passenger Attack

Type 2: Driver Attack

Attacks end at money machines, maxing out daily limits on all cards.

COA 2: Prevention

Use ATMs inside malls, banks, and hotels.

Do not talk to or pick up strangers.

COA 3: Response

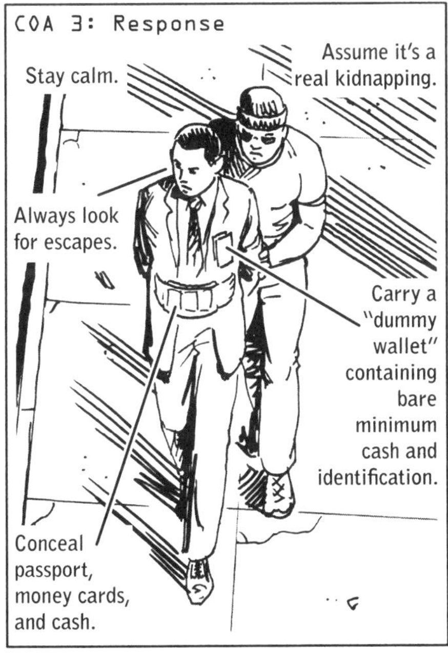

Stay calm.
Assume it's a real kidnapping.
Always look for escapes.
Carry a "dummy wallet" containing bare minimum cash and identification.
Conceal passport, money cards, and cash.

BLUF: Express kidnappings are becoming more and more violent.

068 Resist an Attempted Abduction

Do not gently acquiesce to an abductor's will. Assume the worst—that unlike a thief, an abductor isn't likely to be satisfied until he has caused you grave physical harm—and act accordingly. Do not let him have his way.

If you have the opportunity to place a 911 call, do so quickly and then place the phone on silent, hiding it on your body. If you cannot place a call, switch your phone to silent at the first opportunity. Law enforcement authorities may be able to use your device as a tracking mechanism if you are indeed abducted and taken to a second location.

But nothing positive can be gained from following a violent abductor to a location that is potentially isolated and set up for optimal restraint, so fight back with everything you've got. Be loud and aggressive. Perpetrators look for easy targets who won't put up a fight, and noise may attract the attention of potential witnesses who'll be able to contact law enforcement and provide descriptions of the perpetrator. If you aren't carrying Mace, use improvised weapons such as keys, pens, purse straps, or charger cords (see page 172) to inflict harm.

If the abductor is brandishing a weapon or overcoming your efforts to fight, surrender temporarily rather than fighting to the point where you are rendered unconscious and completely powerless. As you are being restrained, take deep breaths and subtly spread limbs, fingers, and wrists in order to create slack and improve the odds of escape. Present your wrists out in front of you to diminish the odds of getting restrained with your hands behind your back, a far less maneuverable position. Attempt escape as soon as possible—the odds will be much better while you're in transit than after you've been taken to a secondary location.

No. 068: Resist an Attempted Abduction

CONOP: Stay conscious, stay alive, and escape as soon as possible.

COA 1: Call 911, silence and hide phone on body.

Silent mode

COA 2: Be LOUD and RUN.

COA 3: Fight. Use improvised weapons.

COA 4: Surrender temporarily.

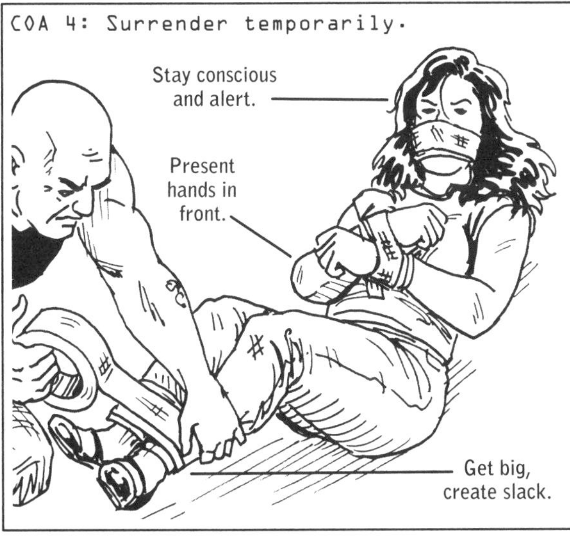
Stay conscious and alert.
Present hands in front.
Get big, create slack.

COA 5: Escape ASAP.

BLUF: If outnumbered or taking life-threatening blows, surrender and escape at the first opportunity.

069 Spot a Concealed Handgun

Individuals who carry a handgun professionally are well attuned to the range of mannerisms that can indicate the presence of a concealed weapon within their vicinity. Civilians, too, can learn to familiarize themselves with these signs and signals. When combined with suspicious behavior, the suspected presence of a concealed weapon should put bystanders on high alert.

Body Language: People carrying handguns tend to subconsciously telegraph the location of the weapon via their body language. They may reflexively palpate the gun to make sure the weapon is still safely in its holster, subtly reposition the weapon prior to sitting or standing, or shift their weight away from nearby bystanders to avoid accidental contact with or theft of the weapon.

Asymmetry: Another telltale sign is asymmetry in clothing. Guns are heavy and bulky, and thus will betray signs of their presence to anyone who's paying attention. An outside-the-waistband holster may cause a visible midline bulge, while an ankle holster may cause a bulge or tightening of the fabric at the lower leg. A gun held in a jacket pocket will weight down one side of the jacket unevenly.

Environment: Hot or inclement weather can make concealed weapons easier to spot. Rain, wind, or sweat can reveal the outline of a gun, which will generally be much easier to hide under multiple layers of cold-weather clothing.

Negligence: Weapons are also frequently exposed due to temporary negligence, flashed or inadvertently dropped as a gunman reaches for his wallet. Dropped weapons are an all-too-common scenario at public urinals, where inexperienced perpetrators may thoughtlessly unzip their pants—thereby releasing the tension that was holding up the holster.

No. 069: Spot a Concealed Handgun

CONOP: Interpret clues in order to spot a concealed gun.

COA 1: Telegraphing

Gun check — Gun adjustment — Hip shift

COA 2: Asymmetry

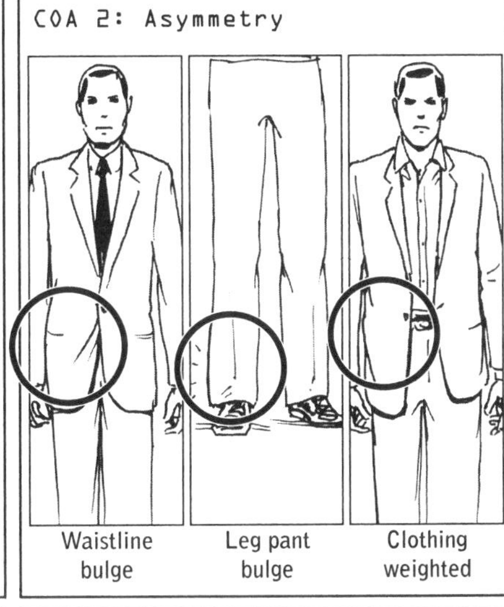

Waistline bulge — Leg pant bulge — Clothing weighted

COA 3: Environment

Rain — Wind — Heat

COA 4: Negligence

Flash — Brandish — Drop

BLUF: Even a well-concealed weapon can be detectable.

070 Spot a Suicide Bomber

Unlike shooters, who can be unarmed or neutralized mid-carnage, suicide bombers strike in a single, deadly blow—a monomaniacal attack so decisive it becomes virtually unstoppable. The only way to fight back is to prevent the device from ever being detonated, disarming bombers before they have a chance to strike. Detection is the name of the game, which is why airline security has become so complex. But as several incidents have demonstrated, you don't need a scanner to detect a potential threat.

The explosive devices that used to be packed in bulky, heavy backpacks are now often strapped onto the bomber's body in belt or vest form, but bombers will still need to wear bulky, heavy layers of clothing to hide the bombs. They are likely to be exhibiting several signs of extreme nervousness, from profuse sweating to a zombie-like sense of tunnel vision. They may seem oblivious to their surroundings, moving through a crowd with an unusual sense of purpose that is the result of prior reconnaissance and a single-minded goal.

Tackling a suicide bomber is a life-threatening proposition, as the bomber could detonate his or her vest or belt at any time. If you're within leaping distance, immediately restrain the bomber's hands so that he or she cannot activate the device. Avoid touching the device. Have all the people around you shut down their mobile phones in order to turn the area into a NERF (non-electromagnetic radiation facility) or Zero RF (zero radio frequency) zone. Explosives and electronics do not mix, and radio frequencies could potentially set off a detonator.

Assume the worst—military-grade explosives with electric blasting caps that could be detonated by any electronic device with Wi-Fi, cellular, Bluetooth, or satellite capability.

No. 070: Spot a Suicide Bomber

CONOP: Identify the projection and demeanor traits of a would-be suicide bomber.

COA 1: Types of Suicide Bombs

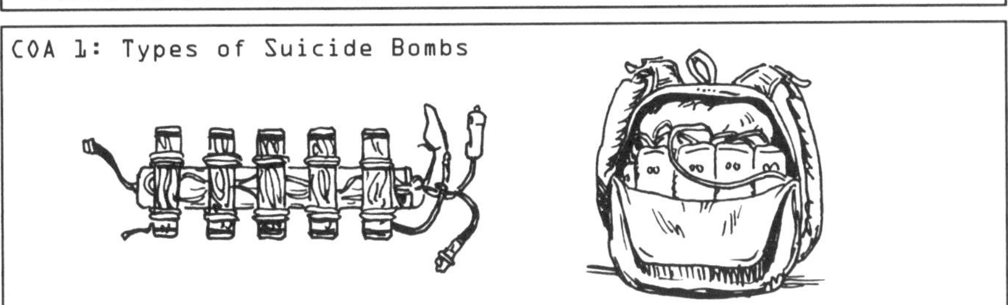

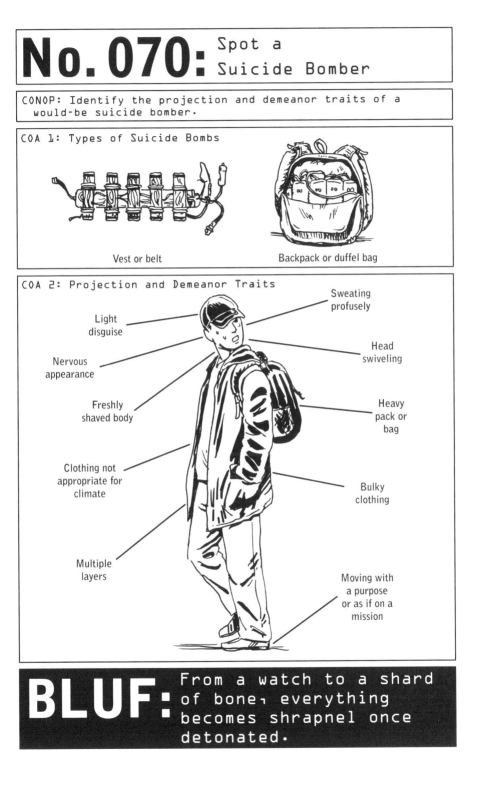

Vest or belt

Backpack or duffel bag

COA 2: Projection and Demeanor Traits

Sweating profusely

Light disguise

Head swiveling

Nervous appearance

Freshly shaved body

Heavy pack or bag

Clothing not appropriate for climate

Bulky clothing

Multiple layers

Moving with a purpose or as if on a mission

BLUF: From a watch to a shard of bone, everything becomes shrapnel once detonated.

071 Choke Out a Bad Guy

An often overlooked form of self-defense, choking out a violent criminal requires neither brawn nor expertise in mixed martial arts. Best employed as a covert attack on an unsuspecting assailant who's just entered a room, the move benefits from the element of surprise—or momentary inattention on the part of an aggressor who might be busy with other victims during a mass shooting scenario.

The goal of the technique is to cut off circulation from the carotid arteries to the brain, causing the aggressor to lose consciousness in a matter of seconds. Slipping an improvised garrote around an aggressor's neck yields a much greater probability of success than a headlock, which requires a significant amount of pressure and some luck. An assailant may be able to hold his breath for several minutes, and a headlock sometimes only succeeds in cutting off airflow. Using an improvised garrote guarantees that, with enough pressure, you'll be hitting both the respiratory tract and the arteries.

All you'll need in order to execute the technique are two pens or pencils and a piece of improvised wire—a single shoelace (preferably Kevlar), the wire from a cell-phone charger, or the Kevlar lanyard from a retractable ID holder. Tying overhand loops into both ends of the wire and inserting pens into the loops yield a two-handled choking system with a grip. Without the handles, you won't be able to exert the necessary amount of pressure.

Loop the wire over the assailant's head, then pull your hands behind his neck to cinch the mechanism in place. Exert as much pressure as possible, and maintain pressure until your opponent collapses. Consciousness will return in under a minute, so quickly use the advantage to run to safety.

No. 071: Choke Out a Bad Guy

CONOP: Induce asphyxiation with an improvised garrote.

COA 1: Collect improvised wire and handles.

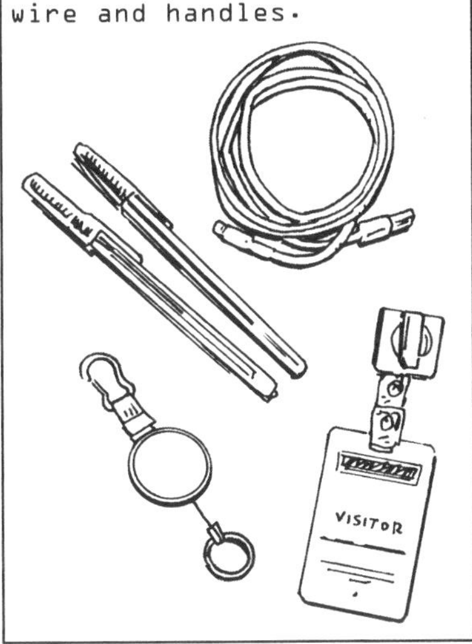

COA 2: Tie overhand loop knots at both ends.

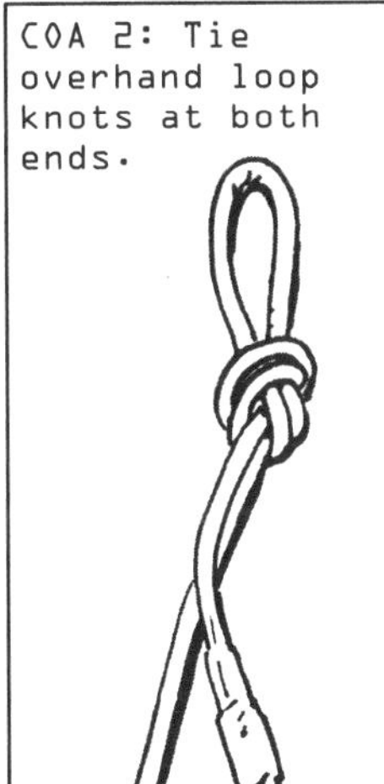

COA 3: Insert pens into loops.

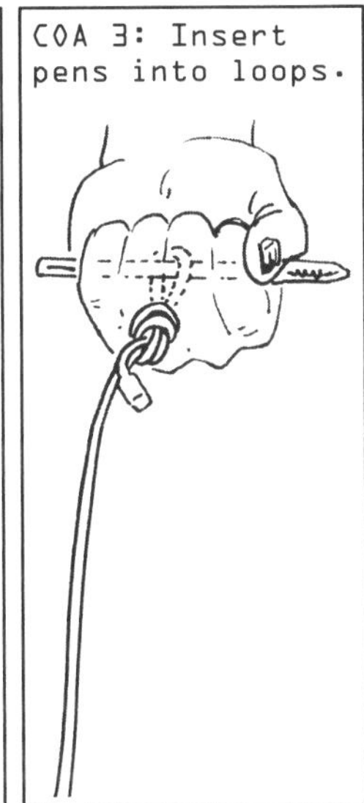

COA 4: Choke out bad guy!

BLUF: Garrotes cut off both air and blood to the brain.

072 Take Out a Hijacker

Today's hijackers make yesterday's airborne vigilantes, with their lists of demands and their penchant for publicity stunts, look practically innocuous.

A suicide bomber isn't using the plane as a form of political leverage, but as an instrument of mass murder. He has no demands that can be immediately fulfilled, and he isn't likely to be talked out of his ultimate goal—mass murder in combination with a suicidal fantasy that promises him untold rewards in the afterlife. Which means that if your flight is overtaken by hijackers, the cost of inaction will almost certainly be death. You certainly may risk personal injury or death by attempting to tackle a suicide bomber, but those outcomes are practically guaranteed if you fail to act. Use the following security guidelines to increase the odds of a successful intervention. Though its passengers weren't able to avoid a tragic outcome, history, in cases such as United flight 93, has shown that passenger action may result in a reduction of carnage at the very least.

Do Not Attempt to Act Alone: Team up with nearby passengers, and assign teams of two passengers to each hijacker. Window-seated passengers are less useful from an immediate-action perspective, due to the difficulty they will have accessing the aisle. Aisle-seated passengers should quietly plan for action with the person sitting opposite them and the two people sitting directly in front and behind them. Those with military or security experience should always select aisle seats in order to be available during a crisis.

Gather an Arsenal: Start by collecting improvised weapons (pitchers of hot coffee, rolled-up newspapers), shields (seat cushions, tray tables), and temporary restraints (power cords, purse straps) from the environment.

Come Up with a Plan: Two to three aisle-seated passengers acting in tandem can create a box around a hijacker as he walks by. To avoid overcrowding, only two people should move into the aisle, while the remaining person stands directly over his or her seat. Assign each person a task. The party with primary access should pounce on the weapon, while the second and third parties should restrain the hijacker's head and body. Control the head, and you've essentially got control of the body. Get the hijacker off balance and onto the ground as quickly as possible, and apply temporary restraints.

Delineate Criteria for Action: For example, you'll spring into action as soon as a hijacker passes you in the aisle, but you'll wait if two hijackers are patrolling the aisles together.

Reinforce Restraints: Once hijackers are restrained, ransack the airplane's medical bags for medical tape and bandages. Layer these over the existing restraints to reinforce the bind.

Quarantine Hijackers: Confine hijackers to rear lavatories, which can be locked from the outside by flight attendants, while you decide what to do.

Shove Them Off the Plane: If pilots and security command forces agree that the hijackers still pose an immediate threat via the possibility of surgically implanted explosives, they may determine that the safest course of action is to jettison them from the flight. After pilots lower the plane to ten thousand feet in order to depressurize the cabin, lead hijackers to emergency exit doors behind the plane's wings. The last thing you want is a hijacker's body flying straight through the engine body as he makes his final exit from the flight.

No. 072: Take Out a Hijacker

CONOP: Prepare, plan, and fight to take back a hijacked plane.

COA 1: Prepare.

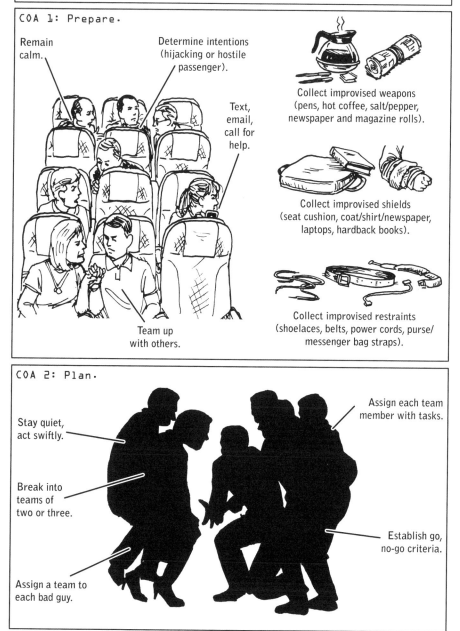

Remain calm.

Determine intentions (hijacking or hostile passenger).

Text, email, call for help.

Team up with others.

Collect improvised weapons (pens, hot coffee, salt/pepper, newspaper and magazine rolls).

Collect improvised shields (seat cushion, coat/shirt/newspaper, laptops, hardback books).

Collect improvised restraints (shoelaces, belts, power cords, purse/ messenger bag straps).

COA 2: Plan.

Stay quiet, act swiftly.
Break into teams of two or three.
Assign a team to each bad guy.
Assign each team member with tasks.
Establish go, no-go criteria.

COA 3: Fight.

Use extreme violence.

One-man: control of weapon, deliver initial blow

Two-man: control of head/body, improvised weapon and shield

COA 4: Restrain.

Restrain hands and feet.

Confine bad guys to rear lavatories.

COA 5: Jettison hijackers.

Request pilots adjust altitude below ten thousand feet and depressurize cabin.

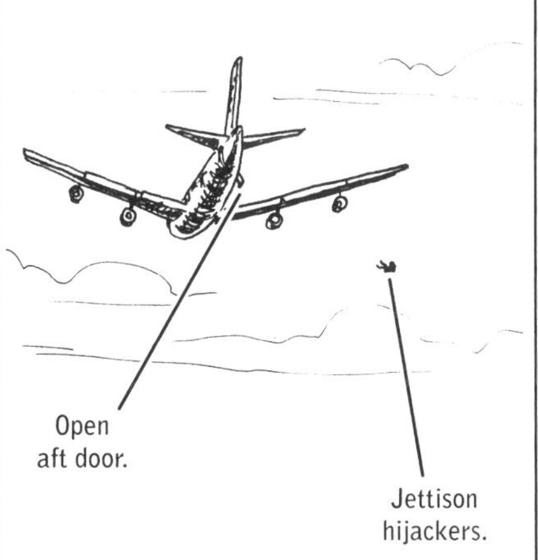

BLUF: Neutralize them before they do the same to you.

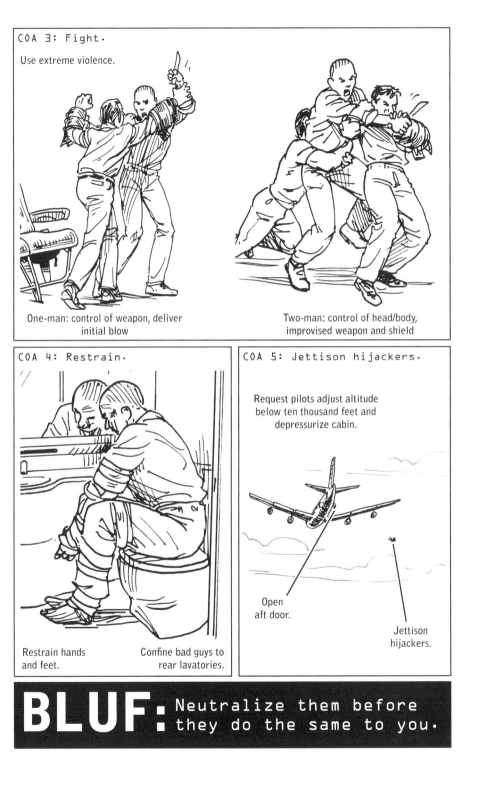

PART VII

DISASTER SURVIVAL

073 Escape a Tsunami

With the power to level entire cities and reshape the course of human history, tsunamis are among the most perilous of all natural disasters. Striking with little warning and causing tremendous devastation, the unfathomably powerful and destructive waves start with seismic activity along faults running deep under the seafloor.

Also sometimes caused by volcanic eruptions, the violent, flooding surges travel at speeds of five hundred miles per hour before piling up against the coastline, rising hundreds of feet into the air, and then crashing onto dry ground with the force of several nuclear bombs.

Though smaller tsunamis are frequent in well-known high-risk zones along the coasts of the Pacific and Indian oceans, the American Northwest is said to be overdue for the kind of giant wave that hasn't been documented in the region for more than a thousand years, so preparation is essential.

Evacuation routes may be marked in high-risk areas, but don't wait until disaster strikes to acquaint yourself with routes to high ground. If you live near or are visiting a high-risk coastline, plan both foot and vehicle routes to landmasses or solid structures 150 feet above sea level or two miles inland. Don't rely on vegetation to keep you safe. Trees will likely be swept away.

Certain regions are equipped with tsunami warning systems based on detection devices placed along the seafloor. In the absence of a warning, heed nature's clues. Any significant earthquake felt along the coast should be cause for concern, as should a rapid fall or rise in shorelines and unusual behavior seen in animals. The amount of time you will have between the earthquake and a potential tsunami depends on the distance of the fault from the shoreline, but you will often have no more than twenty minutes to get to high ground. Move swiftly, for time is of the essence.

No. 073: Escape a Tsunami

CONOP: Understand the indicators and response to a massive oceanic wave.

COA 1: Understand the science.

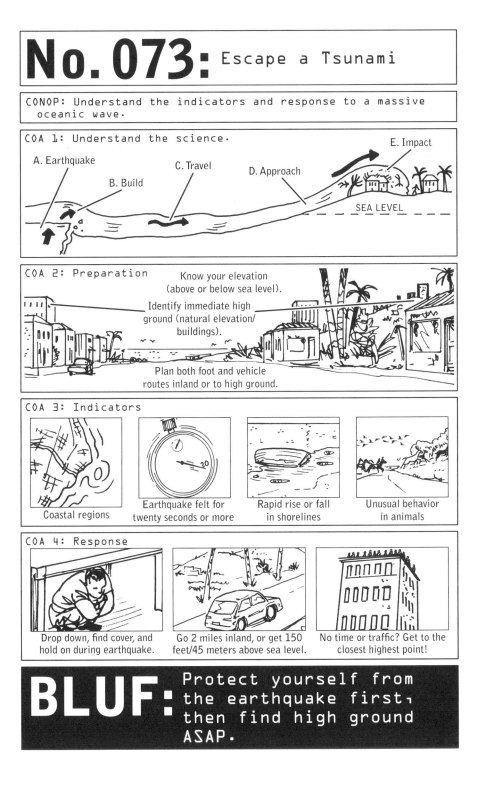

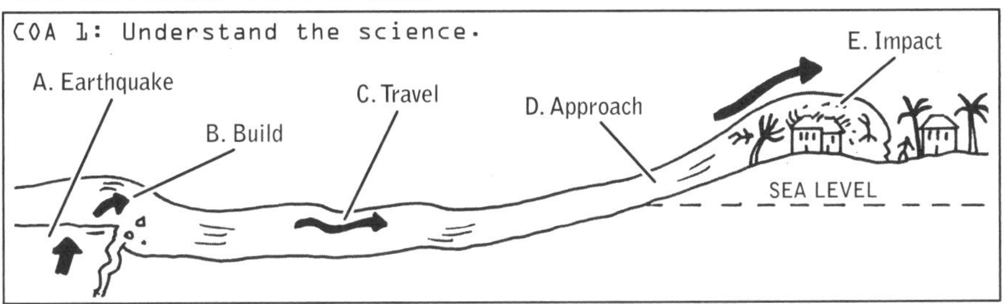

COA 2: Preparation

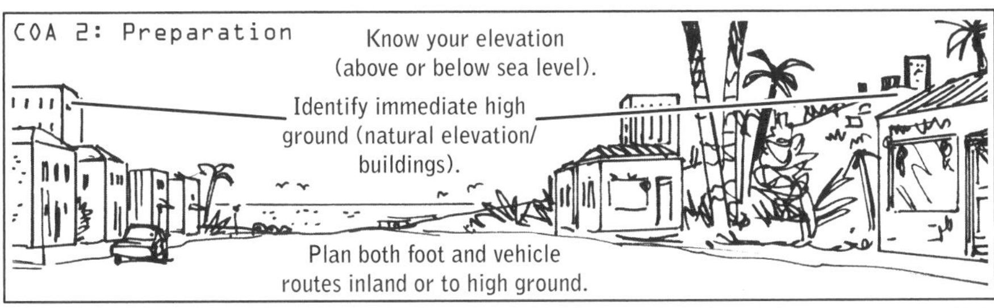

Know your elevation (above or below sea level).
Identify immediate high ground (natural elevation/ buildings).
Plan both foot and vehicle routes inland or to high ground.

COA 3: Indicators

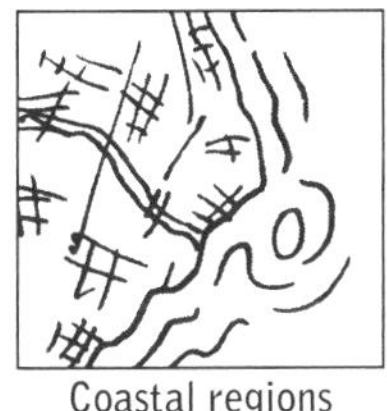
Coastal regions

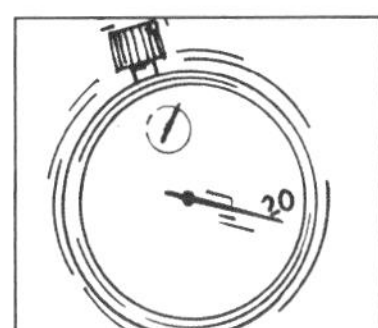

Earthquake felt for twenty seconds or more

Rapid rise or fall in shorelines

Unusual behavior in animals

COA 4: Response

Drop down, find cover, and hold on during earthquake.

Go 2 miles inland, or get 150 feet/45 meters above sea level.

No time or traffic? Get to the closest highest point!

BLUF: Protect yourself from the earthquake first, then find high ground ASAP.

074 Survive an Avalanche

Though occasional incidents involve mass casualties, avalanches claim only some 150 lives per year. But many more non-fatal incidents go unreported. To avoid landing in either category, abstain from skiing, rock climbing, or snowmobile riding on heavily powdered, backcountry slopes that haven't been groomed or detonated in order to purposely precipitate avalanches in advance of human activity. Talk to locals in order to identify known avalanche zones and the general probability of avalanches in the area. Pay attention to the weather—a foot or more of fresh snow can pose a risk factor, as can rain.

If you are caught in the midst of an avalanche while on a steep, barren slope, quickly move to its flanks while you still can. Snow will be funneled down the center of the slope, potentially carrying less momentum and mass on its sidelines. If an avalanche starts below your feet, jump upslope of any crack you might be able to see in the top layer of snow.

If you cannot avoid the oncoming rush, grab onto any solid fixture you can reach (tree, rock formation, telephone pole), or lie down and try to "swim" with the moving snow so that you don't receive the impact at a perpendicular angle.

Being buried in snow isn't dissimilar to being buried in sand. You may not be able to move or breathe once the precipitation comes to a halt, so if you can, create an air pocket by placing your hands in front of your face as you're still moving. Determine which way is up by sensing the direction of the blood flow to your head or lighting a lighter, if movement is available. Punching an air channel from your face up toward the surface of the snow will put you closer to a full breath when a rescue team starts digging.

No. 074: Survive an Avalanche

CONOP: Employ lifesaving tactics to survive an avalanche.

COA 1: Preparation

Know the causes: a foot or more of fresh snow; rain; explosions; earthquakes; foot and vehicle movement.

Talk to locals.

Pay attention to weather.

Always have a buddy.

Carry a beacon.

COA 2: Land Burial

1. Avoid center and move to flanks (skiing or snowmobiling).

2. Jump upslope of a visible crack.

3. Grab something (like a tree or rock).

4. Ditch your gear (skis, poles, packs).

5. Swim on top (try to stay on surface of snow waves).

6. Create an air pocket (put your hand in front of face).

7. Determine "up" (blood flow to head, light a lighter).

8. Punch upward (break surface, make dig shorter).

BLUF: Avalanches are frequently caused by skiers, rock climbers, and snowmobilers.

075 Survive an Earthquake

Of the twenty thousand earthquakes that rock the globe each year, about fifteen will be major seismic events. But all too often, even civilians who live in earthquake-prone areas tend to take a blasé attitude toward preparation. Given that some of the safety protocol has changed over the years, a review is in order.

Identify Safe Zones

The outdated notion of rushing for the nearest doorway has been around since the nineteenth century, when the safest spots in California's adobe clay homes *were* the wood-framed doorways. But doorways won't cover you from projectiles, and these days most homes are fully wood-framed.

True safe zones include sturdy pieces of furniture, such as tables and desks, and structurally sound spaces like the inside corners of rooms and interior walls.

Stay away from glass windows or surfaces.

Be Earthquake Proof

Earthquake-proof your home by latching large, heavy pieces of furniture to the foundation of your home.

Secure bracing wire to a ceiling joist to support hanging light fixtures and fans, and use earthquake-proof picture hooks and putty to affix framed art and photographs to your walls.

Large wall-hanging mirrors and televisions should be bracketed to studs and hung on closed hooks.

Prepare to Evacuate

In addition to the more extensive earthquake kit commonly recommended to residents of geologically active zones (tools, a gallon of water per person per day, and a week's worth of food), a go-bag is a worthwhile precaution.

There's no telling what types of secondary emergencies an earthquake might create—from a collapsed foundation to floods, fires, or violent riots—so it's best to be prepared for sudden egress.

If possible, create several iterations of the go-bag, stashing one in your car, one in the master bedroom, and one in the kitchen or living room.

Stop and Drop

During an earthquake, follow the most widely recommended piece of safety protocol: Stop, drop or cover, and hold on.

Drop to the ground before the earthquake drops you.

Seek cover if possible, holding on to the object you're sheltering under to prevent it from rolling away.

Do not run outside, where toppling trees and power lines can pose grave danger.

If you are in bed, stay there, and cover your face with a pillow to protect yourself from projectiles and glass. If you are in your vehicle, stop once you are clear of underpasses or large trees and remain in your vehicle.

If you are trapped under large pieces of debris, or have fallen down into a basement or subterranean sinkhole, move slowly so as to avoid causing further structural collapse. If your go-bag is nearby, use your whistle to call for help. Tapping on pipes or rebar may produce sounds loud enough for emergency responders to hear.

In coastal areas, earthquakes may be a precursor to a tsunami (see page 180), so once the shaking has stopped, get to higher ground as quickly as possible.

No. 075: Survive an Earthquake

CONOP: Review the proper response to an earthquake.

COA 1: Preparation

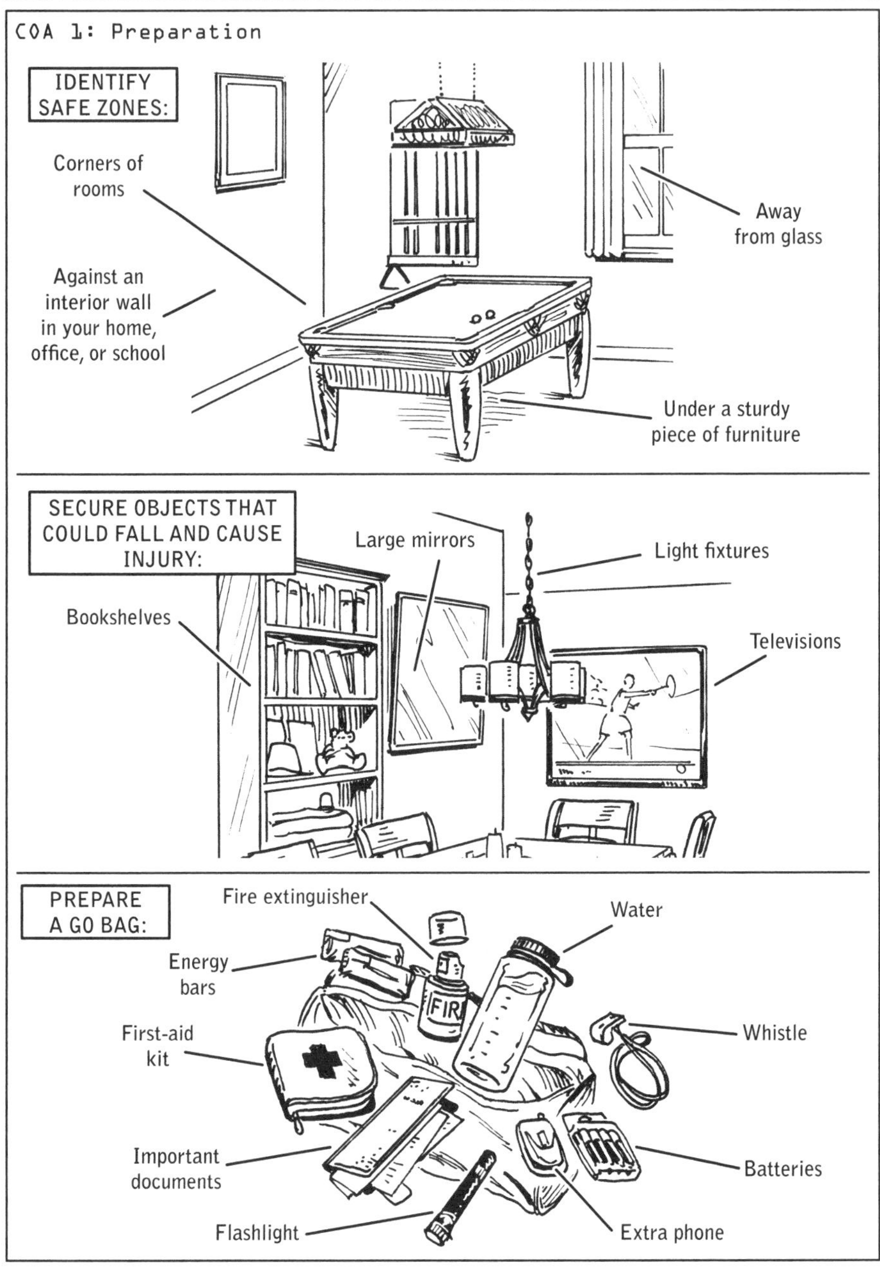
IDENTIFY SAFE ZONES:
Corners of rooms
Against an interior wall in your home, office, or school
Away from glass
Under a sturdy piece of furniture
SECURE OBJECTS THAT COULD FALL AND CAUSE INJURY:
Large mirrors
Light fixtures
Bookshelves
Televisions
PREPARE A GO BAG:
Fire extinguisher
Water
Energy bars
First-aid kit
Whistle
Important documents
Batteries
Flashlight
Extra phone

COA 2: During an Earthquake

If in bed, cover head with pillow.

If in vehicle, stop and stay in vehicle.

If outside, move away from buildings, streetlights, and utility wires.

COA 3: After the Earthquake

BLUF: Drop, cover, and hold on.

076 Survive a Thunder Snow Blizzard

Whether you're caught in an old-fashioned blizzard or a rare occurrence of thunder snow—the combination of thunder and snow that strikes when a cold front moves in over a rising mass of warm, humid air—there's nothing novel about the types of precautions most likely to ensure your safety.

Winterize Your Home and Vehicle

In regions where extreme winter weather conditions are common, be prepared. Stock your house and closets with rock salt, sand, shovels, wood, and weather-appropriate gear. Stash emergency blankets, a wool hat, and pocket heaters in the trunk of your car.

Have your car winterized, making sure your mechanic checks your exhaust system for leaks and crimped pipes. Your mechanic should also replace air filters; check brakes for wear and fluid levels; install good winter tires with adequate tread; check oil; ensure the heater, defroster, and thermostat are working properly; check antifreeze; clean and check the battery and ignition system; replace worn-out windshield wipers; and assess all lights.

Know When to Go

To avoid getting stranded on the road, err on the side of caution when making the decision to drive in a blizzard. Avoid driving on unplowed roads. If conditions look questionable, they probably are. A vehicular death caused by driving in low-visibility conditions is most often a death that would have been preventable through the use of one simple tool: human judgment. If conditions rapidly worsen while you're already on the road, don't feel the need to soldier through. Though emergency conditions set off a kind of fight-or-flight response that launches drivers into frenzied attempts to drive through or away from storms, sometimes the safest course of action is to do nothing—i.e., pull over and wait out the storm.

Wait Out a Storm

If you do become stranded in a remote area, do not attempt to hike your way to safety unless you know the area well and have on appropriate clothing (see page 41 for more on cold-weather gear). Remain in your car. Blizzard conditions will severely reduce visibility and increase the chances of your getting lost while being completely exposed to the elements.

To avoid the risk of carbon monoxide poisoning and conserve your battery, only run your engine and heater for ten minutes of every hour. If you aren't traveling with a trunkful of warm layers and/or blankets, stack seat covers and floor mats on top of you as insulation. At night, leave the dome light on so that your car is visible to other drivers. Hazard lights will burn up your battery.

In the event that you feel the signs of hypothermia beginning to set in, use your stash of emergency pocket heaters to warm up your core (see page 150); if your body temperature has dropped past a certain point, warming your fingers or feet first could cause a dangerous rush of blood to the heart.

No. 076: Survive a Thunder Snow Blizzard

CONOP: Understand and implement counter-blizzard tactics.

COA 1: Preparing Your Home

1. Rock salt for walkways
2. Sand for traction
3. Shovels for clearing areas
4. Wood for stoves and fireplaces
5. Warm clothes

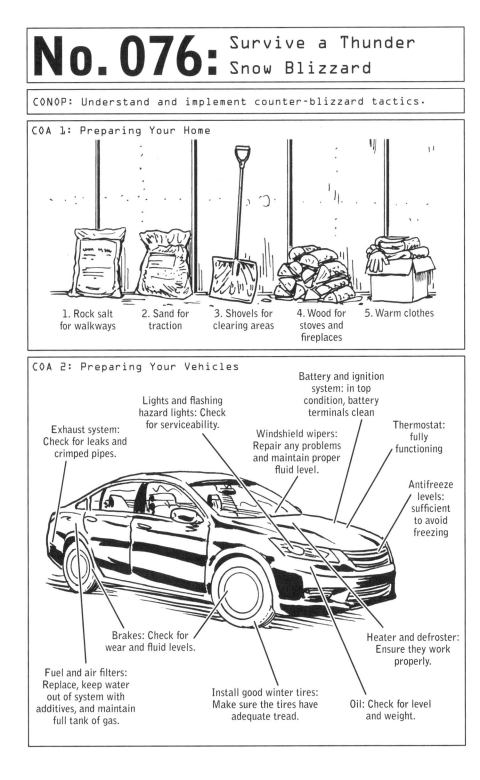

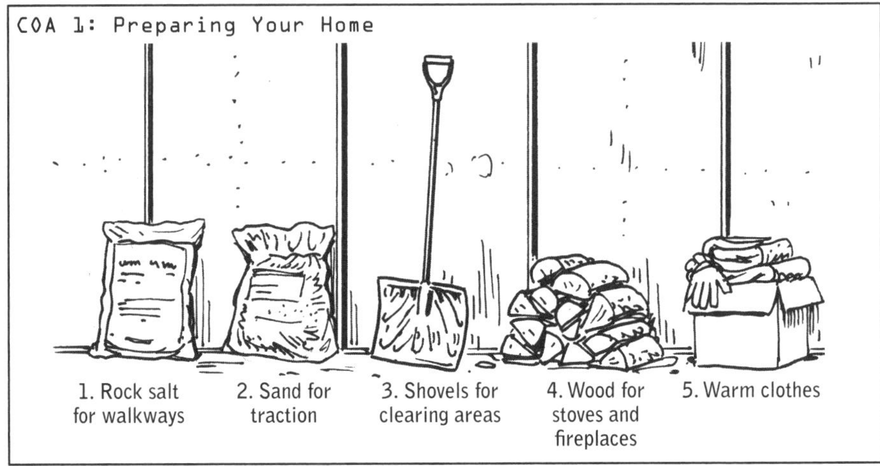

COA 2: Preparing Your Vehicles

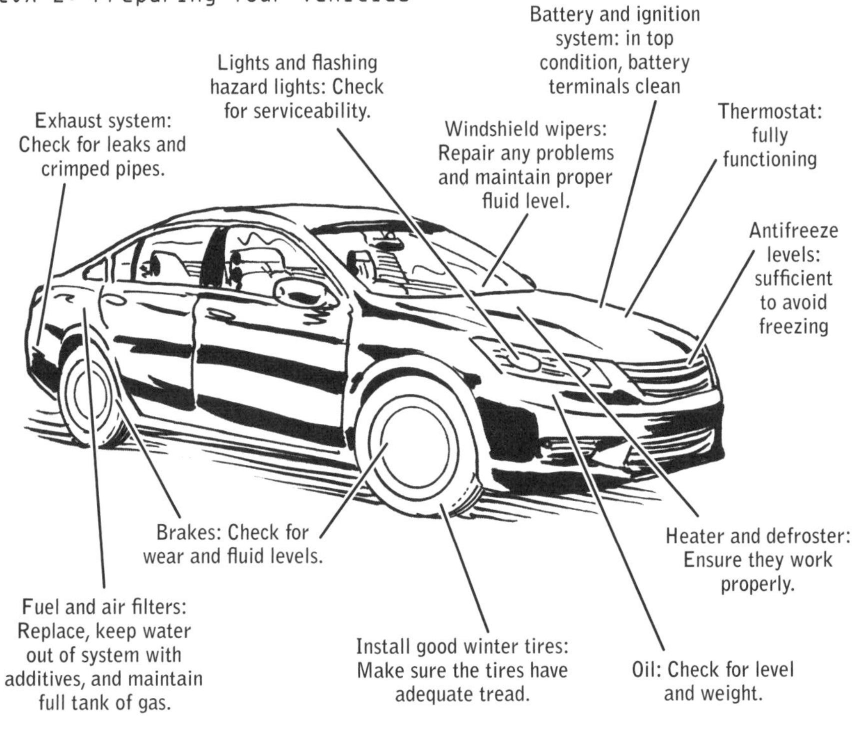

Battery and ignition system: in top condition, battery terminals clean
Lights and flashing hazard lights: Check for serviceability.
Exhaust system: Check for leaks and crimped pipes.
Windshield wipers: Repair any problems and maintain proper fluid level.
Thermostat: fully functioning
Antifreeze levels: sufficient to avoid freezing
Brakes: Check for wear and fluid levels.
Heater and defroster: Ensure they work properly.
Fuel and air filters: Replace, keep water out of system with additives, and maintain full tank of gas.
Install good winter tires: Make sure the tires have adequate tread.
Oil: Check for level and weight.

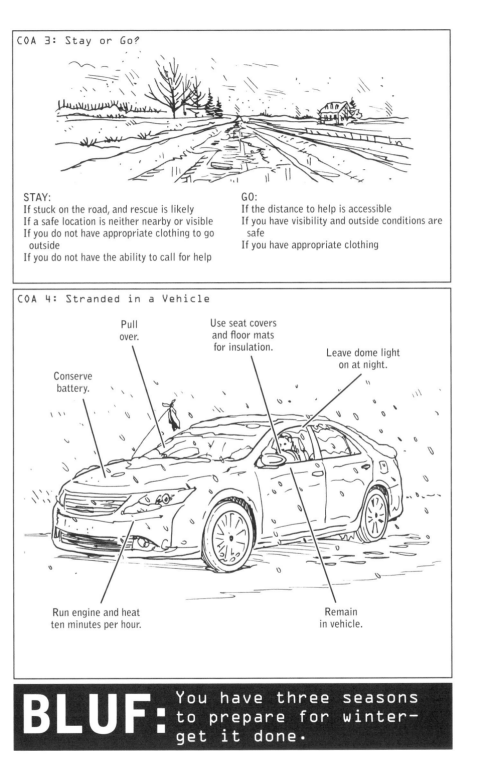

COA 3: Stay or Go?

STAY:

If stuck on the road, and rescue is likely
If a safe location is neither nearby or visible
If you do not have appropriate clothing to go outside
If you do not have the ability to call for help

GO:

If the distance to help is accessible
If you have visibility and outside conditions are safe
If you have appropriate clothing

COA 4: Stranded in a Vehicle

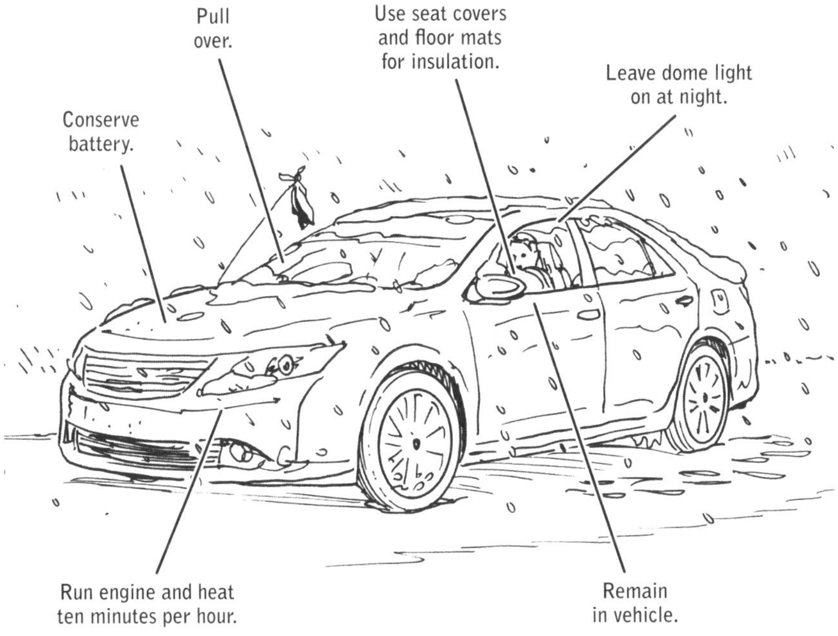

Pull over.

Use seat covers and floor mats for insulation.

Leave dome light on at night.

Conserve battery.

Run engine and heat ten minutes per hour.

Remain in vehicle.

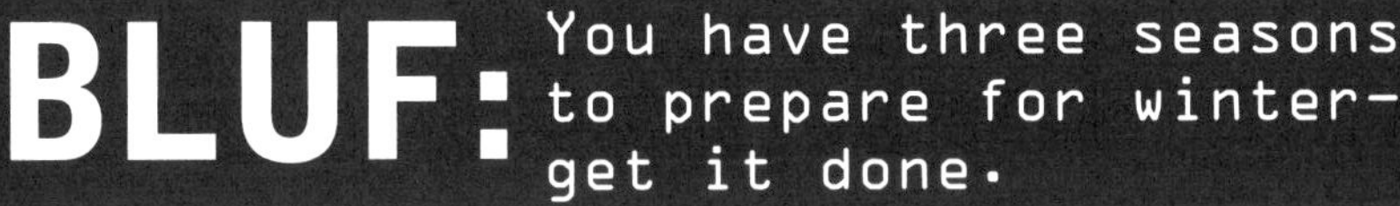

BLUF:
You have three seasons
to prepare for winter-
get it done.

077 Survive Tornadoes and Hurricanes

No natural disaster strikes more fear in the heart of the average civilian than the threat of an impending hurricane, touted for days if not weeks in advance by weather forecasters as a potentially cataclysmic event. But while history has shown the importance of heeding hurricane evacuation warnings, the unannounced danger posed by tornadoes tends to have even deadlier ramifications.

The world may face ten hurricanes in any given year, but the U.S. alone sees upward of a thousand tornadoes—the American Midwest famously being the world leader in the violent weather system. And while severe hurricanes can create mass casualty scenarios, on average tornadoes claim more lives, their deceptively smaller radius camouflaging their sudden powers of destruction. They are the lone wolves of the weather systems.

Heed Evacuation Warnings

The principal danger with hurricanes is not wind but flooding, making timely evacuation crucial. Residents of high-risk areas may take a casual attitude to such warnings after years of false alarms, but they shouldn't—for it only takes one big flood to sweep away an entire city's infrastructure.

In the event of a tornado, there may be very little time to react, which is why the fast and violent winds tend to claim more lives. Where hurricanes are easily spottable by satellite as they gather their strength over oceans, tornadoes can form in minutes, given the right atmospheric conditions. Contrary to popular belief, they are not always visible, and their path of destruction may spread for more than a mile beyond their cyclical funnel.

Follow the Right Protocol for Your Location

Your location will determine the best safety protocol in response to a tornado. In addition to standard preparedness supplies, be sure to include a wrench and pliers in your go-bag so that you can safely shut off gas and water valves in the event of leakage.

Know When to Shelter in Place: Do not attempt to shelter in a mobile or prefabricated home. Unless your home is safely bolted to the ground, you risk severe harm by staying in place. Find a solid structure and hunker down.

Go Low, Go Central: Staying away from windows and doors, make your way to the centermost and lowest point in the building. Keep doors and windows closed. The outdated practice of opening windows to avoid a pressure vacuum can result in strong winds lifting the roof clear off a home's foundation.

Strap In: If you are outdoors, sheltering inside a car may be your safest bet. Vehicle glass is built for impact, unlike household windowpanes. Strap on a seat belt in case the car is thrown by the force of the tornado.

Do Not Attempt to Outrun a Tornado: A tornado has unlimited energy—you do not. It also has an unpredictable path. Use what time you have to hunker down as safely as possible. Seek low ground, lying down against ditches or depressions that may provide some measure of protection against projectiles.

No. 077: Survive Tornadoes and Hurricanes

CONOP: Know what to do when high-speed rotating winds strike.

COA 1: Hurricane vs. Tornado

HURRICANE
Where: Over water
Size: Hundreds of miles wide
Duration: Three weeks
Speed: One hundred eighty miles per hour
Occurence: Ten per year
Warnings: Days

TORNADO
Where: Over land
Size: One-quarter mile wide
Duration: Less than one hour
Speed: Three hundred miles per hour
Occurence: Eight hundred to a thousand per year
Warnings: Fifteen to thirty minutes

COA 2: Prepare an emergency supply kit.

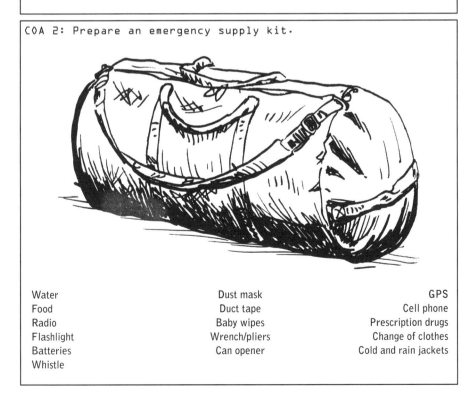

Water
Food
Radio
Flashlight
Batteries
Whistle
Dust mask
Duct tape
Baby wipes
Wrench/pliers
Can opener
GPS
Cell phone
Prescription drugs
Change of clothes
Cold and rain jackets

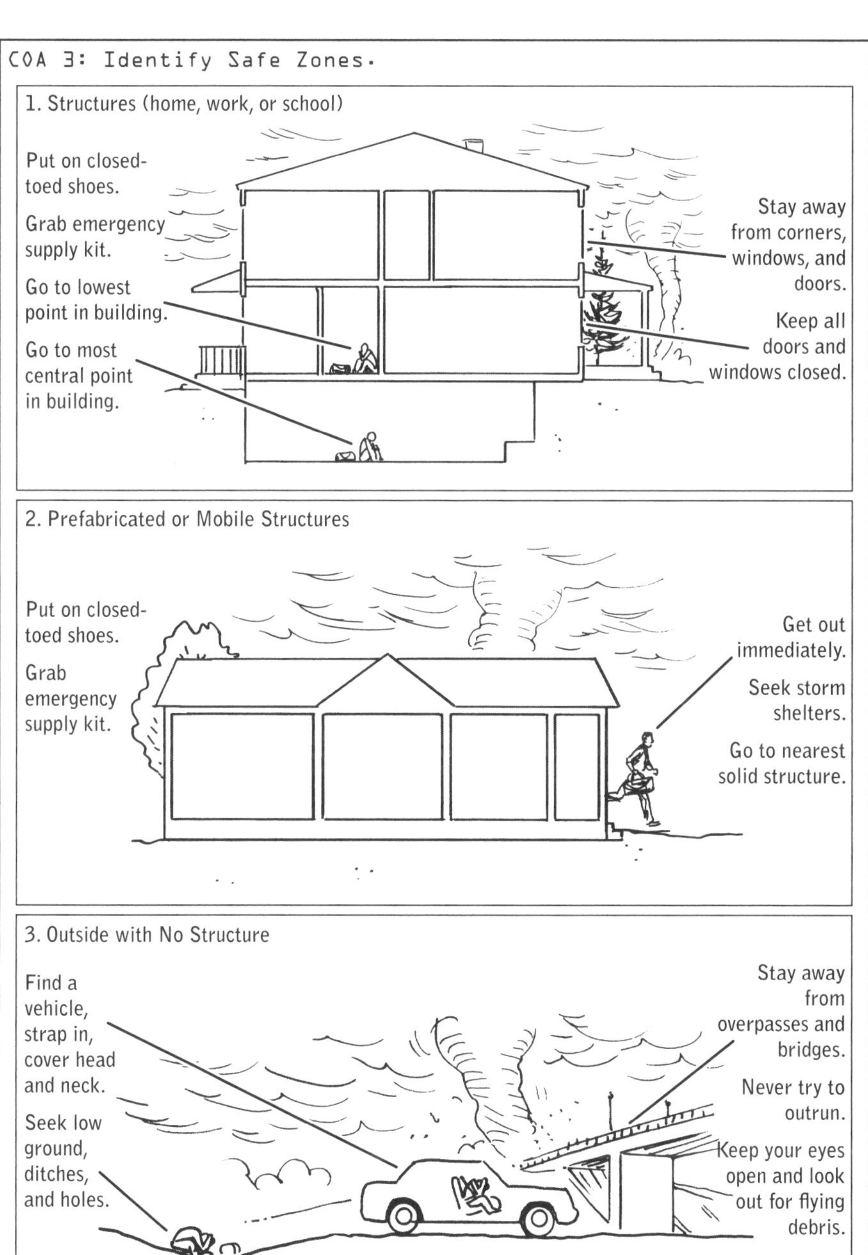

BLUF: Never try to outrun a tornado.

078 Survive a Sinkhole Fall

There are many reasons civilians should be more open to carrying a whistle as part of their EDC. The risk of being trapped under huge chunks of aging infrastructure, without the ability to signal to potential rescuers, is just one.

There's no such thing as solid ground in an urban landscape, where the apparently rock-solid pavement we drive across and stack skyscrapers over is somewhat of an illusion. For beneath that topmost layer lies an entire network of underground transportation, water mains, and sewage lines.

In reality, there are vast pockets of open space beneath our feet. And if we apply too much pressure to the surface, or an aging infrastructure causes a water main or sewage line to rupture, vast and gaping sinkholes can be the result.

There's no way for civilians to anticipate such an occurence, and when solid ground gives way beneath your feet, there's nothing to do but fall. The real question is how to survive.

If you are driving, do not attempt to exit until your vehicle comes to a halt—cars are built to withstand impact, so you may stand a better chance of survival by remaining strapped in. To learn how to escape a car whose doors are jammed shut, see page 198.

If you are sucked into a sinkhole while on foot, practice a parachute landing fall (PLF) to protect your bones. Squeezing your arms and legs together along the midline as pictured, bend your knees. Upon impact, fall to the side, so that the impact is sequentially distributed along your joints and spine, from the ankle through the knee and hip. Roll backward. Landing with straight body positioning and joints risks breaking the feet and harming the spine.

No. 078: Survive a Sinkhole Fall

CONOP: Know what to do when the ground collapses beneath your feet.

COA 1: Understand how sinkholes form.

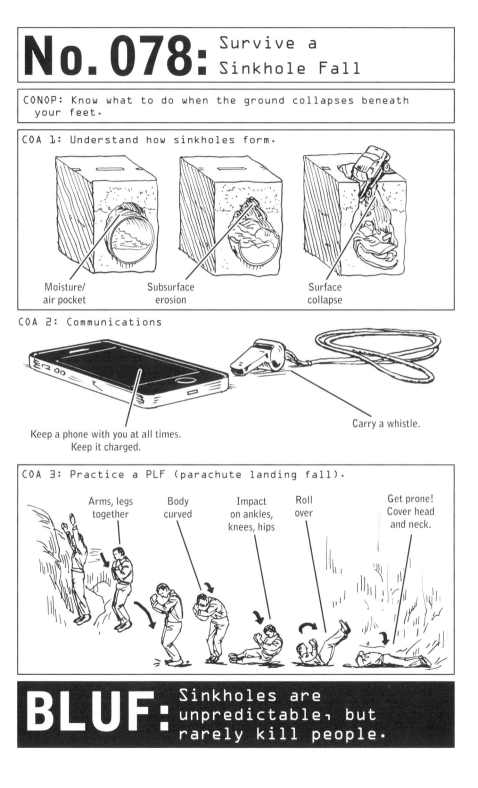

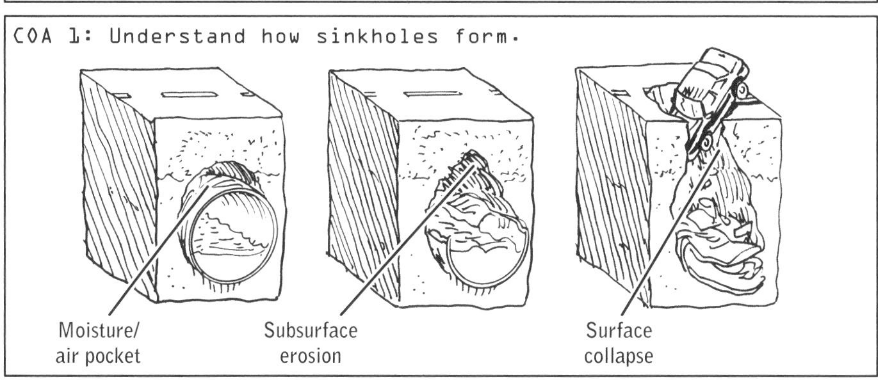
Moisture/
air pocket
Subsurface
erosion
Surface
collapse

COA 2: Communications

Keep a phone with you at all times.
Keep it charged.
Carry a whistle.

COA 3: Practice a PLF (parachute landing fall).

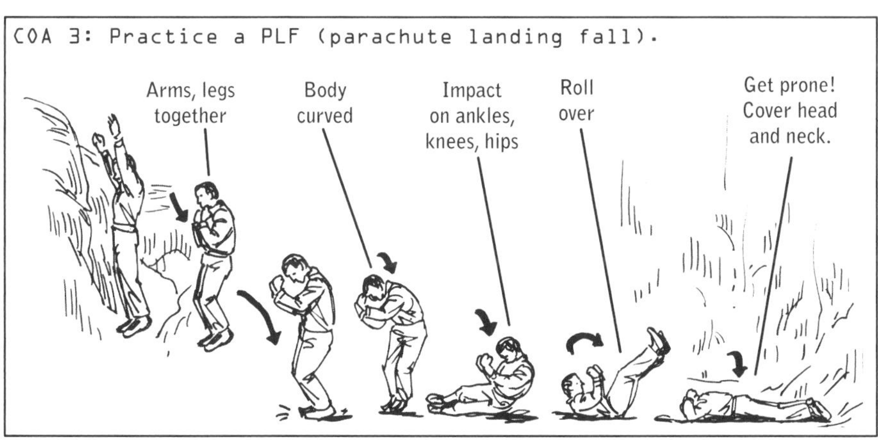
Arms, legs together
Body curved
Impact on ankles, knees, hips
Roll over
Get prone! Cover head and neck.

BLUF: Sinkholes are unpredictable, but rarely kill people.

079 Escape a Flooding Vehicle

Rule of the road: Never attempt to drive through flooding waters high enough to enter your vehicle's tailpipe. Doing so could potentially flood the engine, causing you to stall and inflicting serious damage on your vehicle.

In the event that you are swept into flooding waters and have enough time to react, prepare to exit your vehicle by opening windows and unlocking doors. Though the electrical function on automatic windows and locks will still function when the vehicle is submerged, the pressure differential may keep windows and doors jammed shut. Car doors may be impossible to open underwater until the interior of the vehicle is fully flooded, so prepare for escape while you still can.

Safety protocol indicates that seat belts should be left buckled until the vehicle comes to a full stop, but a particular situation may dictate otherwise. Keep a knife or razor blade in a closed compartment inside the vehicle in order to cut yourself free should the seat belt lock, a real possibility if you are stuck upside-down and the weight of your body jams the closure mechanism.

Do not attempt to break through your car's windshield, as it's double-paned and designed to withstand impact. Kick out a side window instead, aiming for the top of the glass, away from the anchors that bolt the pane down into the door.

Car windows can be difficult to break. Jamming a headrest spoke or knife down between the glass and the door may create a fulcrum that causes the pane to shatter. If you have an emergency glass punch tool, aim it at the corners of the glass.

No. 079: Escape a Flooding Vehicle

CONOP: Use orderly procedures to escape a flooding vehicle.

COA 1: Avoid floodwaters.

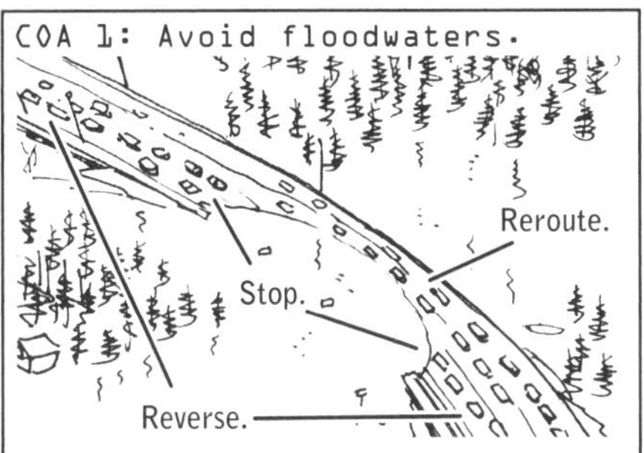

COA 2: Set up exits.

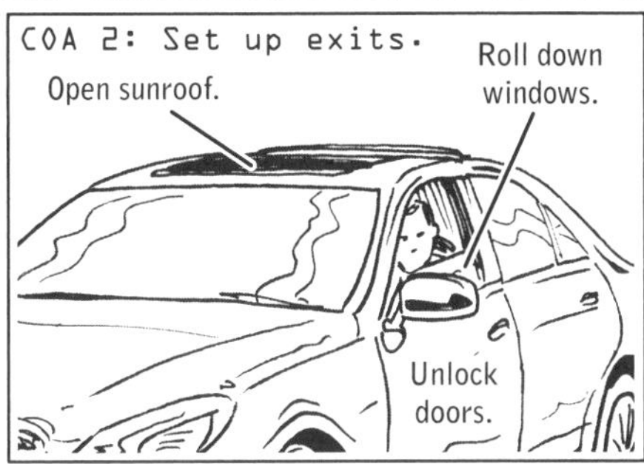

COA 3: Remove seat belt.

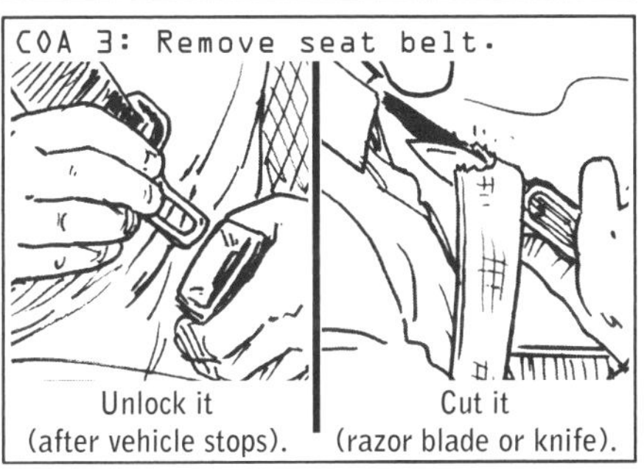

Unlock it (after vehicle stops).
Cut it (razor blade or knife).

COA 4: Exit vehicle ASAP.

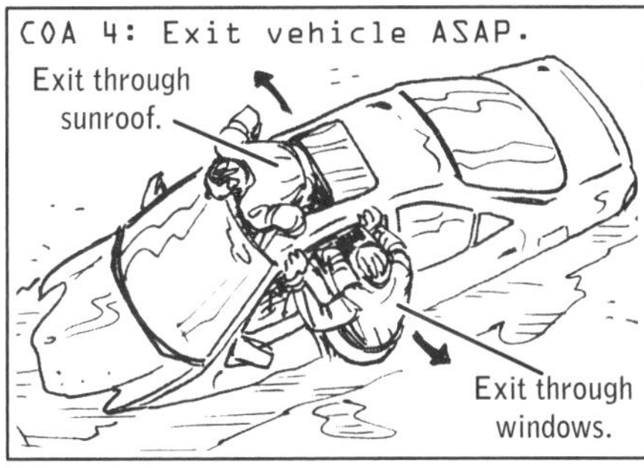

COA 5: Break a window.

KICK IT OUT.

BREAK IT (headrest).

SHATTER IT (glass punch tool).

BLUF: Exit a flooding vehicle before you enter a watery grave.

080 Walk Away from a Runaway Train

We may think of tragic derailments as the province of subpar rail systems in undeveloped countries, but recent history has proven otherwise. Train accidents are often the result of human error, and even a momentary lapse in attention has the potential to catapult a fully functioning rail system into fiery disarray.

A lack of passenger seat belts is disturbingly common among all modalities of public transportation—rail, bus, and underground metro—in most parts of the world. But given how instrumental these simple devices are in saving lives, the survival-minded civilian would be well advised to BYO belt. On airplanes, seat belts make the difference between passengers who survive serious turbulence without injury and those who exit the aircraft with broken bones or worse. (In at least one documented instance, the lone fatality of a plane crash was the single passenger *not* wearing a seat belt.)

Prep Your DIY Seat Belt

Using only a carabiner or two and either a length of one-inch tubular nylon cord, a purse or messenger bag strap, or a tie-down strap (also known as a cargo strap), a passenger can easily create a lifesaving seat belt in a matter of seconds (see illustrations). Attaching the strap to a carabiner using a waterman knot will create an adjustable, non-slipping loop that will allow the belt or cord to be used as a tether.

The safest way to travel is to strap yourself into a seat, an immovable anchor that will prevent you from becoming a human projectile upon impact. But if a seat is not available, you can still increase your survivability by strapping yourself to a balancing pole. Attaching yourself to a hard metal surface may sound less than desirable, but any injuries you may suffer as a result are likely to pale compared to the potential for being ejected out of the compartment upon impact. As the saying goes, when it comes to vehicular accidents, it's not the speed that kills you, it's the sudden stop—the moment when the vehicle comes to a halt and your body continues at the former speed of transit.

Single-point Anchor: To execute a single-point anchor, simply girth-hitch the belt or strap to the pole, attaching the carabiner to your belt buckle or purse strap.

Single Anchor: To create a seated lap belt around a single anchor, hook or girth-hitch the belt to the hardware beneath your seat on either side of your body, creating a semicircle around your legs. If there is no secondary anchor point available, it may be possible for you to hook the belt back onto itself in a full circle around your legs and the seat.

Double Anchor: To create a seated chest belt around a double anchor, hook or girth-hitch a belt to the hardware beneath the seat on one side of your body, and above the seat, to the handhold over your opposing shoulder, on the other.

Configurations will vary depending on the particular vehicle. Modify accordingly.

Bringing a DIY seat belt to a public transportation scenario may seem absurd. But when you consider survival a possible upside, a few curious glances from fellow passengers may be worth the tradeoff. And who knows—you may inspire other passengers to belt up for a safer ride themselves.

No. 080: Walk Away from a Runaway Train

CONOP: Convert everyday items into lifesaving seat belts.

COA 1: Items to be converted into seat belts:

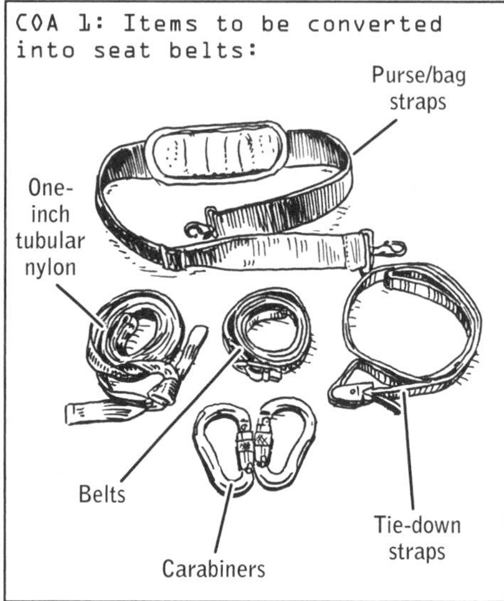

COA 2: Tie a waterman knot.

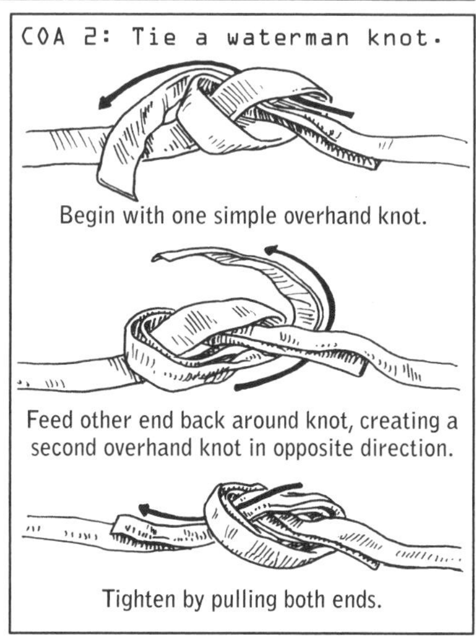

Begin with one simple overhand knot.
Feed other end back around knot, creating a second overhand knot in opposite direction.
Tighten by pulling both ends.

COA 3: Single-Point Anchor (Pole)

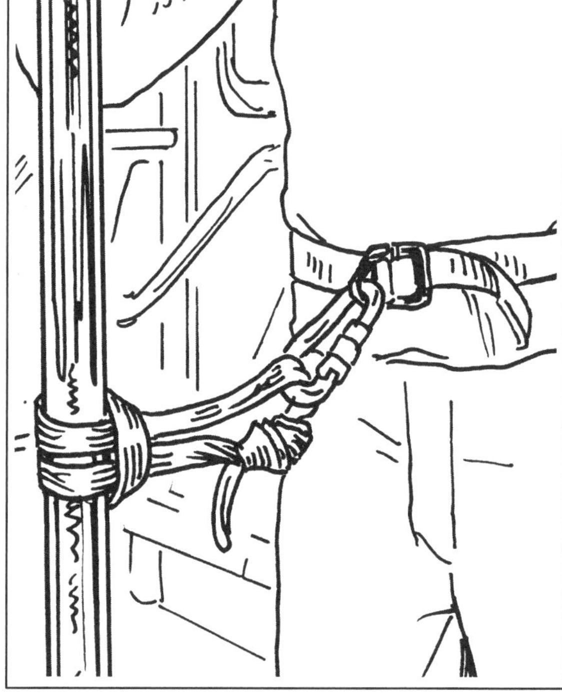

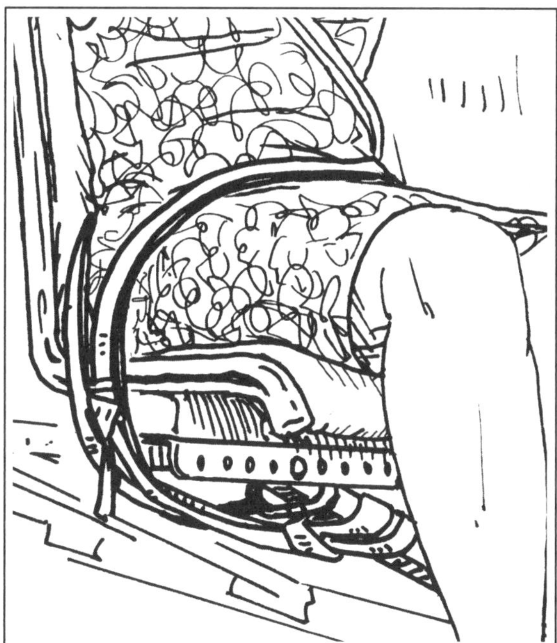

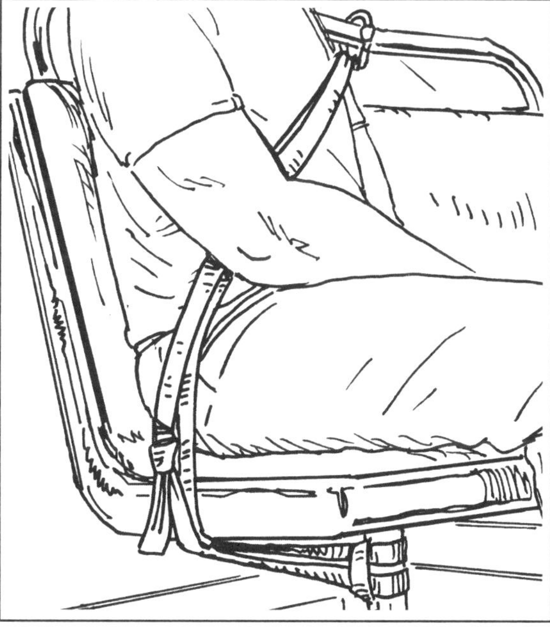

BLUF: Seat belts may prevent passenger ejection at one hundred miles per hour.

081 Escape a Skyscraper Fire

Denizens of corporate America tend to grumble through fire drills with barely disguised contempt, anxious to return to their desks and get on with their days. But the reality is that these drills, considered a nuisance by most, represent only a fraction of the preparation office workers *should* endure. From bolt bags to evacuation routes to emergency protocol, there is more to fire preparation than what is currently served up.

Build a Bolt Bag: A baseline requirement furnished by too few offices is an emergency bolt bag distributed to one of every five employees. Contents should include food and water, but also visibility and signaling essentials such as flashlights, Sharpies, Chem-Lights, and whistles, along with several dust masks.

Know Your Escape Routes: Be diligent about memorizing the location of primary and secondary fire escapes on your floor. Ordinary stairwells, though preferable to elevators, aren't built to code and may be larded with flammable materials. Elevators are generally designed to drop to the first floor and then disengage once a building's fire alarm or sensor is activated, but they should be avoided at all costs. The hot metal boxes can become death traps during a fire, whether they're stuck and slowly baking their passengers or depositing them straight onto a ground floor that's completely ablaze. Devoid of flammable materials, fire stairwells are also ventilated and pressurized to keep out smoke-filled air.

Take a close look at evacuation routes, snapping a photograph so they're stored on your phone. In the event of an emergency, know that you may have to be flexible. If fire blocks your path to exit, you may have to zigzag across floors and down the building in order to get to safety.

Be a Force for Good: Team up with others as you exit. The more eyes, ears, and brains on deck, the better.

Mark your movements as you travel, so that first responders and other emergency evacuees can follow your path. Designate one or two members of your group to mark your path with Sharpies, ChemLights, or Post-it notes. Assume others may be crawling through smoke, so place markings knee-height or lower.

And remember: Calm is just as contagious as panic. Be a viral agent for good.

Use Available Supplies: If you have no choice but to travel through fire, avail yourself of a corporate building's ready water supply. Should you have access to one of the fire hoses on your floor, use it to clear a path. Or head to the nearest bathroom, remove heat conducting jewelry, accessories, and electronics, and completely soak your clothing and hair in water. Roll down sleeves and button up collars to obtain as much coverage as possible. Cover head, face, and hair with a wet cloth and a dust mask.

Whenever you encounter a door, check for heat conduction before opening. A very hot door signals the strong possibility of a hallway engulfed in flames.

No. 081: Escape a Skyscraper Fire

CONOP: Escape and survive fire within vertical environments.

COA 1: Build an emergency bolt bag.

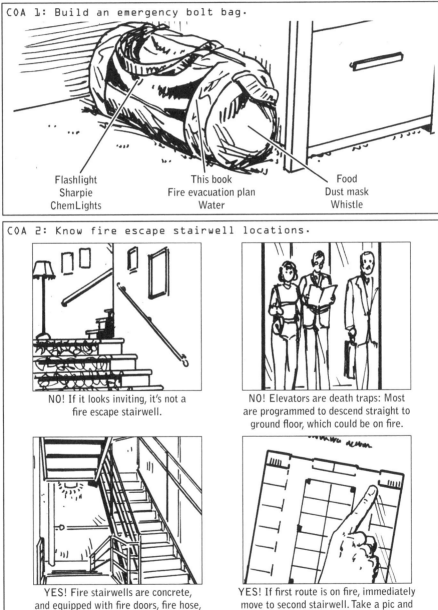

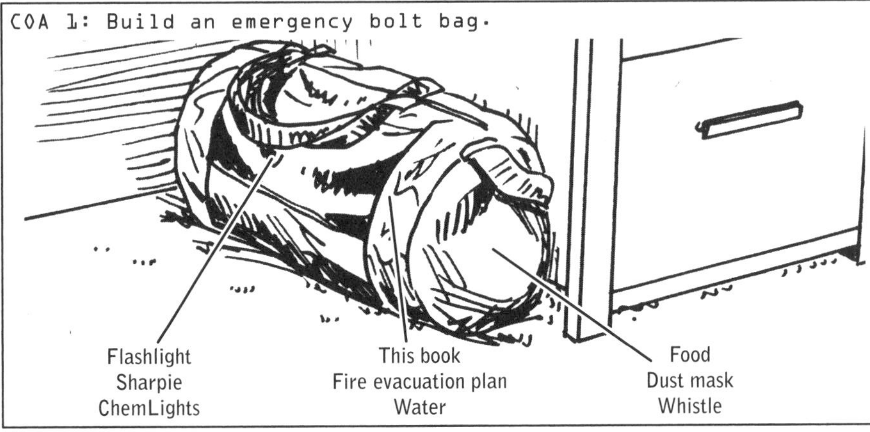

COA 2: Know fire escape stairwell locations.

NO! If it looks inviting, it's not a fire escape stairwell.

NO! Elevators are death traps: Most are programmed to descend straight to ground floor, which could be on fire.

YES! Fire stairwells are concrete, and equipped with fire doors, fire hose, and/or wall hydrants.

YES! If first route is on fire, immediately move to second stairwell. Take a pic and store evacuation routes on your phone.

COA 3: Call and signal for help.

Use a cell phone to call 911. Don't assume someone else did.

Grab your bolt bag.

Team up with others and stay together.

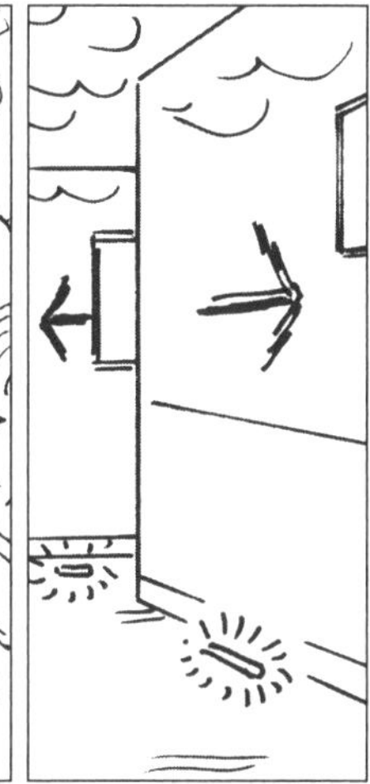

If separated, mark walls with arrows and drop ChemLights in direction of travel.

COA 4: Moving Through or Near Fire

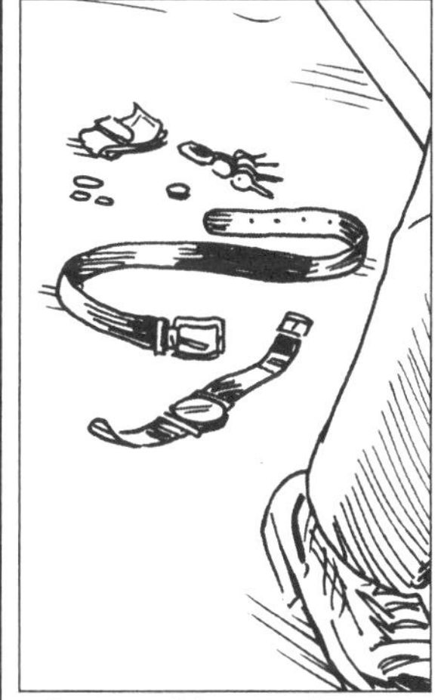

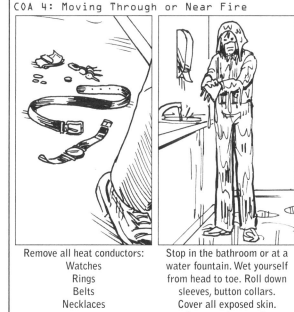

Remove all heat conductors:
Watches
Rings
Belts
Necklaces

Stop in the bathroom or at a water fountain. Wet yourself from head to toe. Roll down sleeves, button collars. Cover all exposed skin. Don Wet dust mask.

Check doors before opening. Use back of hand and touch door from top to bottom. Use caution when touching door knobs. Open doors slowly and look for fire or smoke.

BLUF: Fire can spread in any direction, so have a multidirectional plan.

082 Escape Social Unrest and Riots

Banned by repressive governments, yet condoned as a fundamental pillar of democracy, protests can turn into chaotic, violent events wherever they take place—even if they start out peaceful. A tiny band of picketers isn't likely to be cause for concern, but when emotionally volatile groups of people gather in large numbers, acts of violence may be the result. Whether you're a willing participant, an observer, or a passerby inadvertently swept up in the crowd, keep an eye on crowd dynamics at all times. A peaceful protest may be hiding pockets of violence at its center.

De-escalating mass violence is very difficult, because aggression tends to spread contagiously in an already agitated crowd. The safest course of action is to bypass violent crowds altogether and identify points of potential danger before they erupt. Avoid the space between groups of protesters with opposing beliefs, the front lines of protests, areas where protesters are massed against barricades, or dividing lines between protestors and law enforcement.

If you are unwittingly caught in a violent protest or riot, think twice before turning to law enforcement for help. Law enforcement officials will be in defensive mode and may reflexively lash out at anyone who approaches. Instead, move to the periphery of the crowd. Seek shelter inside or on the backside of buildings. Get to elevated ground. Skirt a large crowd rather than attempting to cross it.

Journalists covering volatile protests should aim to blend in with crowds and seek out safe havens in which women and peaceful protesters congregate to keep each other safe. Flow with the crowd rather than walking against the grain. Avoid the center of the crowd, where chaos tends to accumulate and violence can go undetected.

Exercise caution and vigilance at any large gathering, as sizable crowds have increasingly become a favorite target of terrorists and lone wolves.

No. 082: Escape Social Unrest and Riots

CONOP: Implement tactics that increase survivability when surrounded by emotionally charged crowds.

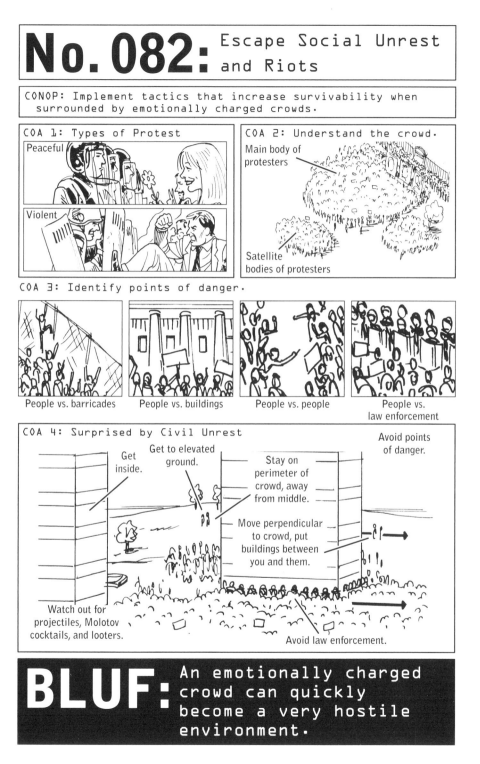

COA 1: Types of Protest

Peaceful
Violent

COA 2: Understand the crowd.

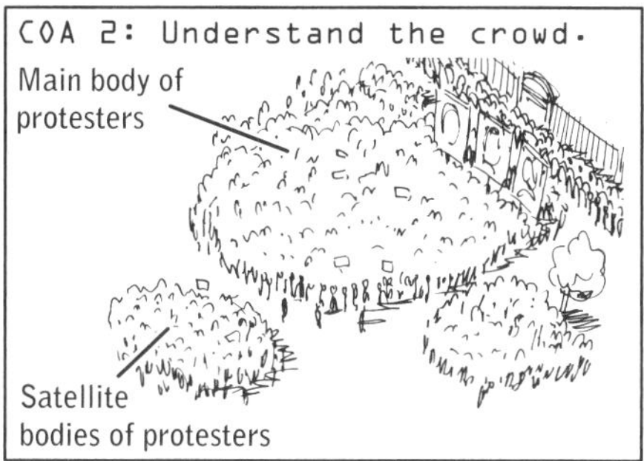

Main body of protesters
Satellite bodies of protesters

COA 3: Identify points of danger.

People vs. barricades

People vs. buildings

People vs. people

People vs. law enforcement

COA 4: Surprised by Civil Unrest

Get inside.
Get to elevated ground.
Stay on perimeter of crowd, away from middle.
Avoid points of danger.
Move perpendicular to crowd, put buildings between you and them.
Watch out for projectiles, Molotov cocktails, and looters.
Avoid law enforcement.

BLUF: An emotionally charged crowd can quickly become a very hostile environment.

083 Survive a Pandemic

As we're slowly starting to learn, the medical advances of the past few centuries may have lulled us into a false sense of complacency regarding our vulnerability to communicable disease. The widespread use of antibiotics in our medical and food systems, along with the porosity of our modern world's international borders, have contributed to the rise of a class of superviruses and drug-resistant pathogens with the ability to travel faster than they can be contained. Though we may think we live in a modern society in which it's no longer possible to perish from a case of the flu, recent outbreaks have shown that belief to be anything but true.

Of course, it's near impossible to imagine epidemics on the scale of those from the past, like the outbreak of Spanish influenza that killed forty million people in 1918. The most widely publicized recent viral outbreak, Ebola, took somewhere in the neighborhood of ten thousand lives. But unknown new variants that emerge before a vaccine is created can hamper the containment abilities of even the most medically advanced facilities.

In the case of a true pandemic, avoiding public spaces will be the safest way to limit your exposure. In the early days of an outbreak, misinformation about communicability is common. Stock up on food and water supplies before shelves are stripped bare, and wash hands religiously before eating and after any expedition or contact outside the household.

Steer clear of public bathrooms, particularly those equipped with hand dryers—these supposedly hygienic contraptions have been shown to send germs ricocheting through the air.

If surgical and dust mask supplies are depleted at the first news of an outbreak, silk ties and scarves may be used as reasonable substitutes. The finely woven material has the ability to filter out foreign particles, but in a pinch you can also use any piece of cloth that has been doused with clean filtered water.

No. 083: Survive a Pandemic

CONOP: Prepare and outlast a global pandemic outbreak.

COA 1: Before a pandemic: Store two weeks of food and water.

Eight hundred calories of dry nonperishable food, per day, per person

Gallon of water per day, per person in household

COA 2: During a Pandemic

Avoid contact with others.

Stay home.

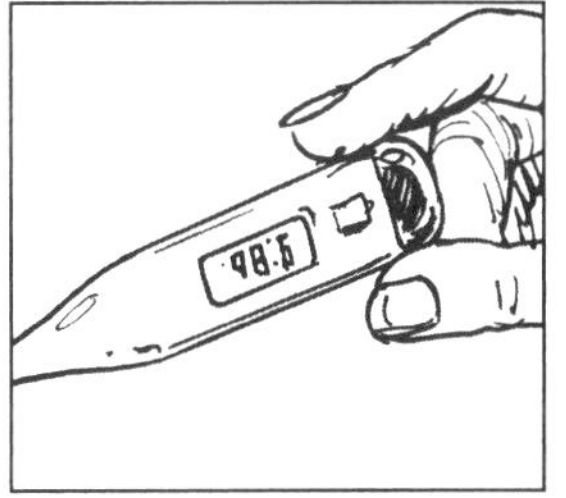

Take temperature.

Cover coughs and sneezing.

Wash your hands.

Stay tuned.

BLUF: Mother Nature is full of unpleasant surprises.

084 Survive a Human Stampede

The stuff of nightmares, human stampedes can happen anywhere from emotionally charged sporting events to peaceful religious pilgrimages. When crowd control is overwhelmed, crushing injuries that lead to fatal suffocation can be the unfortunate result.

If you are caught in an evolving stampede, do not let feelings of panic cause you to lose control over your personal space. Widen your stance and keep your knees bent to ground your weight. Travel via shuffle step, shifting weight by dragging your feet in order to minimize the amount of time spent on one leg. Avoid getting pushed to the ground at all costs—it will be very difficult to get back up again once you're pushed beneath a rushing tide of panicked people. Keep your arms up in fighting stance, not so that you can punch people, but to create a shield. This defensive posture will protect your head and chest from crushing injury while preserving a bubble of space in which you can breathe.

While the rest of the horde beelines for the exit, seek out and exploit gaps in the crowd. Others may be so single-minded in their quest for release that they fail to notice pockets of breathing room around them. Move from gap to gap. Keep moving. Do not attempt to stand your ground. The rush of bodies will make it very difficult to stay on your feet.

Avoid barricades and walls, solid surfaces without give. Better to be crushed against a human body, which at least contains soft tissue.

If, despite your efforts to stay upright, you are pushed to the ground, immediately assume the tornado position—knees bent, spine curved over, hands clasped behind neck and elbows tucked in. You will be protecting your head and neck and carving out breathing space. A completely prone body is far too easy to step on.

No. 084: Survive a Human Stampede

CONOP: Employ crowd-control tactics to survive human stampedes.

COA 1: Fighting Stance

COA 2: Fill the gaps and keep moving.

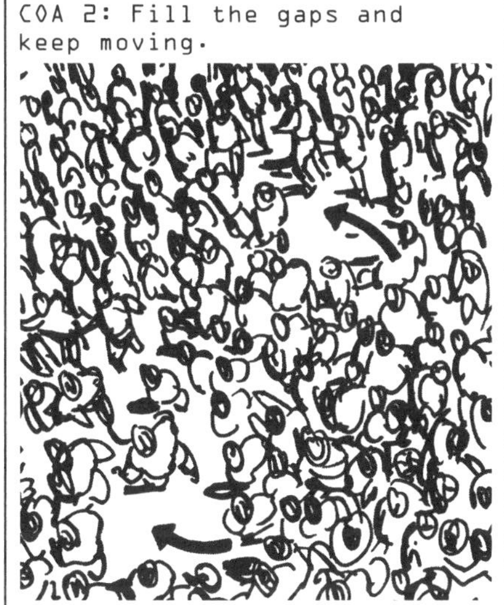

COA 3: Avoid barricades and walls.

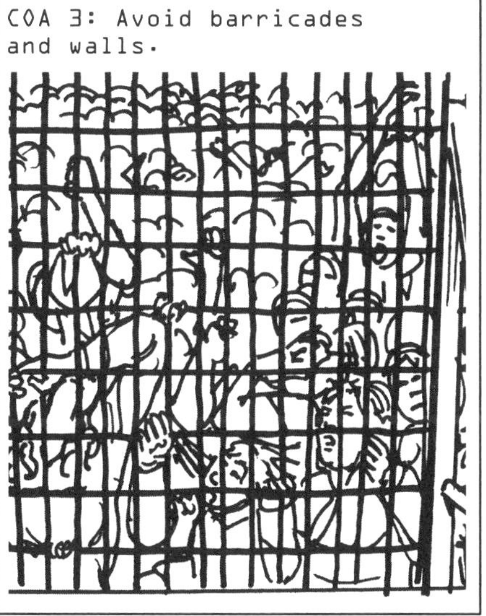

COA 4: Tornado Position

BLUF: Stay on your feet. Do not fall down!

085 Escape a Stadium or Theater Shooting

Characterized by high fatality and injury rates, shootings in crowded, contained public spaces are volatile and extremely dangerous. A density of targets, the potential for bottlenecks, and a lack of clarity about emergency response protocol create a ripe environment for one or more armed aggressors to do serious harm. As with all crisis scenarios, survival depends partly on preparation and response—and partly on dumb luck. The level of security in any given public space is not under your control, but you *are* the sole owner of your personal preparation and response.

Identify Exits and Choke Points

Take note of standard and emergency exits in any public space. But also consider unconventional exit paths such as stadium balconies. Dropping down to a seating area or walkway below yours may result in injury, but could be worth the risk if standard pathways have become target points for the shooter's rifle sights.

Rather than instinctually following the herd, identify potential choke points and think through alternative pathways in advance of a crisis scenario so that you're able to decisively execute an exit plan without excess forethought when emergency strikes. But look before you jump—do not attempt to exit from stadium high points. And hit the deck before you move, dropping down to a crouch at the first sign of gunfire and identifying the shooter's direction before proceeding. The fight-or-flight instinct may cause those around you to blindly run when the first shots are fired, but the proper response is to get low as quickly as possible.

Seek Cover and Crawl to Safety

Locate the shooter in the room or stadium before you attempt to run to safety. The last thing you want to do is accidentally run in the shooter's direction. Do not blindly head for the emergency exits. Shooters may have snuck into theaters through improperly closed emergency exit doors.

Use available materials, furnishings, and structures as protection. Due to the fact that movie theater and stadium seating rows are built out of concrete, chairs may provide both concealment and a lifesaving form of cover, depending on the angle of the shooter. Stay low as you crawl between seat rows. Keep your eyes on the shooter at all times, adjusting your path depending on his whereabouts.

Listen and Watch

Take advantage of lulls in gunfire, when the shooter may be changing magazines, to gain serious ground toward exiting. If the shooter is within arm's reach, use such a lull to attempt to take him down (see page 149).

Do not box yourself in by hiding in a dead-end zone such as a bathroom stall. The best choice for a contained space is one with a solid door that can be barricaded (see pages 141–45).

Playing dead may or may not have some chance of success, but prioritize escape or tackling the shooter (see page 154) over surrender. Be brave, be bold, be violent.

No. 085: Escape a Stadium or Theater Shooting

CONOP: Survive an active shooter in contained populated environments.

COA 1: Preparation

Identify the exits.

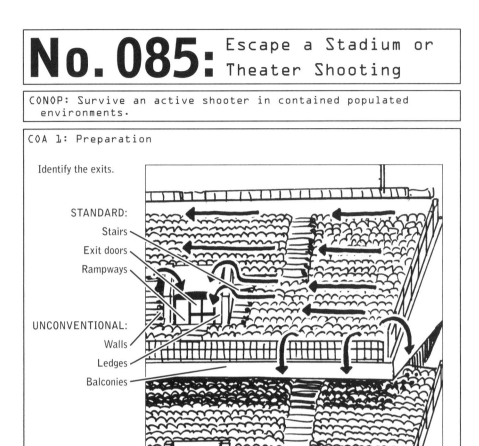

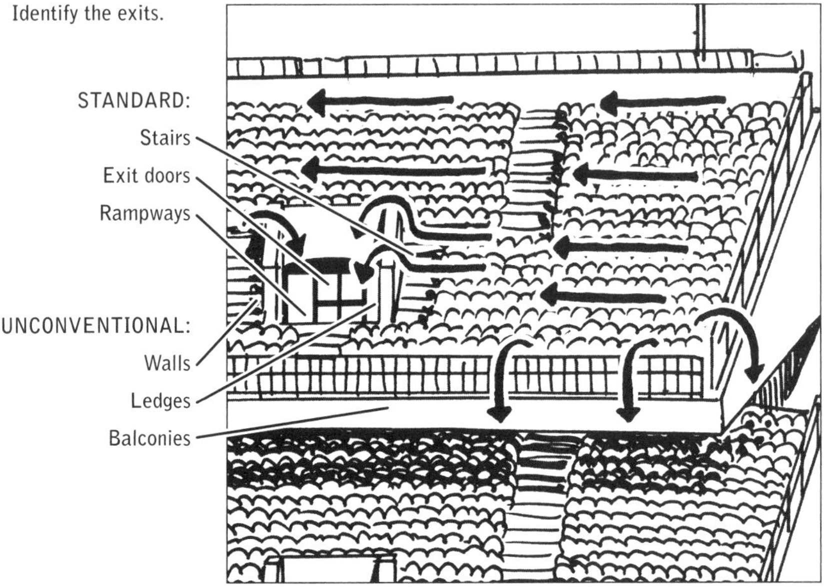

STANDARD:
Stairs
Exit doors
Rampways
UNCONVENTIONAL:
Walls
Ledges
Balconies

Identify choke points.

Stairs
Transitions
Landings

Check the exits.

Emergency exit doors should be tightly shut.

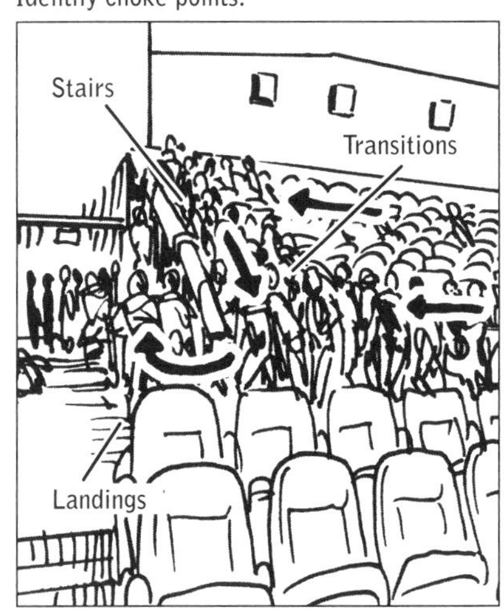

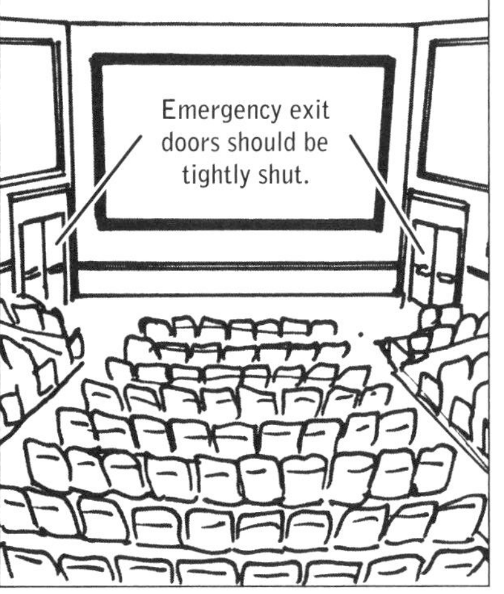

COA 2: Response

IDENTIFY SHOOTER!

Above/from behind Below/in front

HIT THE DECK!

Use chairs to conceal your position.

CRAWL!

Toward cover and unconventional/ standard exits

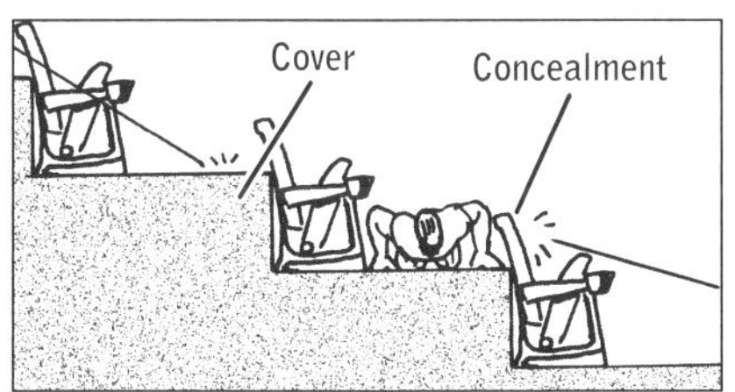

Keep low to use concrete steps for cover.

KEEP EYES ON SHOOTER AT ALL TIMES.

BLUF: Get out of sight, crawl toward cover and exits.

086 Survive an Inspired Terrorism Attack

A climate of severe global instability indicates that acts of terrorism and their copycat offspring aren't going anywhere anytime soon. But whether an attempted mass shooting is inspired by the propaganda of an organized group or the disturbed fantasies of a lone individual, the results tend to look much the same. At least within the U.S., these acts of violence still tend to center around gunfire rather than suicide vests or pipe bombs.

Your response to any sign of gunfire should begin with hitting the deck. "Run, hide, fight" is the order of operations for civilians caught in a cross fire, running being the first option, and fighting the last. But before you run, drop and take cover. Squat or move to hands and knees rather than lying down, as most ricocheting bullets follow the path of the floor. So that you don't accidentally run toward live fire, do not attempt to escape before you've established the direction of the shooter.

When you do escape, run from cover to cover. Choose sources of cover over concealment when hiding. Cover consists of materials that stop or slow bullets—concrete, steel, dense wood, and granite. Concealment options such as curtains, Sheetrock walls, or aluminum trash cans won't stop bullets, but might help you escape the notice of an assailant who's revved up on adrenaline and psychotic delusions. When running through areas with no sources of cover, travel in a zigzag pattern to create a challenge for a shooter who is likely to be inexperienced.

If you're hiding in a confined space, lock down and barricade doors (see pages 142 and 144). Steer clear of the line of the doorway, the "fatal funnel" through which the majority of bullets fly.

If all else fails, fight. Team up, grab improvised weapons, and assign tasks. Fight with extreme violence and aggression. Your life depends on it.

No. 086: Survive an Inspired Terrorism Attack

CONOP: Employ proactive tactics to survive an inspired terrorism attack.

COA 1: Hit the deck! Take cover.

COA 2: Identify where shots are coming from.

COA 3: Run away from shooter.

COA 4: Hide behind cover or concealment.

COA 5: Lock down if in confined space.

COA 6: Fight if all else fails.

BLUF: In the U.S. alone, there are approximately twenty mass shootings per year.

087 Survive Long-term Captivity

Long-term solitary confinement in a windowless subterranean warren, far outside the reach of law enforcement or rescue, would be enough to make most human beings crack. Yet survivors of prolonged episodes of captivity report monumental and sometimes surprisingly successful efforts at preserving their mental acuity and psychological equilibrium under even the most unimaginable conditions. Though most captives assume they are completely powerless, a combination of internal habits of mind and external behaviors can improve both their survivability and their odds of escape.

Despite the complex and dark matrix of feelings captors will inspire, they become the other half of a captive's primary relationship during captivity—a relationship the smartest of captives learn to nurture and manipulate. Establish a rapport with captors over time, developing individual bonds with the most sympathetic among them. Use small talk to extract information about the outside world and to humanize yourself to captors—while making the most of your limited access to social contact, an essential component of psychological stability. And remember: Your captor is human, too. You're both going through the same ordeal, though you may be on different sides of the bars. The more quickly you can humanize yourself to the person on the outside, the better chance you'll have of cultivating an asset who'll advocate on your behalf for basic survival needs and improvements in quality of life. But be very strategic about when and how you ask for favors. You are engaged in a mental game of chess, using your dependence to create a sense of responsibility without arousing suspicion or the sense that your captor is being taken advantage of.

Captors from other cultures may hold long-entrenched beliefs about the inferiority of captives, who may be seen as dogs, heathens, intrinsically evil, and essentially subhuman creatures. Wild or erratic behavior will only confirm their prejudices. Regardless of poor treatment on their part, do your best to maintain a polite

No. 087: Survive Long-term Captivity

Implement daily habits to increase odds of survivability during long-term hostage situations.

COA 1: Establish rapport.

Talk about family.
Ask for food and water.
Ask what's going on in the news.
Ask about the weather.

COA 2: Create dependence.

Be polite when provided food and water: be appreciative.
Be a good listener: Let captors vent, be understanding.
Maintain dignity: Don't beg, cry.

COA 3: Maintain survival mindset.

Observe captor habits: Note vulnerabilities.
Stay physically active: Stretch and do body weight exercise.
Stay mentally active: Plan escapes, outline your biography.
Take one day at a time.

COA 4: Collect tools for escape.

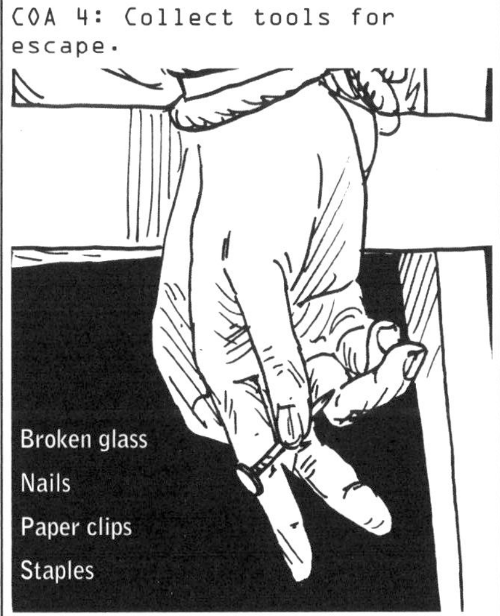

BLUF: The more human you are, the more difficult it is to rape or kill you.

and collected external facade. A crying, whimpering, or outwardly angry prisoner becomes a prisoner who is all too easy to neglect or ignore, where a prisoner who gratefully accepts food is one who is more likely to be regularly fed.

Do not fall into the trap of assuming your captivity will end in either rescue or death, a mindset that makes it all too easy to slip into passivity while ignoring the third option, escape. Staying physically and mentally active will both improve your odds of survival and make it more likely that you will be able to seize the opportunity for escape when it arises.

And arise it will. Take advantage of the natural accumulation of complacency in your captors. On day forty of your captivity, they will not be nearly as attentive as they were on day one. Unlike the wardens of organized, ultramodern prison facilities, captors aren't generally working in airtight security contexts. There *will* be holes in their routines and structural vulnerabilities in their detainment compounds, and the watchful captive will observe, catalog, and exploit these security gaps over time. Staying focused on this constant state of information collection will have the beneficial side effect of keeping the captive mentally alert.

Watch, wait, and plan. Collect tools and ideas. An empty room is not as empty as you think. Gather nails and splinters from furniture, scrape paint chips off the wall, break pieces of metal away from air vents.

There's no telling what a particular escape path may look like, but any routine that involves temporarily moving you out of the containment space is an opportunity to gather intel or make a run for it. Use glimpses of external facilities to catalog information that may be useful for escape. Where are the exits? Where are guards stationed? When are guards' mealtimes?

A locked door that is temporarily opened presents an opportunity to tamper with the strike plate, the part of a lock into which the deadbolt enters. Each time you pass through the doorway, surreptitiously pack the strike plate with a balled-up wad of paint stripped from the wall. Eventually, you will have created a situation in which the deadbolt isn't fully seated and can easily be pushed back into the door with a nail or other piece of thin metal debris.

PART VIII

SIGNALING FOR HELP

088 Send a Distress Signal by Day

Carved in sand or etched in rock, old-school distress signals carry a whiff of the outdated desert island adventure tale. But when technology fails and options are limited, they may represent your only possible means of communicating with search and rescue teams or passersby.

Whether you're leaving signals in the aftermath of a crisis in an urban environment or you're stranded in a desolate rural setting, your strategies will depend on how you are most likely to be found. If you've been separated from a group or know that an on-foot search and rescue team represents the most likely rescue scenario, use text or symbols to leave a physical trail marking your direction of travel. Date- and time-stamp your messages if you can. Every expedition pack should include Sharpies and duct tape in bright colors that contrast the natural environment, but if you're traveling light or caught unaware, you can make a trail out of found natural objects or use your clothing and urine to create a scent trail for rescue dogs.

Distress signals meant to catch the attention of aircraft or watercraft must leave a much larger signature, whether by means of smoke, glare, or SOS messaging. A large fire lit during the day will benefit from the addition of pinecones, rubber, or petroleum- or plastic-based products. These will create plumes of black smoke, particularly useful in a snowy environment in which white or gray smoke may not be visible. A laminated ID card, the bottom of a can, or a shard of glass can all be pointed toward the sun and flashed toward passing aircraft to create an attention-getting reflective glare.

Oversize distress signals carved into sand and snow must contrast with the environment. Fill the carved-out lettering with leaves and grass, rocks, or other materials to create differentiation.

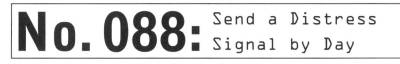

No. 088: Send a Distress Signal by Day

CONOP: Communicate and signal for help during daylight hours.

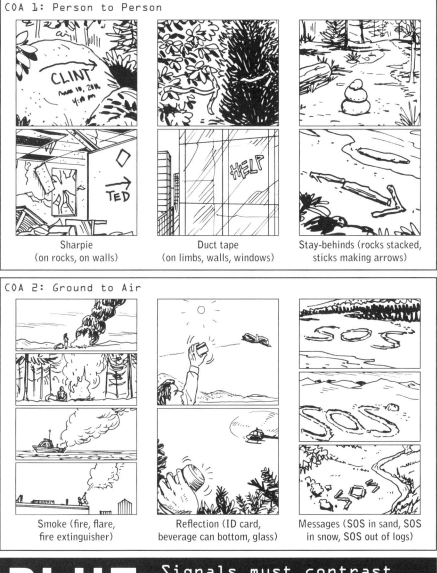

COA 1: Person to Person

Sharpie
(on rocks, on walls)

Duct tape
(on limbs, walls, windows)

Stay-behinds (rocks stacked,
sticks making arrows)

COA 2: Ground to Air

Smoke (fire, flare,
fire extinguisher)

Reflection (ID card,
beverage can bottom, glass)

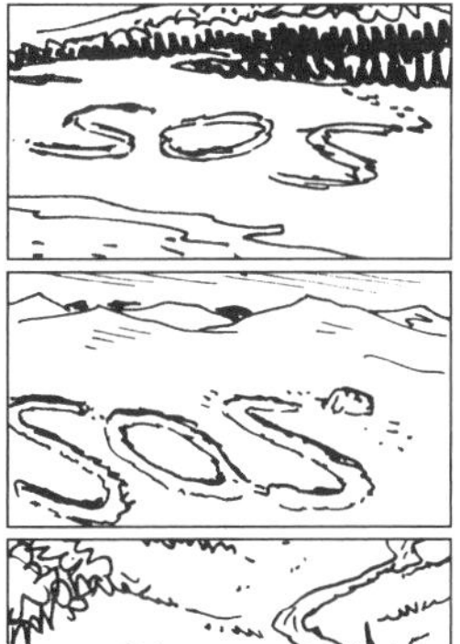

Messages (SOS in sand, SOS
in snow, SOS out of logs)

BLUF: Signals must contrast their background to be effective.

089 Send a Distress Signal at Night

A multitude of unpleasant scenarios may call for the use of nighttime distress signals. But while emergencies may feel more harrowing in the dark, the good news is that you have a great many signaling options available to you after sundown.

To signal person-to-person, a flashlight can be pointed directly at passing cars, through neighbors' windows, or down to emergency responders. Set a flashlight to strobe or use your hand to create an SOS flicker.

The panic button on your vehicle will not only set off the alarm but also get hazards and headlights flashing. If you're trapped in a commercial building during a power outage, the building's battery-operated emergency lights can be unscrewed from the wall and used to signal out a window. Use your hand or a piece of paper to create an emergency flicker.

When signaling from ground to air, you'll need to increase the signature of your light source for it to be seen from a great distance. A flashlight can be turned into a buzz saw of light particles whirring above your head or used to lasso a passing aircraft. Point the beam of light at the aircraft, then illuminate your coordinates by sweeping the light down toward the ground (scattering the light particles so they create a wider and more visible footprint) and back up to the aircraft. Alternating between these two positions may catch the attention of aircraft even if pilots aren't looking for you.

Both light and fire can be set up in the triangular pattern that is the universal symbol for rescue—whether you're using bundles of ChemLights, upright flashlights, or a trio of campfires. The latter can be particularly useful in a jungle environment where a triple canopy prevents visibility from above. When waterways are the only pieces of land that aren't covered in trees and brush, light fires aboard rafts tied down with vine or rope.

No. 089: Send a Distress Signal at Night

CONOP: Communicate and signal for help at night.

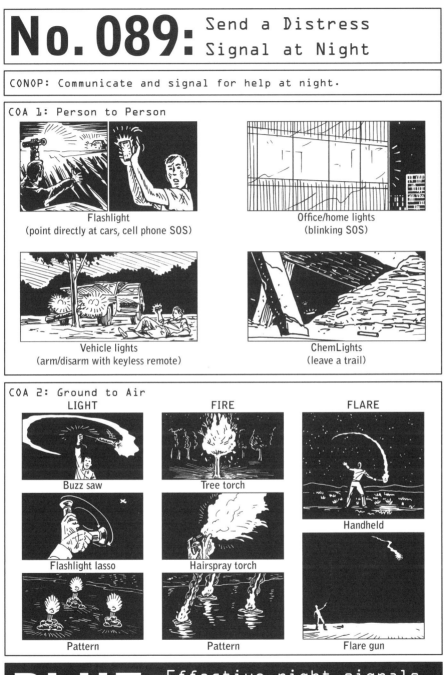

COA 1: Person to Person

Flashlight
(point directly at cars, cell phone SOS)

Office/home lights
(blinking SOS)

Vehicle lights
(arm/disarm with keyless remote)

ChemLights
(leave a trail)

COA 2: Ground to Air

LIGHT

Buzz saw

FIRE

Tree torch

FLARE

Handheld

Hairspray torch

Flashlight lasso

Pattern

Pattern

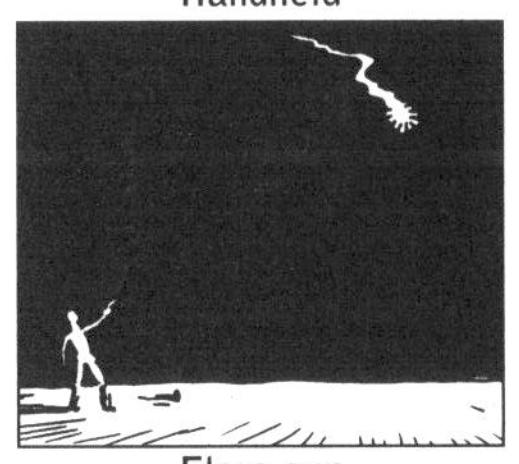

Flare gun

BLUF: Effective night signals must outshine ambient and background lighting.

090 Send a Distress Signal on a Smartphone

The unparalleled convenience of our portable communication systems arms modern civilians with both an endless source of entertainment and a sophisticated personal safety device. With the touch of a finger, you have the power not only to occupy a small child for hours but also to immediately summon a team of first responders to your exact location. If the battery runs out before you get the call out, however, the lifesaving potential of your device will be significantly diminished.

To preserve battery life during emergencies, place your ringer on silent, turn off Wi-Fi and Bluetooth, lower illumination, and shut down any nonessential apps. Turn on location services in your general settings to enable law enforcement authorities to track your phone.

Be clear, calm, and direct in your communications with emergency dispatchers. Though 911 operators will default to keeping you on the phone, once you've communicated the information and answered their questions, politely explain that you need to conserve battery life and would prefer to end the call. If you don't know your cross streets or coordinates, use visible landmarks and businesses to give a dispatcher the best possible sense of where you might be.

If your signal is too low to place a call, send a text. Text-to-911 capability is only supported in certain areas, so follow up an attempted text to 911 with a mass text to loved ones and anyone you know in the vicinity. Follow the general format outlined opposite, being sure to add a request for confirmation texts (not calls) in response.

If the signal completely fails, use your phone to send reflective distress signals during the day (see page 224) or illuminated signals at night (page 226). As an option of last resort, a dead phone can be used to start a fire (page 68).

No. 090: Send a Distress Signal on a Smartphone

CONOP: Utilize a smartphone to facilitate survival and rescue.

COA 1: In Range

Call 911.
Voice Procedures: I am stranded. I am/am not injured. Battery low. My location is ______. Location marked with ______. My emergency is________. My name is ______. My number is__________. Next of kin is ___________. Phone number is ____________.

Mass text: This is not a joke. I am stranded. I need help. I am/am not injured. Battery low. My location is___. Location marked with ___. My emergency is________. My name is ______. My number is__________.

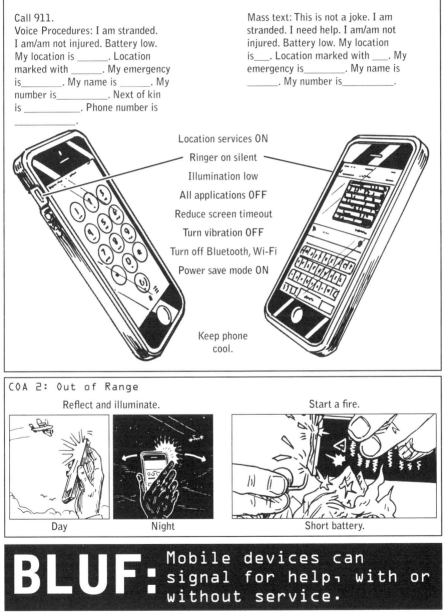

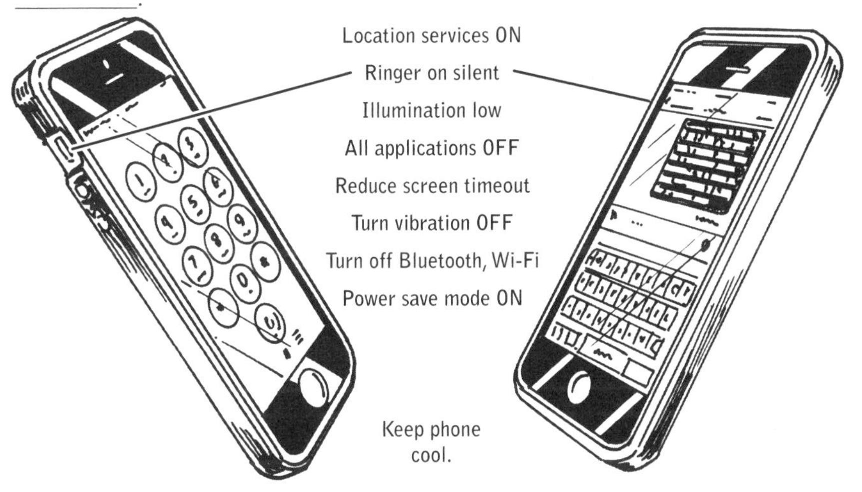

COA 2: Out of Range

Reflect and illuminate.

Day

Night

Start a fire.

Short battery.

BLUF: Mobile devices can signal for help, with or without service.

091 Leave a DNA Trail

Plotting your escape (see page 220) and outlining your memoirs aren't the only useful ways to spend your time while in captivity. Through a series of simple, undetectable measures, you can also endeavor to leave a trail of your own DNA behind—while simultaneously collecting your adversary's blood, skin, and hair. Leaving behind a swath of your genetic data creates a bread-crumb trail for law enforcement officials to follow if you've been moved to a second location. And collecting your adversary's data has obvious benefits for both investigators and prosecutors.

In the worst-case scenario, if you do not survive the ordeal, your trail of evidence may at least lead to a future conviction. An act of resistance, the consequences of which could ultimately lead to justice being served, your actions will serve as an invisible but potent message scrawled on the walls: "*I was here.*"

Smear your skin, hair, sweat, urine, and blood in spots that are difficult to clean or that may be overlooked by a criminal hastily covering his tracks: corners of room, walls, air vents, and door hinges. Law enforcement officials *will* find these markers of your forced detention.

Use violent or nonviolent contact with your adversary to collect his genetic material and store it on your body. Skin and blood cells trapped under your fingernails will generally stay there. Wipe body fluids on the underside of your hair or under your armpits to ensure that they aren't rubbed off by repeated contact or washed away in the event that your captor forces you to shower. If he does, discreetly attempt to wash around collection areas.

Employ these measures even in the event that you find yourself temporarily restrained in the trunk of a car. There's no telling what the future holds.

No. 091: Leave a DNA Trail

CONOP: Leave trace evidence and DNA for law enforcement to find.

COA 1: At the scene: Leave your blood, urine, hair, fingernails, skin behind.

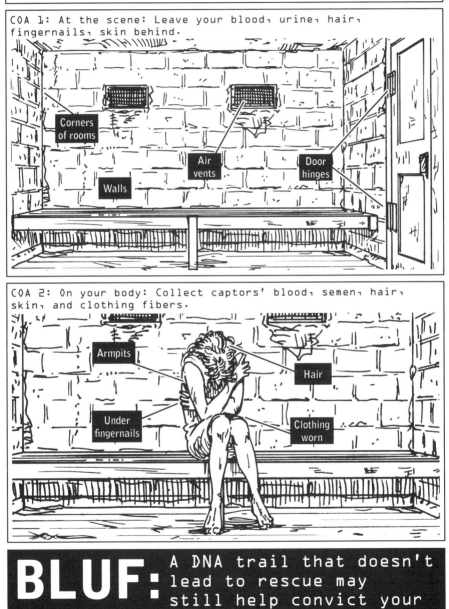

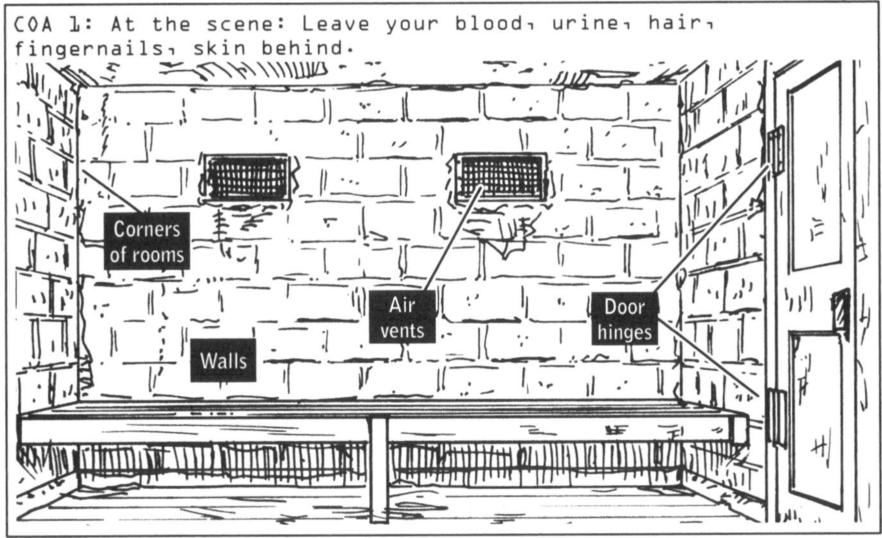

COA 2: On your body: Collect captors' blood, semen, hair, skin, and clothing fibers.

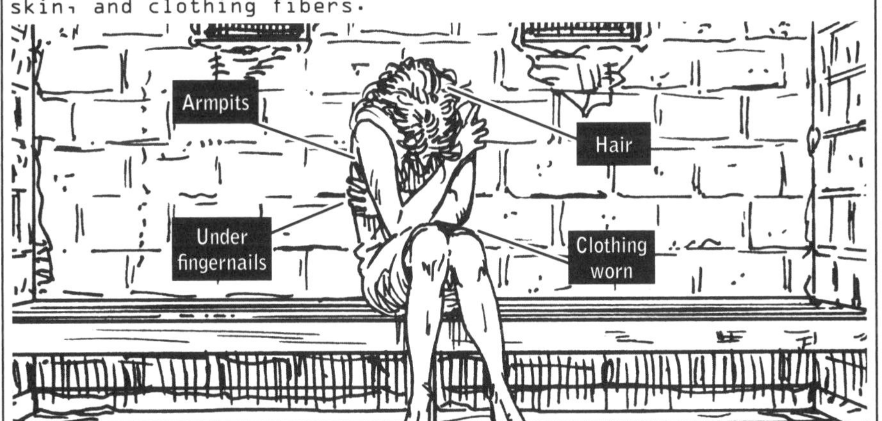

BLUF: A DNA trail that doesn't lead to rescue may still help convict your captors.

PART IX

EMERGENCY MEDICINE

092 Primary Assessment

Whether they are the result of urban or natural disaster or mass violence, catastrophic events with multiple victims strain the limits of our comprehension. Even civilians trained in basic first-aid may be at a loss when it comes to a response. But if you're lucky enough to survive a mass casualty scenario unscathed, or to arrive late enough to bypass the event, following a triage protocol once you've called 911 is the most effective way for you to help.

Determine Level of Consciousness

Start by determining the victims' levels of consciousness. Announce your name, then call out a simple series of commands: "I'm here to help. Get up and come toward me if you can. If you can't, raise your hand or shout."

No rule of triage is ironclad, but generally, victims who are ambulatory should be treated after those who are conscious but unable to move. Unconscious or unresponsive victims are your last priority. If one victim is bleeding out and another is unconscious, staunching the blood loss is the most effective use of your time.

On the other hand, though your first instinct may be to run to the victim who's audibly screaming for help and spend the bulk of your time attending to him or her, the ability to scream demonstrates an ability to breathe. There may be someone nearby with a chunk of debris lodged in his or her throat, minutes away from a herniation of the brain.

Use the ABC Method

Check to see if a victim who is not alert can respond to the sound of your voice. If not, prod the victim to see whether he or she can respond to sensory stimuli. If there is no response, the victim is unconscious.

Difficult decisions like these are the reason triage protocol has responders use the ABC (airways, breathing, circulation) method.

To employ, check airways immediately after determining level of consciousness (LOC), followed by breathing and circulation.

Assess Airway: Assess the victim's airway by listening for breath. If you don't hear breath, use your hand to open the victim's mouth. Look for any visible obstruction that could be preventing airflow; if you spot something, carefully attempt to remove the object; if not, use your index finger to do a shallow sweep (too deep and you'll engage the gag reflex).

Assess Breathing: Assess breathing by observing the movement of the lungs. Are both lungs moving? Does one move less than the other? Put your ear to the person's chest and see if you can hear the breath moving in and out of the chest cavity. Simultaneously, you can assess blood pressure by placing your index and middle fingers just to the left or right of the person's Adam's apple. A pulse at the neck is good, a pulse at the wrist is very good, and a pulse behind the knee indicates excellent circulation.

Assess Circulation and Control Bleeding: Once you've assessed the airways and lungs, move on to circulation. Identify serious wounds and apply pressure or a tourniquet (see page 238) to stanch blood flow.

Mouth-to-mouth and CPR can be lifesaving methods of resuscitation, but in a mass casualty scenario, a generalized triage must take precedence over techniques that will tie first responders down to the least responsive victims for long periods of time. Following triage best practices will enable you to help more people, as well as provide valuable information to the first emergency workers to arrive on the scene.

No. 092: Primary Assessment

CONOP: Properly assess an injured or unconscious person.

COA 1: Call 911. Ensure the situation is safe. Note exact time.

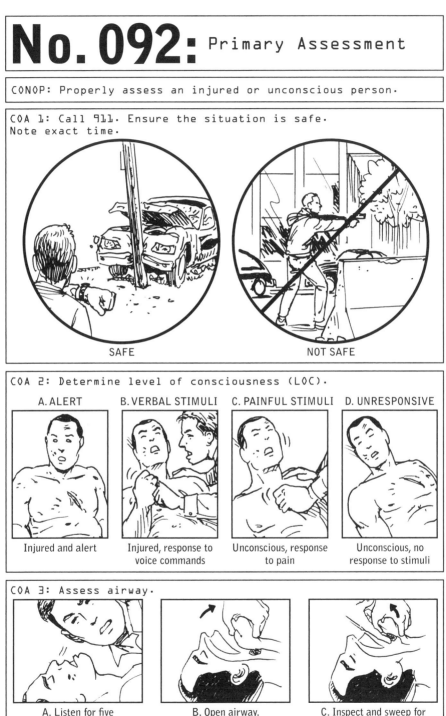

SAFE

NOT SAFE

COA 2: Determine level of consciousness (LOC).

A. ALERT

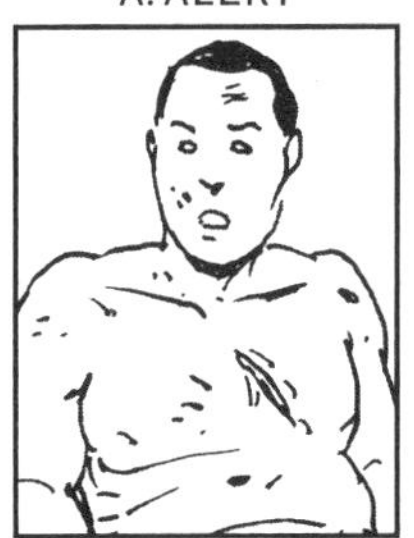

Injured and alert

B. VERBAL STIMULI

Injured, response to voice commands

C. PAINFUL STIMULI

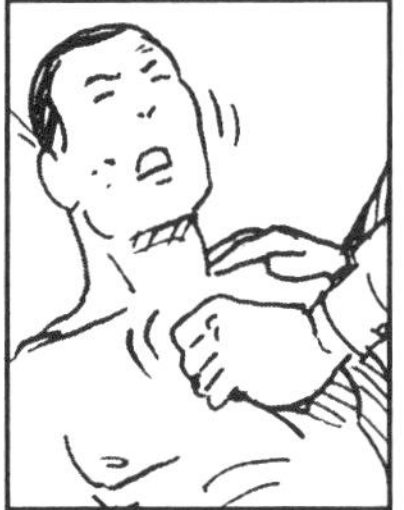

Unconscious, response to pain

D. UNRESPONSIVE

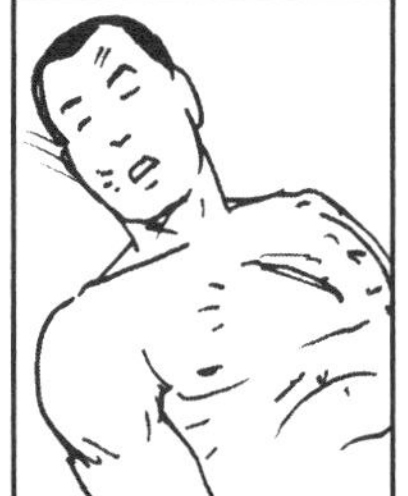

Unconscious, no response to stimuli

COA 3: Assess airway.

A. Listen for five to ten seconds.

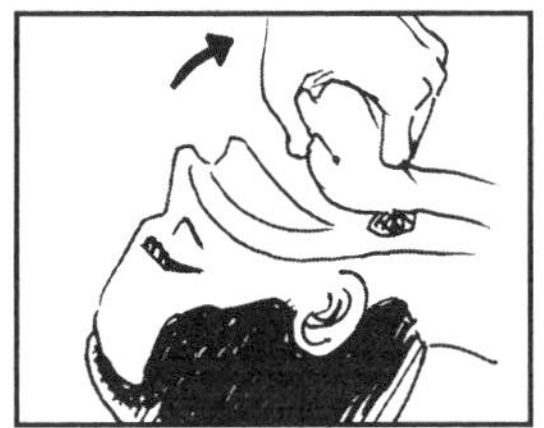

B. Open airway.

C. Inspect and sweep for obstructions.

COA 4: Assess breathing.

A. Observe chest for rise and fall.

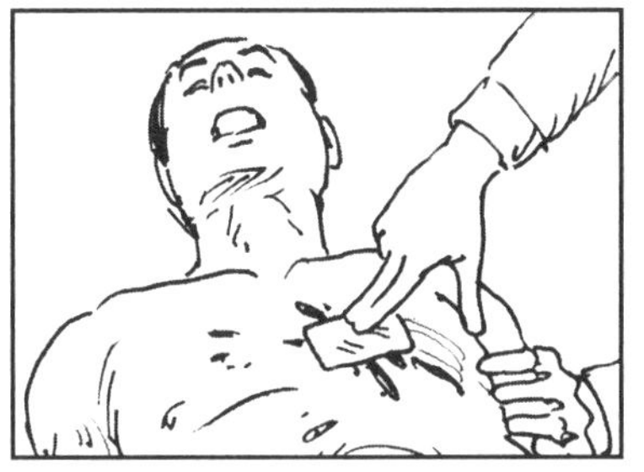

B. Occlude anterior chest wounds.

C. Occlude posterior chest wounds.

COA 5: Assess circulation.

A. Identify and control major bleeding.

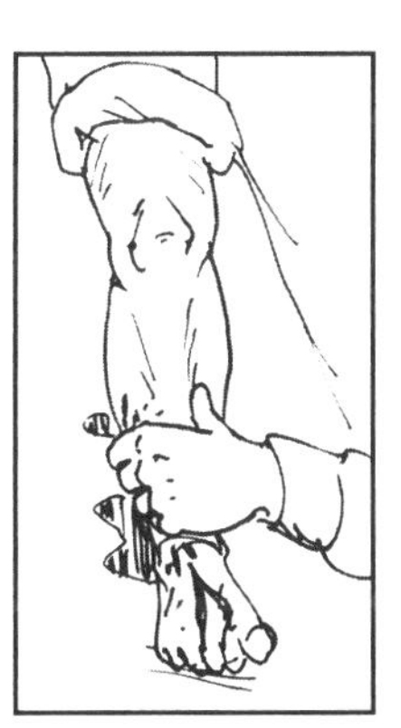

B. Apply direct pressure to wound.

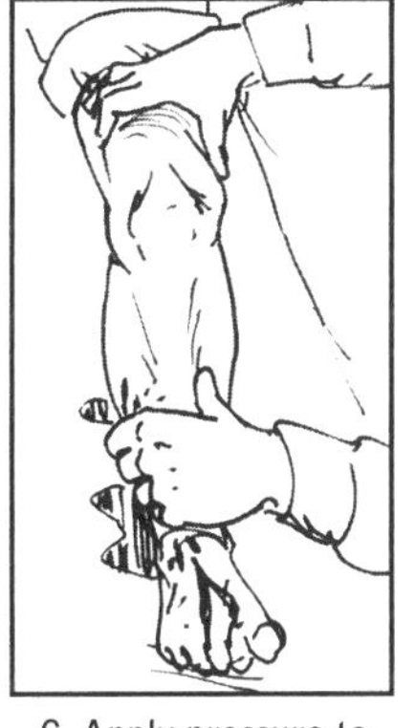

C. Apply pressure to pressure points.

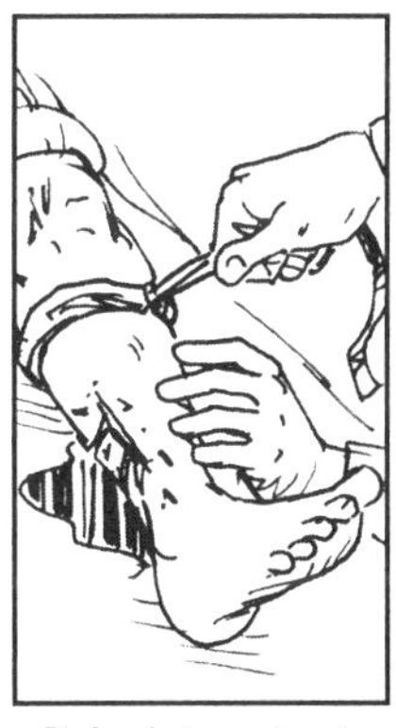

D. Apply tourniquet.

BLUF: Ensure the scene is safe for you before you try to save a life.

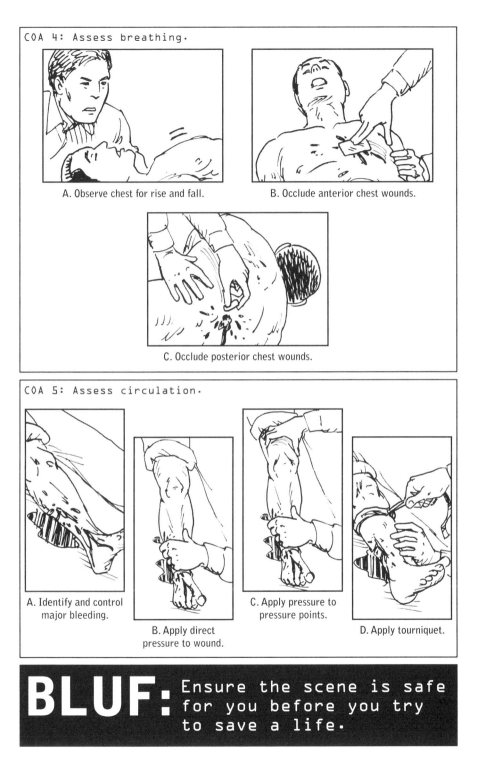

093 Stop the Bleeding

Panic may be a natural response to the sight of major blood loss, but swift action can mean the difference between life and death. Any civilian who is witness to a catastrophic injury has the power to halt blood loss and stave off organ failure, using only his or her bare hands.

Direct pressure is the first line of action. Act quickly, particularly if the blood is bright red—arterial blood loss can quickly lead to organ failure. Immediately place the heel or palm of your hand directly on the wound and apply a significant amount of pressure. Use your body weight. Your goal is to choke off the artery by pressing it down against the bone. If the injured person isn't yet on the ground, help him or her down so that you aren't working against gravity.

If you can't stop blood loss using direct pressure, try applying equally intense force to one of the vascular pressure points illustrated opposite. Choose the point just above the injury site. If you don't see an abrupt slowdown in blood flow, try again in the general vicinity. Use the heel or blade of your palm on large muscle masses or if the injured person is overweight.

If none of these options successfully control the bleeding, use a shirt, a pair of pants, or a belt as a tourniquet. Tie off the limb above the wound, as close to the wound site as possible, and get the injured person medical attention ASAP. Left on too long, a tourniquet will cause tissue death to healthy parts of the limb and may lead to amputation.

Once blood loss has been controlled, bandage the injury and elevate the injured area above the heart if possible. In all cases, get help immediately.

No. 093: Stop the Bleeding

CONOP: Use pressure points to control bleeding.

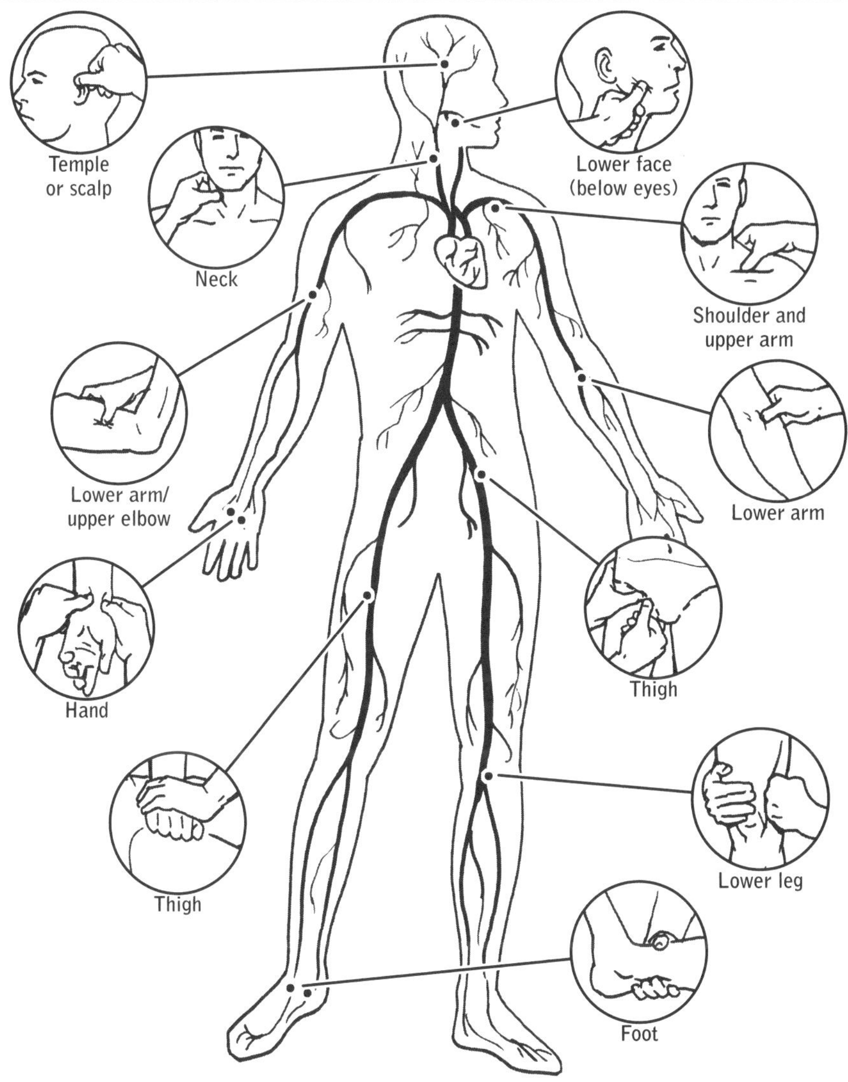

BLUF: If direct pressure to wound is unsuccessful, combine with pressure points.

094 Treat Gunshot Wounds

More than seventy thousand people are treated for gunshot wounds each year in the United States alone, yet most civilians know little to nothing about how to help a shooting victim before emergency workers have arrived. In the event that the victim is hit in a life-threatening location like the brain, heart, or lungs, fatality may result before medical intervention can be undertaken. But blood loss from wounds in other locations can sometimes be managed through the use of direct pressure, indirect pressure, or a tourniquet. (See page 238 for more detail on these techniques.)

In a pinch, combine direct pressure with the use of a shirt, a tampon, or a menstrual pad to slow the bleeding. Feminine hygiene products are designed to absorb large quantities of blood, and if you actually insert a tampon into the wound you may be able to clot bleeding at the source.

Internal trauma may be extensive, particularly if the bullet has hit organs or arteries. But again, there is little a bystander can do about internal injuries. What you *can* do is look for an exit wound, so that you're controlling the bleeding on both ends. Be thorough, as exit wounds may not appear in logical places. Bullets can bounce around inside body cavities and travel along bone, so that a gunshot to the knee results in an exit wound at the pelvis.

Don't be deceived by a small wound. Though a 9mm bullet may cause less cavitation (penetrating tissue trauma) than a round of buckshot, the latter has less velocity—and thus may be slightly less likely to have lethal consequences, depending on where it lands and the distance of the shooter.

Attempt to keep the victim calm. Gunshot victims frequently go into shock, their blood pressure dipping as their bodies enter a kind of emergency conservation mode. Cover the victim with a blanket to mitigate against heat loss. Do not attempt to move the victim if there is any chance of a spinal injury.

For gunshot wounds to the chest, see page 242.

No. 094: Treat Gunshot Wounds

CONOP: Understanding and treating gunshot wounds.

COA 1: Life-threatening locations:

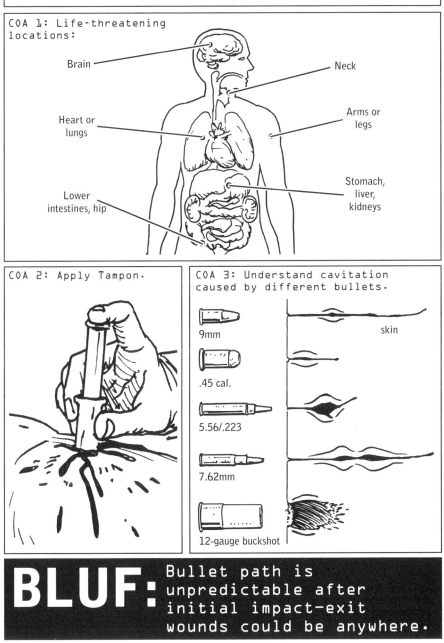

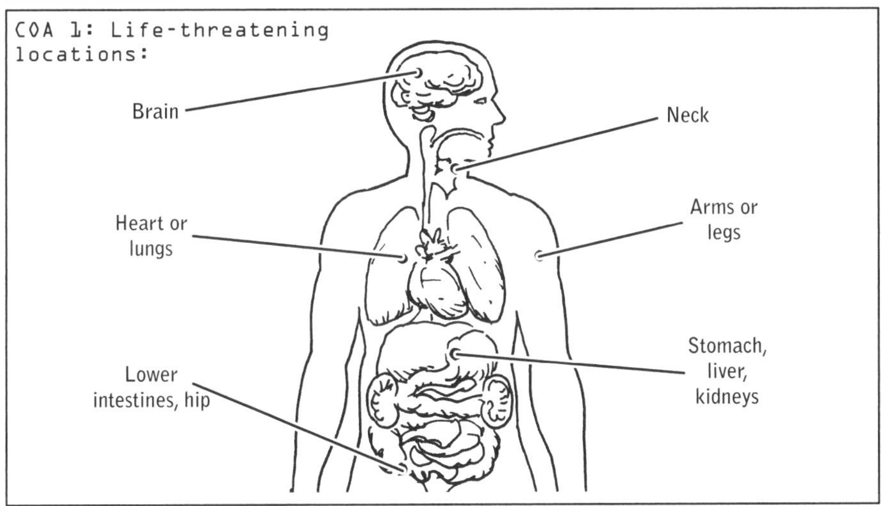

COA 2: Apply Tampon.

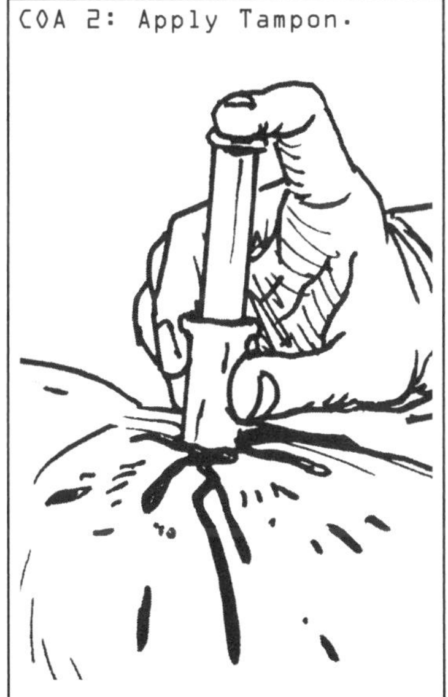

COA 3: Understand cavitation caused by different bullets.

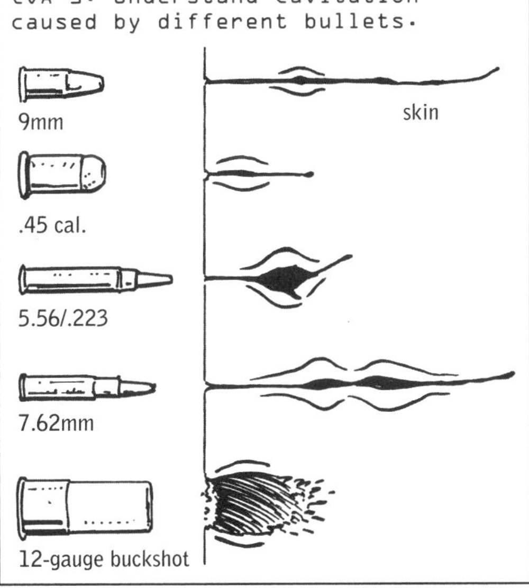

BLUF: Bullet path is unpredictable after initial impact—exit wounds could be anywhere.

095 Occlude a Sucking Chest Wound

Whether it's the result of unfortunate contact with a sharp piece of mechanical equipment or being at the wrong end of a knife or bullet, a puncture wound that lands anywhere near the chest cavity poses a grave risk not only to the heart, but also to the lungs. There is little a bystander can do about a wound to the heart other than perform CPR and call for help. While penetrating injuries to the heart don't necessarily result in death, they certainly do require a surgical team.

But a chest wound that threatens the lungs can be temporarily managed by a bystander waiting for emergency services to arrive, with a technique based on the standard operating procedures used by paramedics and military medics.

Rather than use bandages to stop the bleeding, the goal with any chest wound is to occlude (seal) the wound to prevent air from entering. Treat any chest wound as if it may have caused a "sucking chest wound," also known as a tension pneumothorax. The lungs are surrounded by a pleural sack, the thin membrane that protects organs from surrounding tissues and bones. If the pleural lining is punctured, air can enter the pleural sack through the wound site, putting pressure on the lung and preventing it from inflating. With every breath the victim takes, more air enters through the wound, and the lung is further compromised.

Use flat, impermeable materials such as credit cards or plastic wrap to create an occlusive seal over the wound, taping the seal down on only three sides so that you leave a flutter valve through which air trapped inside the pleural sack can escape. When the victim takes a breath, the chest's expansion will put pressure against the occlusive dressing, preventing air from entering at the wound site.

No. 095: Occlude a Sucking Chest Wound

CONOP: Treat a sucking chest wound and prevent a tension pneumothorax.

COA 1: Identify a tension pneumothorax.

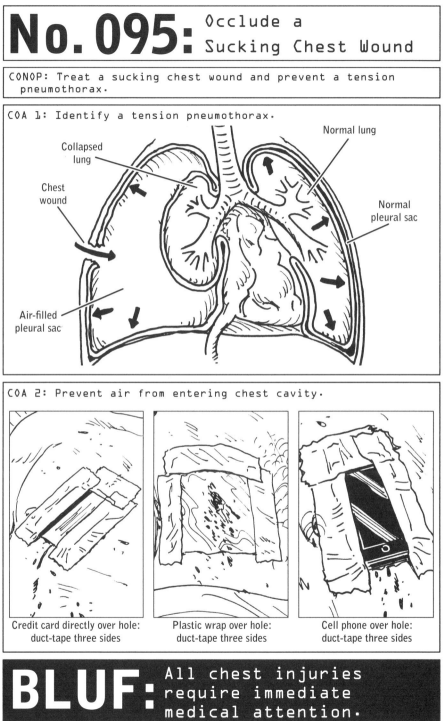

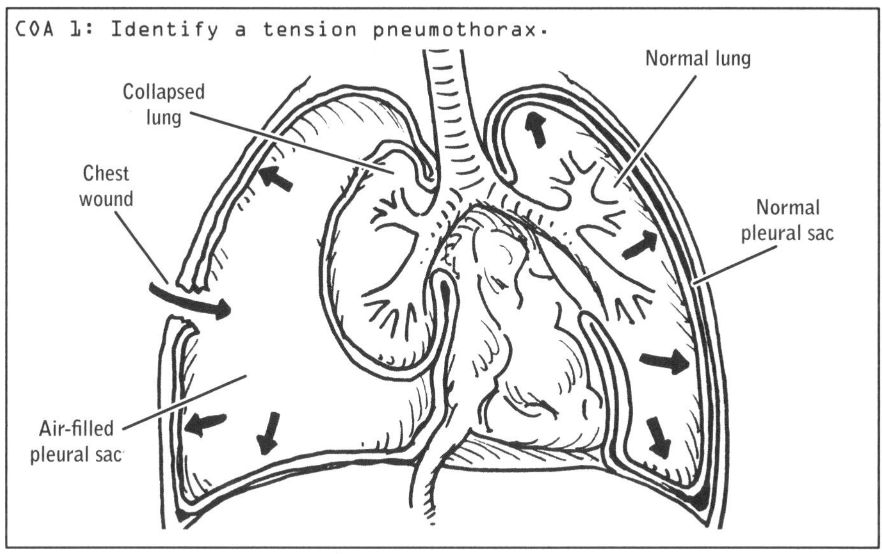

COA 2: Prevent air from entering chest cavity.

Credit card directly over hole: duct-tape three sides

Plastic wrap over hole: duct-tape three sides

Cell phone over hole: duct-tape three sides

BLUF: All chest injuries require immediate medical attention.

096 Treat Foreign Object Impalements

Never, ever attempt to remove a sizable foreign object that has penetrated the skin to a significant depth or may have struck near major arteries, vessels, or organs. This misguided attempt to play good samaritan could result in severe tissue damage or worse. If the foreign object has breached a vessel or artery, its removal could cause sudden and profuse bleeding. Even in the case of an impalement to the foot, the very common result of the mishandling of kitchen knives or other sharp implements, the foreign object should never be removed on site. Removing the object without proper medical equipment and knowledge can cause further tissue, vascular, or arterial damage.

If the victim has impaled him- or herself on a large or fixed object and adequate tools are available, cut the victim free. Fire trucks are stocked with electric saws, so wait for emergency services to arrive if you can't free the individual safely.

If the object is anywhere near the chest cavity, the most useful thing a bystander can do, after calling 911, is create a seal around the impalement. Chest impalements risk puncturing a lung—a "sucking chest wound" or tension pneumothorax being the life-threatening result. Air that enters the chest cavity through the wound depresses the lung, preventing the victim from taking a full breath. With every exhale, more air enters through the wound, further decreasing the victim's lung capacity. To prevent air from entering the wound site, seal the area around the object with a combination of credit and ID cards and duct tape.

Once the impalement has been sealed, brace the object to prevent it from moving around or slipping further inside the body. Surround the protruding end of the object with a pyramid of rolled up gauze or socks, then tape down. For more detail on how to manage a sucking chest wound, see page 242.

No. 096: Treat Foreign Object Impalements

CONOP: Properly treat and secure impaled objects.

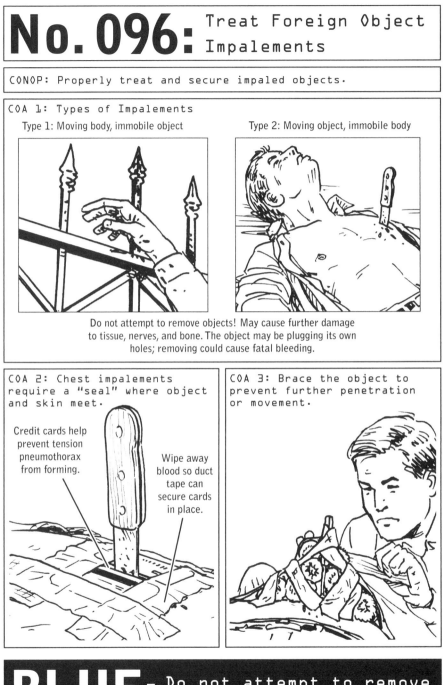

COA 1: Types of Impalements

Type 1: Moving body, immobile object

Type 2: Moving object, immobile body

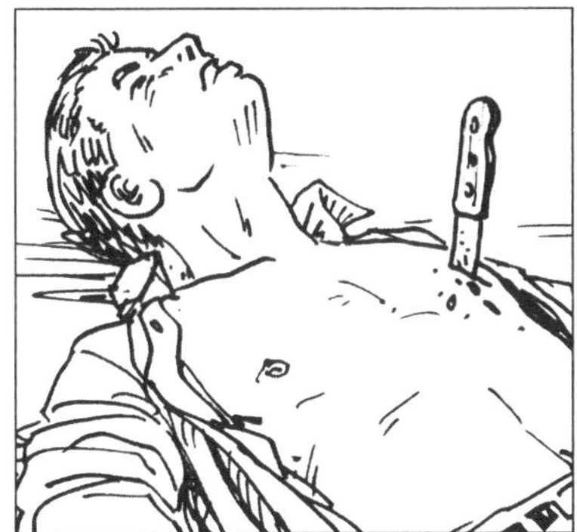

Do not attempt to remove objects! May cause further damage to tissue, nerves, and bone. The object may be plugging its own holes; removing could cause fatal bleeding.

COA 2: Chest impalements require a "seal" where object and skin meet.

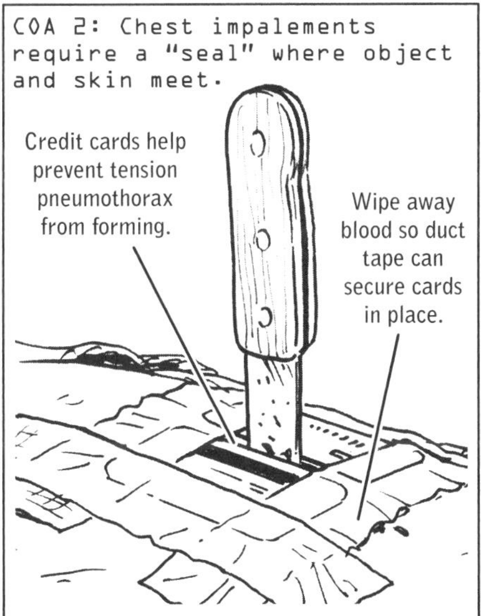

Credit cards help prevent tension pneumothorax from forming.
Wipe away blood so duct tape can secure cards in place.

COA 3: Brace the object to prevent further penetration or movement.

BLUF: Do not attempt to remove impaled objects!

097 Suture a Cut

If you're within hours of a hospital, cleaning and tightly bandaging a cut should provide sufficient protection against infection. But if the nearest medical facility is more than twenty-four hours away and adequate materials are available, temporarily suturing a cut that is over a quarter inch in length may be advisable. Avoid attempting to suture messy nonlinear wounds, crater-like injuries, or extremely deep lacerations. These complex wounds are likely to require deep cleaning and possibly skin grafting. Avoid closing up a wound you can't adequately clean with boiled, cooled water and/or alcohol—sealing contaminating agents into a closed environment is even more likely to breed infection than leaving a wound open to the external environment.

While the notion of piercing the epidermis or skin with a needle and thread will be off-putting to most civilians, the skill is achievable by anyone with even minimal sewing experience.

To determine what type of stitch to use, consider its placement and shape (see illustrations). Interrupted stitches are time-consuming and may be challenging to those with thicker or less dexterous fingers, but they provide a tight seal and can be adapted to jagged lacerations. Continuous stitches are the fastest and easiest option, but they can leave gaps in a wound or loosen up over time. Lock-stitch sutures, in which the needle is looped upward through the preceding stitch after each horizontal loop, are a step more secure than continuous stitches but tend to scar.

Because the skin of the scalp is thin and stretched very tight, stitching it will prove difficult to impossible. Instead, a viable improvised suture can be made by knotting pieces of hair together over the wound and super gluing the knots.

Medical tape can be used to bypass the needle altogether. Butterfly the tape by pinching pieces at their center to protect the oozing portion of the wound. Secure tape on either side of the wound.

No. 097: Suture a Cut

CONOP: Use everyday material to suture a wound.

COA 1: Types of Suture Knots

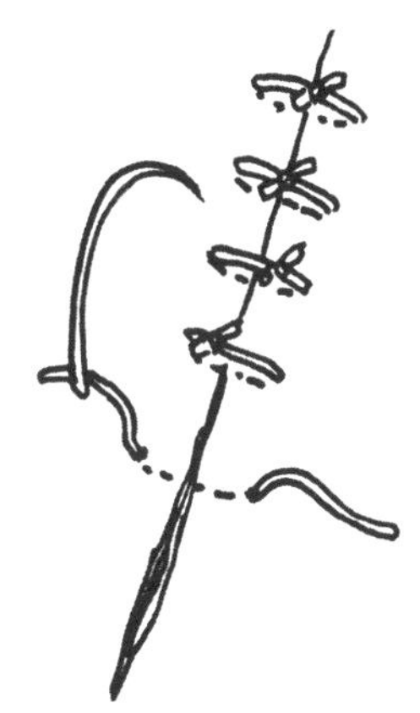

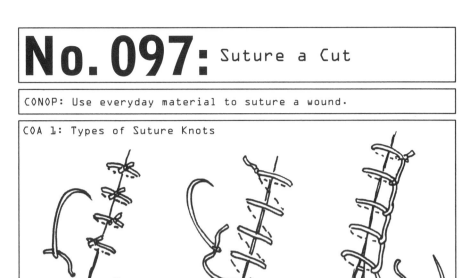

Over-and-over sutures (interrupted)

Over-and-over sutures (continuous)

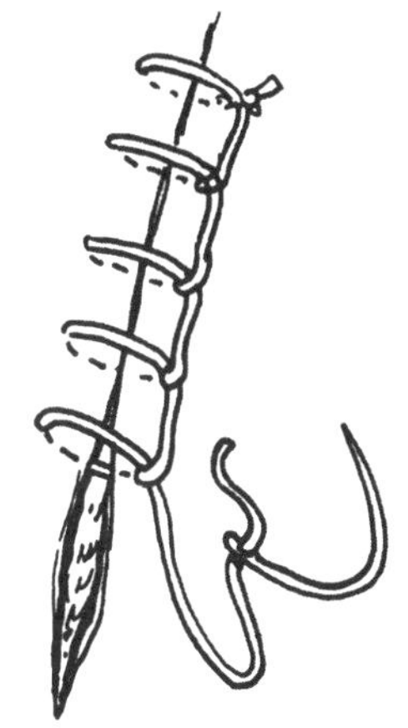

Lock-stitch sutures

COA 2: Improvised Suture Material

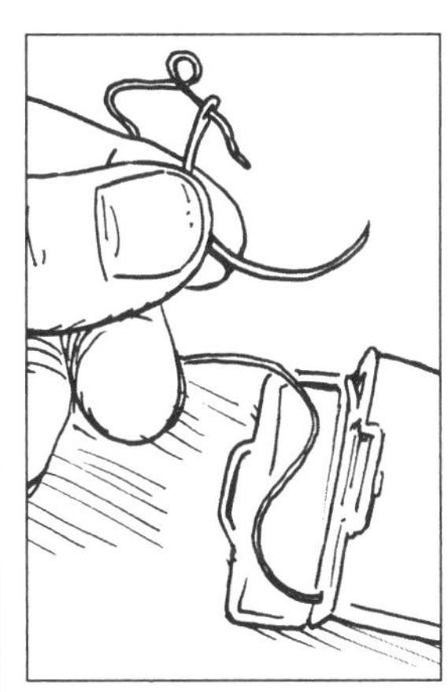

1. Dental floss and bent sewing needle

2. Super glue

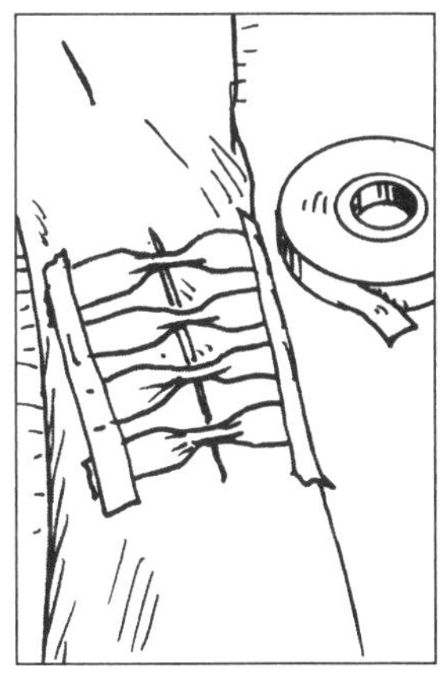

3. Tape

BLUF: All bleeding eventually stops.

098 Treat Minor Burns

You may think you're already familiar with the basics of burn treatment and fire safety. Stop-drop-and-roll if you catch on fire, smother the affected party in a blanket if you're a bystander. But if you've ever applied an ice pack to a burn wound in search of relief, a review of fundamentals is in order—ice can cause frostbite to recently burned skin and also prohibits healing.

Most burn care follows the same initial protocol, whether the burn is thermal (caused by direct contact with heat or flame), a scald (caused by exposure to hot liquid or steam), chemical (caused by contact with a corrosive chemical substance or weapon), or electrical (caused by exposure to a live electrical current).

Second- or third-degree burns of any type must be treated as emergencies—second-degree burns reach down to the deeper layers of the skin, and third-degree burns may cause severe, irreparable damage to ligaments, tendons, bones, and internal organs. Both render victims extremely susceptible to serious infection. Internal burns, whether to the lungs or the digestive system, must be treated by medical professionals; any time a corrosive substance is ingested, get the victim to the hospital or a poison control center as soon as possible. Chemical burns to the skin should also be treated immediately, though they may not produce symptoms or sensations until hours after contact.

Only first-degree burns, which affect just the epidermis, the most superficial layer of skin, can safely be treated at home. Run cold water over the affected area (or dip in a cold river or stream), then apply a pain-relieving antibiotic ointment or the time-tested home remedies of yellow mustard or soy sauce. Their effectiveness has not been proven by medical studies, but the anecdotal and experiential evidence is strong. Keep burns clean and dry to avoid infection.

For information on smoke inhalation and escaping a burning building, see page 204.

No. 098: Treat Minor Burns

CONOP: Understand and treat burns.

COA 1: Causes of Burns

1. Thermal

2. Scald

3. Chemical

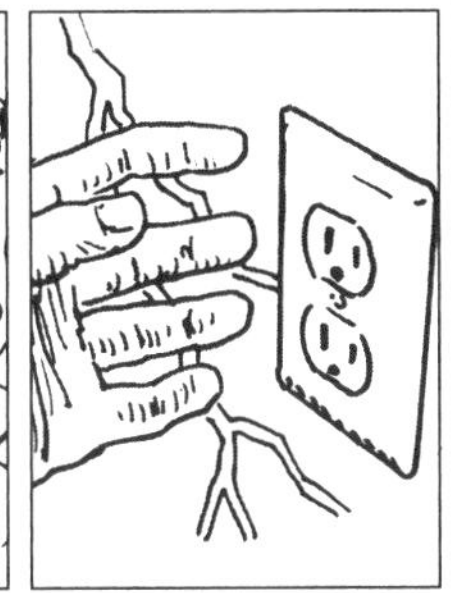

4. Electrical

COA 2: Types of Burns

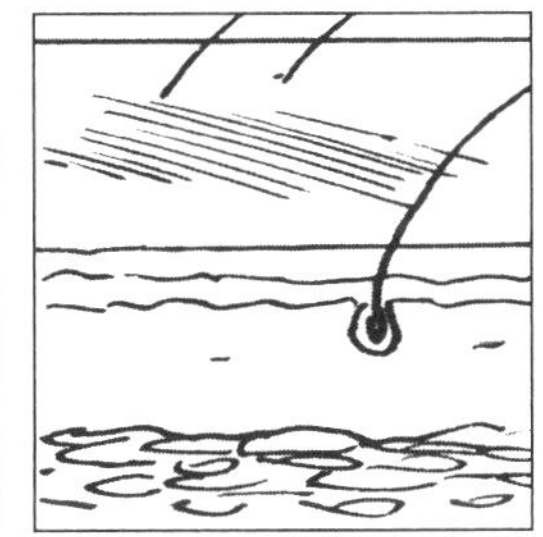

1. First degree

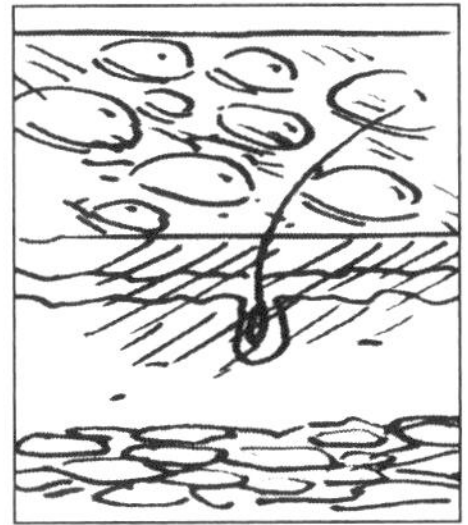

2. Second degree

3. Third degree

COA 3: Treatment of Burns

1. Stop the burning process.

2. Stop the swelling.

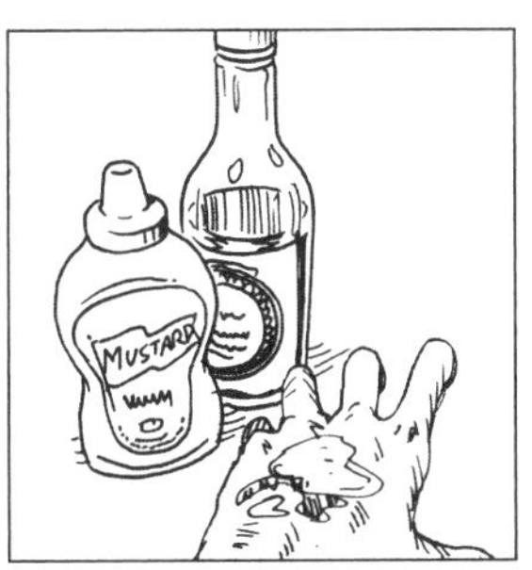

3. Stop the pain.

BLUF: Treat burns with cold water, not ice.

099 Splint Fractured Bones

Painful and slow to heal but generally not life-threatening, broken bones are among the most common of childhood injuries. But when they occur far from civilization or medical facilities, they can certainly become a threat to survival.

If your location means you'll be moving yourself or the victim of a broken bone to a medical facility on your own, splinting the bone will help reduce pain. More important, immobilizing the injured limb may prevent the jagged end of the bone from shredding tissue, arteries, or veins inside the body. The breaking of the bone itself can result in significant blood loss, as the blood marrow inside the bone is dispersed throughout the body, and in combination with broken vessels may be responsible for severe internal bleeding. For these reasons, any broken bone must be treated as soon as possible. Do not exert pressure on the fracture site.

The goal in splinting is to temporarily immobilize the broken bone by taping the length of the limb to a rigid, stabilizing object, the "splint." Splint the bone above and below joints on either side of the injury site. For a break at the shin, extend the splint from the ankle past the knee.

When combined with duct tape, folded-up newspaper, ski or hiking poles, sticks, and even pillows can be called into service as temporary splints. Once you've splinted the limb straight, further immobilize the injury site by taping or wrapping the limb against the body; arms should be nestled against the torso, legs pinned together.

For hip fractures, tape the legs together at the thighs.

For broken ribs, gently attach the arm on the injured side to the body and avoid movement, as a broken rib in motion can puncture a lung.

No. 099: Splint Fractured Bones

CONOP: Utilize everyday objects to splint broken bones.

COA 1: Types of Fractures

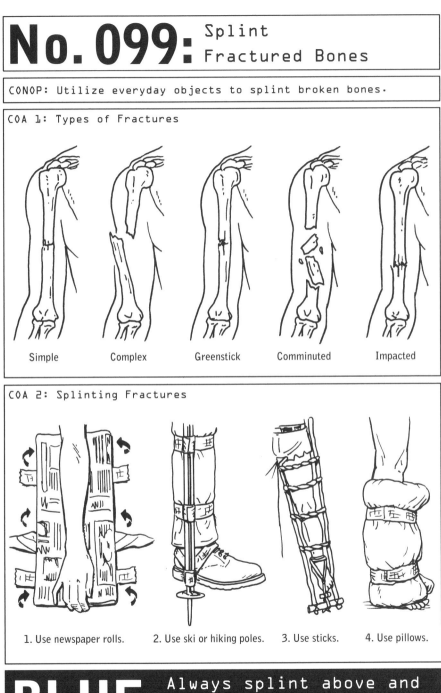

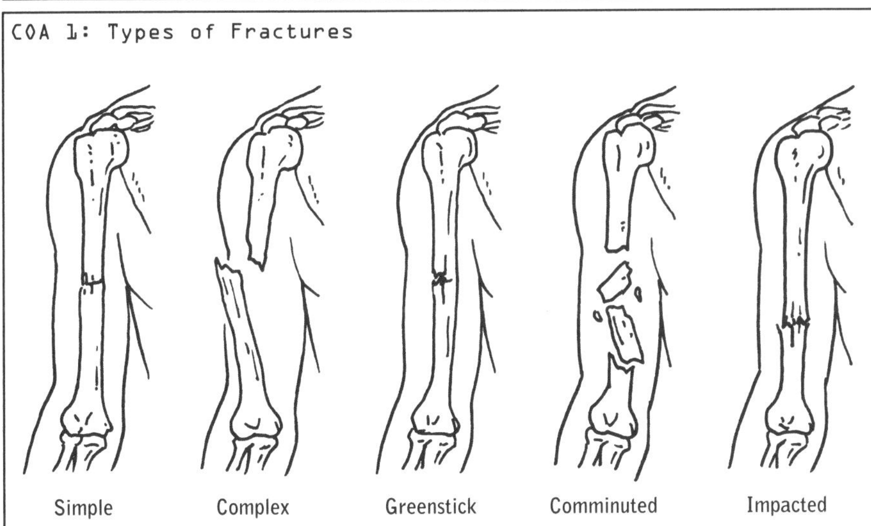
Simple
Complex
Greenstick
Comminuted
Impacted

COA 2: Splinting Fractures

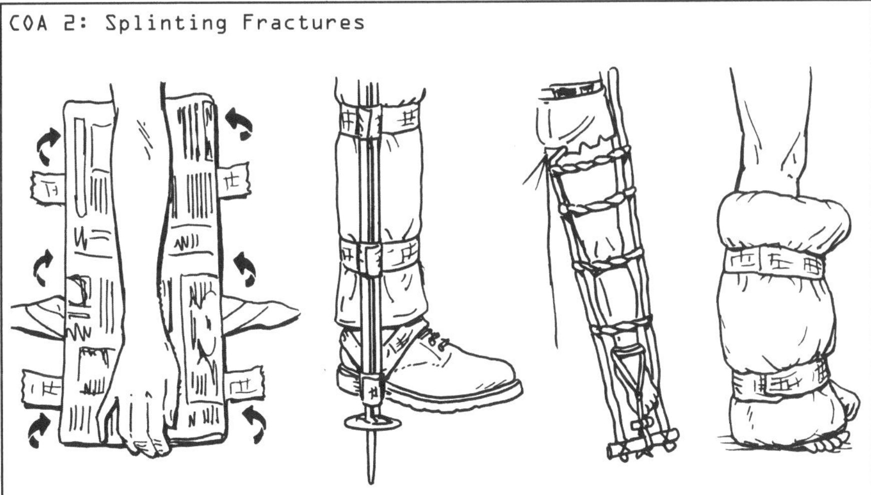
1. Use newspaper rolls.
2. Use ski or hiking poles.
3. Use sticks.
4. Use pillows.

BLUF: Always splint above and below the fracture, from joint to joint.

100 Perform a Cricothyrotomy

Like many emergency medicine skills, a cricothyrotomy is only to be performed by an untrained bystander as a method of last resort. Creating an alternate airway by punching a hole through the cricothyroid membrane should be attempted only when a massive trauma such as a vehicular collision has mangled the victim's upper airway or a foreign object has lodged in his or her airway and cannot be removed—and after an attempt to sweep the airway and a Heimlich maneuver have both failed, emergency services have been contacted, and the victim has lost consciousness due to lack of airflow. Continue to attempt the Heimlich maneuver as long as the victim is gasping, choking, wheezing, or displaying any other audible breathing attempts. Describe the victim's symptoms to the 911 operator, and only proceed if the dispatcher agrees that the procedure is necessary.

In a test of the efficacy of bystander cricothyrotomies, 57 percent of junior doctors and second-year medical students with no prior experience operating on airways were able to successfully perform simulated interventions, using only a scalpel and a ballpoint pen. This study, supported by a small number of documented interventions, suggests that though the rate of success for civilian bystanders would be much lower, the use of these tools does offer some hope in situations where the only other alternatives are irreversible brain damage or death. Severe brain damage and/or complete brain death can occur after a mere three to seven minutes without oxygen, so time is of the essence when dealing with airway obstructions.

Begin by quickly preparing your tools. You'll need a sharp knife to make the incision, and a durable straw-like tube or pen barrel to create the airway. The thicker the pen, the better the chance that its barrel will create a viable airway. Studies have identified the oversize durable straws found in sports bottles as a better choice. But most of us are more likely to have a pen in a purse or back pocket—and

No. 100: Perform a Cricothyrotomy

CONOP: Perform a "cric" to provide an alternate airway.

COA 1: Locate and "pinch" skin directly above cricothyroid membrane.

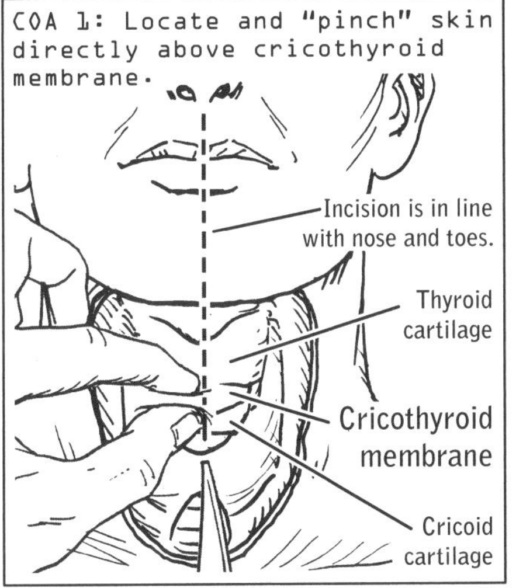

COA 2: With a knife, cut pinched skin in line with neck.

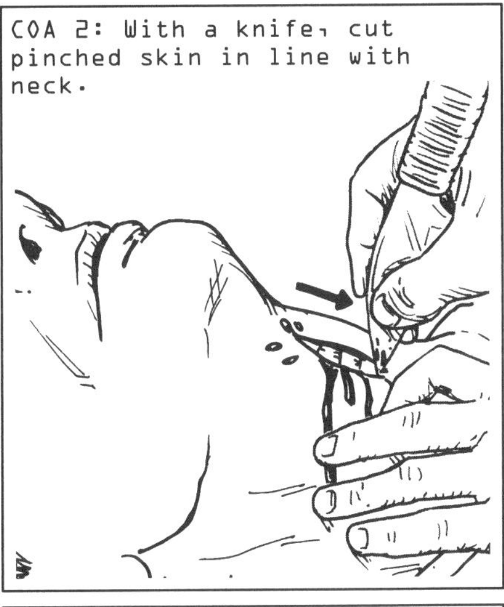

COA 3: Puncture membrane with knife point.

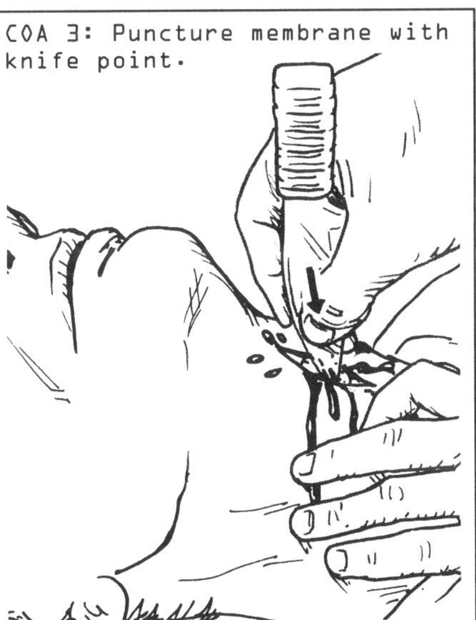

COA 4: Remove ink cartridge and both ends of writing pen and insert into punctured membrane between thyroid cartilage and cricothyroid membrane.

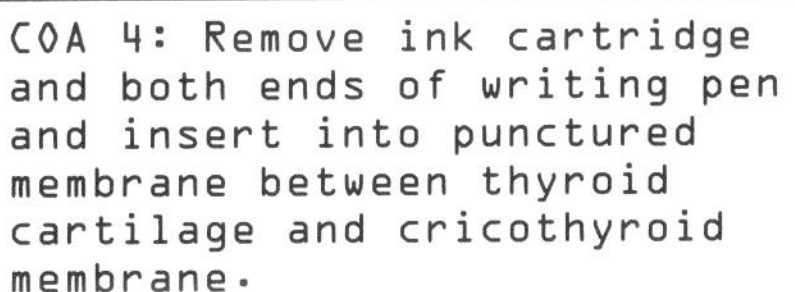

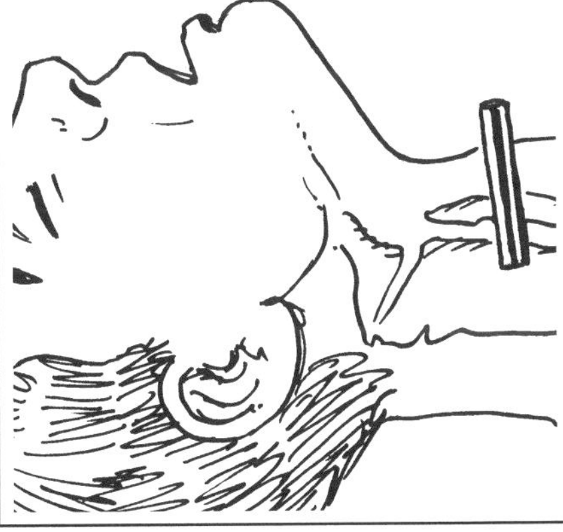

BLUF: Cricothyrotomies should only be performed when all other attempts have failed.

a situation in which a victim may be near death calls for the use of the best available option. More extensive first-aid kits may contain endotracheostomy or ET tubes, and these are the obvious first choice. If using a pen, remove and discard the ink cartridge and the top and bottom parts of the pen, so that all you are left with is the barrel.

Palpate the neck to locate the Adam's apple, a lump formed by the angle of the thyroid cartilage as it surrounds the larynx. If it isn't visually prominent, slide your fingers down the victim's neck. The first solid protrusion is the Adam's apple, and you want to aim for the space just below it—the cricothyroid membrane that connects the thyroid cartilage to the cricoid cartilage. After an initial cut through the skin, you'll be punching through this membrane in order to clear a new pathway to the trachea.

The skin at the neck is very thin, which means that you need to be extremely careful in performing the initial cut. Slice too deep and you could be lacerating deeper layers of tissue and cartilage. The jugular veins and carotid arteries lie just to the side of the cervical vertebrae, so your cut must be centralized. Cut too low, and you'll be slicing into the thyroid gland. To ensure that your first cut slices only through the skin, pinch the skin just below the Adam's apple and pull it away from the throat. Make a perpendicular, quarter-inch horizontal cut in the loose skin.

Now the underlying membrane will be exposed. Aiming at the indentation between the two rings of cartilage (the thyroid and the cricoid), use the tip of your knife to puncture the membrane. A small, shallow incision is all that is needed; the system will work more efficiently if there's a tight seal around the breathing tube. Though there will be some blood, typically this maneuver should not result in profuse blood flow.

Force the barrel of the pen or ET tube into the incision. To quickly check the airway, look for misting, feel for airflow, or suck on the tube to confirm airflow. Administer two to three breaths through the tube. If the intervention was successful, the victim should thereafter begin to breathe through the airway on his or her own.

If breathing does not resume and a pulse is not discernible, begin to perform CPR.

Index

About the Author

Clint Emerson, retired Navy SEAL, spent twenty years conducting special ops all over the world while attached to SEAL Team Three, the National Security Agency (NSA), and the elite SEAL Team Six. A graduate of the American Military University in Virginia with a B.A. in Security Management, he spent a portion of his time in the special operations community with a Special Mission Unit (SMU), developing and implementing specialized skills in support of operations in various hostile environments targeting high value individuals. A counterterrorism and surveillance expert, Clint has received numerous awards for bravery and leadership, including a bronze star.

Emerson is the founder of Escape the Wolf, a company focused on workplace violence prevention and response, threat identification and crisis management. The author of the *New York Times* bestselling book *100 Deadly Skills*, he continues to catalog self-defense skills while developing unique, durable tools and products for personal and home security.